JAMES SALTER

BOOKS BY JEFFREY MEYERS

BIOGRAPHY

A Fever at the Core: The Idealist in Politics

Married to Genius

Katherine Mansfield

The Enemy: A Biography of Wyndham Lewis

Hemingway

Manic Power: Robert Lowell and His Circle

D. H. Lawrence

Joseph Conrad

Edgar Allan Poe: His Life and Legacy

Scott Fitzgerald

Edmund Wilson

Robert Frost

Bogart: A Life in Hollywood

Gary Cooper: American Hero

Privileged Moments: Encounters with Writers

Wintry Conscience: A Biography of George Orwell

Inherited Risk: Errol and Sean Flynn in Hollywood and Vietnam

Somerset Maugham

*Impressionist Quartet: The Intimate Genius of
Manet and Morisot, Degas and Cassatt*

Modigliani

Samuel Johnson: The Struggle

The Genius and the Goddess: Arthur Miller and Marilyn Monroe

John Huston: Courage and Art

Robert Lowell in Love

Resurrections: Authors, Heroes—and a Spy

CRITICISM

Fiction and the Colonial Experience

The Wounded Spirit: T. E. Lawrence's Seven Pillars of Wisdom

A Reader's Guide to George Orwell
Painting and the Novel
Homosexuality and Literature
D. H. Lawrence and the Experience of Italy
Disease and the Novel
The Spirit of Biography
Hemingway: Life into Art
Orwell: Life and Art
Thomas Mann's Artist-Heroes

BIBLIOGRAPHY
T. E. Lawrence: A Bibliography
Catalogue of the Library of the Late Siegfried Sassoon
George Orwell: An Annotated Bibliography of Criticism

EDITED COLLECTIONS
George Orwell: The Critical Heritage
Hemingway: The Critical Heritage
Robert Lowell: Interviews and Memoirs
The Sir Arthur Conan Doyle Reader
The W. Somerset Maugham Reader

EDITED ORIGINAL ESSAYS
Wyndham Lewis: A Revaluation
Wyndham Lewis by Roy Campbell
D. H. Lawrence and Tradition
The Legacy of D. H. Lawrence
The Craft of Literary Biography
The Biographer's Art
T. E. Lawrence: Soldier, Writer, Legend
Graham Greene: A Revaluation

EDITED LETTERS
Remembering Iris Murdoch: Letters and Interviews
The Mystery of the Real: Letters of the Canadian Artist
Alex Colville and Biographer Jeffrey Meyers

JAMES SALTER

PILOT | SCREENWRITER | NOVELIST

JEFFREY MEYERS

LOUISIANA STATE UNIVERSITY PRESS

BATON ROUGE

Published with the assistance of the Pelican Book Club

Published by Louisiana State University Press
lsupress.org

Manufactured in the United States of America
First printing

Designer: Barbara Neely Bourgoyne
Typeface: MillerText
Printer and binder: Sheridan Books

Cover photograph reproduced courtesy of the Estate of James Salter.
Interior photos are by Valerie Meyers.

Cataloging-in-Publication Data are available from the Library of Congress.
ISBN 978-0-8071-8116-4 (cloth: alk. paper) — ISBN 978-0-8071-8168-3 (pdf)
ISBN 978-0-8071-8167-6 (epub)

CONTENTS

Photographs follow page 104.

Only those things preserved in writing
have any possibility of being real.

—SALTER, *All That Is*

PREFACE AND ACKNOWLEDGMENTS

I knew James Salter during the last decade of his life, visited him twice on Long Island and received 80 letters from him. My friendship and knowledge of his life provide many new insights about the personal, literary and historical background of his work. This appreciative book, the first full-length study in 26 years, is intended to introduce him to new readers, and show his achievement as a writer of novels, stories, screenplays, memoirs and travel essays. I discuss Salter's family and friends, the significance of his book and chapter titles; characters' names and cultural allusions; literary influences, especially Ernest Hemingway and Scott Fitzgerald; development of his fictional style and techniques; awareness of weather and light; supreme delineation of sexual ecstasy; recurrent themes of war and love; strange career. His lyrical evocation of people and places, of luxurious decadence and the danger of death, are unsurpassed in contemporary literature. Salter had an extraordinary range of experience as West Point graduate; fighter pilot in the Korean War; downhill skier, rock climber and mountain climber; screenwriter and film director; connoisseur of food and wine; world traveler and sophisticated observer.

I am pleased to acknowledge the generous help I received when writing this book. I met Nina Salter; interviewed his twin children, Claude Salter and James Owen Salter; and had illuminating letters from William Benton, Geoff Dyer, Dana Gioia, Lyndall Gordon, Richard Greene, Edward Hirsch, Christopher MacLehose, Tom McGuane, Jack Shoemaker, Donald Sultan, Paul Theroux and Colm Toibin. Archives provided valuable information: Andrew Isidoro at Boston College for Salter's correspondence with Graham Greene; Humanities Research Center, University of Texas: correspondence with Saul Bellow, Joe Fox, Robert Ginna, Peter Glenville, Peter Matthiessen, Michael Mewshaw, Irwin Shaw and Diana Trilling; New York Public Library: correspondence with George Plimpton; as well as Denver University, Duke University, Horace Mann School, Pacific Film Archive and West Point. To get Graham Greene's comment on *Light Years* I wrote to the Birmingham Public Library, British Library, Islington Library (London), Kensington Central Library (London), Leicester University, National Library of Scotland and Reading University. It's been a pleasure to work with my editor James Long. My wife, Valerie, expertly edited this book and compiled the index.

CHRONOLOGY

1925 June 10: Born James Arnold Horowitz in Passaic, New Jersey, only child of George Horowitz (1898–1959), a West Point graduate and real estate investor, and Mildred Scheff Horowitz (1904–2000). Grows up in Manhattan.

1938–42 Attends Horace Mann School in Riverdale, New York. Publishes poems in the school's literary magazine.

1942 Plans to attend Stanford or MIT. Father insists he enter West Point.

1944 Publishes two stories in *The Pointer*.

1945 Graduates early from West Point and enters Air Force as a pilot. On V-E Day, May 8, 1945, gets lost and crashes his plane into an empty house in Great Barrington, western Massachusetts, but is not injured.

1946–47 Forced to fly transport planes in Hawaii, Philippines, Okinawa and Japan. Aide to General Robert Travis.

1947 Promoted to first lieutenant. Harper gives some encouragement but rejects his first novel.

1948 Honolulu. Cuts himself on coral reef in Marianas. Hospitalized for blood poisoning in Peking.

1948–50 Earns master's degree in international relations at Georgetown University in Washington.

1950 First trip to Europe.

1951   Trains as fighter pilot in Korean War. Marries Ann Altemus (1927–2015) in Fort Myer, Virginia. Spring: Aide to General Robert M. Lee during atomic bomb testing at Eniwetok.

1952   February–July: Flies F-86 Sabre jet on more than 100 combat missions against Russian MIGs in Korea. March 14: near-fatal mechanical accident. July 4: gets first kill.

1952–53   Serves in fighter squadrons, mainly at McGuire Air Force Base in New Jersey.

1954–57   Stationed in Bitburg, Rhineland, Germany, as squadron operations officer and member of aerobatics team.

1955   Daughter Allan Conrad is born.

1956   *The Hunters*, edited by Joe Fox.

1957   Daughter Nina Tobe is born. Receives $60,000 for film rights of *The Hunters*.

1957   July 3: Resigns from Air Force with rank of lieutenant colonel. Lives in Grandview and New City on the Hudson River, north of Manhattan.

1958   *The Hunters* film, starring Robert Mitchum and Robert Wagner, directed by Dick Powell.

1959   Briefly sells swimming pools. Meets filmmaker Lane Slate. First visit to Aspen, Colorado. February 8: death of father.

1961   *The Arm of Flesh*.

1961–62   During the Berlin Crisis—partition of the city and erection of Berlin wall—he's recalled to active duty as squadron operations officer in Chaumont, Lorraine, eastern France. Leads aerial aerobatic team. February 1962: hospitalized for hepatitis in France. Friendship with Irwin Shaw.

1962   Changes his name, and those of his wife and children, to Salter. May: twins James Owen and daughter Claude Cray are born. Writes and directs with Lane Slate a 12-minute documentary *Team, Team, Team*.

1963–64   He and Slate make documentary series *Circus* for NET-TV.

1965   In Rome for research on his screenplays *The Appointment* and *Three*.

1967   Publishes *A Sport and a Pastime* with George Plimpton's Paris Review Editions. Gets poor reviews. Sells only 3,000 copies.

1967–69   Family lives near Grasse, in Provence, France.

1968   Attends winter Olympics in Grenoble, France, with Robert Redford for research on *Downhill Racer*.

1969   Annus mirabilis. Writes script for *The Appointment* starring Omar Sharif and Anouk Aimée, directed by Sidney Lumet. Writes script for *Downhill Racer*, starring Redford and Gene Hackman. *Three*, written and directed by Salter, starring Charlotte Rampling and Sam Waterston. Buys house in Aspen, population 2,500, and spends winters there. Begins correspondence with editor Robert Phelps that continues through the 1970s.

1970   To Corsica on film project with director Stanley Donen. In *The O. Henry Prize Stories*, 1970, 1972, 1974 and 1984.

1971   Documentary *The Artist in America: James Salter*. Meets Kay Eldredge (b. 1948).

1972   Fails to get Guggenheim fellowship for *Light Years*.

1973   Summer: friendship with Saul Bellow in Aspen.

1975   *Light Years*. Divorce from Ann.

1976   January: breaks his shoulder skiing. Autumn: begins living with Kay. Travels to France and Italy.

1977   Redford commissions screenplay of *Solo Faces*. Salter takes up mountain climbing.

1978   July: to Tahiti on film project with screenwriter Lorenzo Semple.

1979   Redford rejects screenplay. Salter publishes *Solo Faces* as a novel, edited by Robert Ginna.

1980   July 20: daughter Allan dies in freak electrical accident. Salter moves
       to Bridgehampton, Long Island.

1082   Award from the American Academy of Arts and Letters.

1983   Writes script for *Threshold*, starring Donald Sutherland and Jeff
       Goldblum.

1984   To St. Croix, Virgin Islands.

1985   March 10: son Theo Shaw born in Paris.

1986   Teaches at Vassar.

1987   Teaches at Iowa.

1988   *Dusk and Other Stories.*

1989   Teaches at Alabama and at Iowa. PEN-Faulkner Award for *Dusk*.

1991   Fails to get MacArthur Fellowship. Teaches at Houston.

1992   *Still Such*, limited edition of prose poem about New York.

1996   Film *Boys* with Winona Ryder, vaguely based on Salter's story "Twenty
       Minutes."

1997   *Burning the Days: Recollections*. Teaches at Williams.

1998   William Dowie, *James Salter* (Twayne). *Burning the Days* wins the
       New York State Edith Wharton $10,000 Citation of Merit; John
       Steinbeck Award; PEN Center USA Award for Creative Nonfiction;
       English Speaking Union Ambassador Book Award.

2000   Humanities Research Center, University of Texas, buys his archive.
       Rewrites *The Arm of Flesh* as *Cassada*. Foreword to reprint of Irwin
       Shaw's *The Young Lions*.

2003   *Light Years* wins the Clifton Fadiman Award for Excellence in Fiction.

2004   *Gods of Tin: The Flying Years*. Alex Vernon, *Soldiers Once and Still:
       Ernest Hemingway, James Salter and Tim O'Brien* (Iowa).

2005   *Last Night: Stories. There & Then: Travel Writing.*

2006   *Life Is Meals*. In Fort Worth invited to fly an F-16. Teaches at Duke.

2007   March: Picador book tour, London and Dublin. June: to St. Petersburg, Russia. October: to Spain.

2007–08   Penguin Modern Classics reissues *The Hunters, Light Years* and *Solo Faces.*

2009   Literary festival in São Paulo, Brazil.

2010   February: to Egypt. PEN-USA Lifetime Achievement Award.

2011   Documentary, *James Salter: A Sport and a Pastime.* Rea Award $10,000 for Short Stories; *Paris Review* Hadada Prize for Unique Contribution to Literature.

2012   March: "As They Were: American Masters Through the Lens of James Salter, Photos 1962–63," Armory Show, New York. April: Back surgery. October: breaks his leg skiing. PEN-Malamud Award for Excellence in Short Fiction.

2013   Last novel *All That Is. Collected Stories.* May: Book tour from Hay-on-Wye to Dublin. Windham-Campbell Literary Prize, $150,000, for Outstanding Achievement in Fiction.

2014   January–February: San Miguel de Allende, Mexico. Teaches at Virginia. F. Scott Fitzgerald Award for Achievement in American Literature.

2015   February–March: San Miguel de Allende. June 10: Maria Matthiessen gives his 90th birthday party. Dies on June 19 while exercising in a gym in Sag Harbor. July 28: Memorial Service in New York. November: *Conversations with James Salter.*

2016   *The Art of Fiction.*

2017   *Don't Save Anything: Uncollected Essays, Articles and Profiles.*

JAMES
SALTER

ONE

A RESTLESS LIFE

James Salter believed "my biography explains, in a way, some of the aspects of the tone of my writing and the point of view of it," as well as his dominant themes of war and love, sex and marriage.[1] His paternal grandfather, an importer of toys, often traveled to Europe on business. He'd once owned a hotel in the resort and racing town of Saratoga Springs, New York, and had lived in the posh Astor Hotel in Times Square when Salter was a boy. Salter wrote me that his paternal grandmother was a crushed and broken figure. Her husband had left her, and she had to take care of her father and her son. That was her whole life.

He added that his father, George Horowitz (1898–1959), graduated as an engineer from West Point in 1918 and served only a few years in the army. Careers seemed unpromising for those who'd missed the war, and the army shrank drastically in size. He was in the reserve and was reactivated in 1940.[2] He served in desk jobs in World War II, some of it in England and India, and retired as a full colonel. Between the wars Salter's father had grandiose plans, took bold risks and made a lot of money in real estate. In his autobiography *Burning the Days* (1997) Salter added that after World War II "was over his father was never able to fit in again. Everything had changed, he said. The vice presidents of banks were no longer able to turn pieces of property over to you. He was operatic. He lived on praise and its stimulus and performed best, only performed, when the full rays were shining on him. . . . He'd lost seventy thousand dollars in the market. He had nothing left. He'd have to give up the apartment, he said, he couldn't pay the rent. Finally, ashamed to be seen, he would lie in bed for hours. His hair was white, his jawline slack."[3] Visits to psychiatrists and shock treatments didn't work. He was finished.

Salter was born in 1925, when Fitzgerald's *The Great Gatsby* and Hemingway's *In Our Time* were published. He remembered his grandfather's toys and his mother's exaggerations. He was pleased when his mother brought him a present and could still remember what she brought. But he couldn't recall that his room was so cluttered with toys that she could scarcely walk into it, as she claimed.[4] His mother, born Mildred Scheff in Washington, D.C., was the youngest of four sisters. She could be difficult as well as bountiful, and made emotional demands that her only child could not satisfy. Reluctant to encounter her forceful presence, he confessed, "I can hardly keep my personality intact at my mother's much less concentrate on anything else."[5] Unwilling to recognize his achievements when he won a literary prize in his sixties, she said, "It isn't too late to go to law school."[6]

When his father was prosperous during the postwar boom, Salter's family lived in a posh neighborhood of Manhattan, on East 86th Street between Madison and Park Avenue. As a child, he played with a boy who became the famous photographer Richard Avedon. Salter's prep school, Horace Mann in Riverdale, was a forty-five-minute train trip uptown from his house. His contemporaries included Jack Kerouac, football star at school and famous novelist; William Buckley, the conservative editor; and John Simon, the fierce critic.

Salter published nine poems in the school magazine in 1940–42, many about death in the current war. Another poem, "Eliot Stanton," imitated A. E. Housman's weariness with life and mournful death in *A Shropshire Lad*: "Like aspirations of the bold, / We came and tilted and grew old. / Now every sabre, lone and grand, / Is poled obliquely in the sand."[7] In two interviews and an essay in *Don't Save Anything* (2017), Salter claimed that he sold two poems to *Poetry* magazine. But his schoolboy efforts were not nearly good enough to get into that competitive and prestigious journal. Searches by three scholars have not found any of his poems published in *Poetry*.

He was young and handsome, and had many sexual adventures. He first fell in love with a girl while still a cadet at West Point: "She was ambitious, beautiful, heartless. . . . A good drinker." But he had to leave her when he sailed for the Pacific and called her for an emotional farewell. "The Captain's Wife" chapter in *Burning the Days* describes a rare instance of his sexual restraint and answers the crucial question in W. B. Yeats' "The Tower": "Does the imagination dwell the most / Upon a woman won or woman lost?"

After graduating from West Point in 1945, Salter flew transport planes in the Pacific until the Korean War in 1951. He fell hopelessly in love with another woman when he was stationed in Honolulu: "We were attracted to one another instantly. We ridiculed one another and adored one another. Her husband was a captain in the Air Force. He was to be my best friend." She was unhappily married and loathed air bases: "Going to the commissary was a horror. She looked down on military life, made fun of the army wives." She told Salter that she was in love with him. Her husband tolerated their attraction to keep her happy and to keep her. Salter said, "I didn't know what to do. I loved her passionately and I knew I would never find a woman like her again." Looking back on his younger self, he quoted Frances Cornford's poem on Rupert Brooke, "A young Apollo, golden-haired, / Stands dreaming on the verge of strife, / Magnificently unprepared / For the long littleness of life." He recalled, "The current was pulling faster and faster. Nothing is as intense as unconsummated love."

After losing his first love, Salter desperately wanted to possess the captain's wife. Everything was perfect except for his unwillingness to betray his best friend: "She was ready to give anything, do anything, and we were held apart by all that was drawing us together: honor, conscience, ideals"—the values of West Point. He had the chaste passion captured on Keats' Grecian Urn, "For ever wilt thou love, and she be fair!" Sensing "the impossibility of our situation, the hopelessness of pretending, she put her mark on me in another way. . . . She chose for me the girl I ought to marry. She saw someone she knew she could be friendly with and who would not be a threat to her."[8]

The captain's wife introduced Salter to the attractive, tall, slim, dark-haired Ann Altemus ("old swamp" in German), two years younger than him, in the lounge of the Moana Hotel in Waikiki. In *All That Is* (2013) he describes his courtship and marriage to a woman he calls Vivian Amussen, giving her the first name of T. S. Eliot's crazy wife, her family name echoing Altemus and Amazon. Ann grew up in the Anglo, privileged, inbred, fox-hunting country around Middleburg, Virginia, where, as Scott Fitzgerald wrote of Long Island in *The Great Gatsby*, "people played polo and were rich together." She rode with her father, followed the hounds and confidently jumped the high hedgerows. She had fine skin and the gift of allure. But she turned out to be an unsuitable wife: shallow and superficial, intellectually limited and meager of utterance.

Ann had graduated from Harcum Jr. College, a proper up-market finishing school in Bryn Mawr, Pennsylvania. But she was bold in pursuit of

Salter and took the train up from Washington to New York "to see a man she had met in a bar, whose background she did not know but who seemed to have depth and originality." In their hotel room she kissed him before he could make the first move, asked if he wanted sex, took off her clothes and then her panties. He was wildly excited and too quick to come; he didn't have a condom and feared she might get pregnant.

Ann's WASP father disapproved of Salter and gave him a cool reception. He didn't object to the marriage, but refused to attend the wedding and didn't even give them a present. In *Burning the Days* Salter described her family's hostility to Jews: "there was something about them that drew hatred and made them reviled, their ancient rituals perhaps, their knowledge of money, their respect for justice. It was not their looks that marked them anymore. They were confident, clean-featured." Salter felt that in Ann's world, "the drinking, the big houses, and cars with mud-crusted boots and bags of dog food lying in back, the self-approval and money, all of it seemed inessential, even amusing." Ann had no interest in his writing and he thought, "how unalike the two of them were, how little they had in common."[9] But her family's disapproval was a stimulus.

Salter didn't write about his wife as he rapturously did about his two lost loves. After the wedding they stopped, unromantically, "for the first, uneasy night in some nameless motel on the road to Florida." The captain's consort continued to enthrall him and Salter's wife tolerated her friend. When she was visiting, the pasha "would come back in the evening and find two women, both amiable, smiling, sitting on cushions on the floor and waiting for him." After Salter had returned from Korea, and had left the Air Force in 1957, they lived in several towns on the Hudson River between West Point and Manhattan. In 1958 he bought a half-converted barn in New City. Instead of renting a quiet room nearby to write in, he spent (like ordinary commuters) two hours a day driving thirty miles each way, crossing the George Washington Bridge and into noisy Manhattan, for literary contacts, social life and possibly sexual distractions.

Unable to support himself as a writer, Salter worked in Hollywood for ten years. In 1969, when three of his screenplays were made into movies, he bought a house for $22,000 in the ski resort of Aspen, Colorado, and kept it forever. Eight thousand feet high, the town had a population of 2,500 and spectacular views of the Rocky Mountains. Interviewers reported that "Salter writes in an old cabin, recently renovated by an architect, with white walls, cedar plank ceiling, [high] windows and pools of natural light. 'It feels a little like being on a sailboat.'"[10] He explained his way of writing (when he is able to write) as well as his study: "I do my best to write the whole thing out one way or another, and then go back and put it in a form that I'm not too dissatisfied with to keep. I don't agonize over a sentence in the first draft or even sometimes in subsequent drafts. The thing to do in my case is to get it down."[11] Recalling his struggles he bitterly concluded, "Early rejections are the most painful except for the late ones."[12]

The biographer of the writer Hunter Thompson, the presiding guru of the local hippies, wrote that in those days "Aspen was a fixed-up old mining town. The main street through town was paved, and nothing else. There were no stoplights. There were no condominiums, and no big hotels or lodges other than the Jerome, which had been there for one hundred years. Everybody was living in these old miner cabins or Victorian houses that had been fixed up. . . . In the late sixties and early seventies everyone was doing copious amounts of drugs. In the Jerome, not only would they sell drugs, but they had the mescaline flavor of the week."[13] Salter had escaped from Hollywood, but the invaders, including Jack Nicholson and Bruce Willis, came to Aspen. In the 1990s Aspen also featured Gay Ski Week when men dressed in drag and called themselves the Aspenettes.

By contrast, the highbrow Aspen Institute for Humanistic Studies invited prominent intellectuals. In 1973 Salter wrote that Lionel and Diana Trilling—he was a professor, she was a critic—were rooted in New York and completely out of their element: "They were not physical people. The altitude bothered them. They were thrown in with a lot of people who had never heard of Lionel Trilling and had never heard of Hawthorne and didn't know about 'authenticity.' I could hardly find anything to talk to them about. They were on an extremely elevated level."[14] Two years later Salter was still awed by the sickly Lionel, who had black circles under his eyes, didn't look well and died in 1975. In her lecture at the Aspen Institute, Joyce Carol Oates said *Moby-Dick* is about chasing a great white whale, which prompted the Trillings to walk out in disgust.

In August 1971 Salter met Saul Bellow, who had the same June 10th birthday and was exactly ten years older. Also invited by the Institute, he called Aspen "the Magic Mountain without TB."[15] Salter told the literary editor Robert Phelps that he was impressed by Bellow, who "has been here and gone. We had frequent dinners, all without contact. He tells people he likes me, I don't know what to make of him. He knows so much, that's one thing that puts me off, and also I know my betters." Salter found a remote study for Bellow and was slightly annoyed when his friend rejected it, but was rewarded by the wit of the famous raconteur: "I tried to find a cabin for him for next year, he wanted more isolation and silence. We drove about eight miles into the woods and looked at one by the Roaring Fork near a ruined bridge where the stagecoach once crossed. Of course, there was no electricity. He turned it down because the sound of the diesel generator was too loud (you couldn't hear it inside the house). It was the princess and the pea, but then he told me some very winning stories on the way back."[16]

Bellow's biographer Zachary Leader quoted extensively from Salter's unpublished journal to illuminate his close friendship with Bellow. Salter wrote that the day after Bellow read *A Sport and a Pastime*, "he came to my house, he came to the door. He had my book in his hand and said, 'Well, I just wanted to talk with you.'" Salter was impressed when he read *Henderson the Rain King*: "I just thought, this is simply gorgeous, a wonderful book. So I esteemed him as a writer—no question about it—because of his position and because of what he had written." He also described *Humboldt's Gift* as "compelling, witty, extraordinarily kind. His treatment of his ex-wife Susan Glassman is incredibly fair." Salter saw the book "naked with its flaws, wanderings, ineptness," but thought it had an "excellent, succinct, *honest*, style."[17]

They met every afternoon at the local swimming pool where Bellow swam like a frog. He was reading Dostoyevsky's *The Idiot*, Chekhov's stories and *The Kreutzer Sonata*, and they talked about Tolstoy's troubled marriage. Bellow's stimulating conversation was defined by "strange silences, almost shyness, his eyes looking to the side as he talks." His talk was "lovely, nicely filled with real detail, sexual, sums of money, names of streets, all in the right proportion with an unfailing sense of humor and style."

In *The Art of Fiction* Salter noted that "women were especially on Bellow's mind at the time since his ex-wife—his third—was suing him for more money" after he'd won the Nobel Prize in 1976. "Getting away from women didn't make much sense since women were his means of ignition." The recently divorced Salter advised Bellow, after his third divorce, about difficult women: "You must calm them, I suggest. The way to calm them, I thought, was to go to bed with them. That does calm them. Not for long, he says." Salter sagely adds, "It must be repeated." He also advised caution: "not to marry again unless you are absolutely certain, unless it is impossible not to." He thought Bellow's "concerns, his sorrows, seem so childish. He will find a woman, I assure him. The world is filled with them," the possibilities are endless. Salter admired Bellow but did not envy him as a man: "I felt he was harried. He was beset by problems of guilt and behavior."[18]

Salter and Bellow then decided to look for and buy a time-share house together in Aspen. As they drove through the wilderness of mountains and old mining towns, Salter's old Volkswagen broke down. While Bellow, out of his urban ambience, sat down to read on the side of the road, Salter, a trained engineer, took out a screwdriver, hammer and tape and quickly repaired the machine.

In October 1973 Salter visited Chicago and Bellow, the perfect guide, drove him to favorite places in the city. Bellow had carefully read a draft of *Light Years* (1975), and pointed out its flaws and weaknesses. He thought Salter idealized his characters without recognizing their faults, and that his great theme—like Bellow's—was the cruelty of women and wives. Salter recalled, "[I met] Saul Bellow in the aquarium. We strolled among the eels and drowsing fishes and then drove to his cousin's bakery, all the while he gave me his reactions and thoughts about my book. I found them exact, well-taken. . . . It would be better if shorter, he said. Its repetitiousness causes it to lose power. I am perhaps a little too indulgent toward the people, and the book would be better if the angles were sharper. . . . He said the book was really about the sexual heartlessness of women—their new role—the *vita nova* for women and they are devastating in it."[19]

Salter was disappointed, but admitted "the accuracy of what he tells me, the knowing, direct appraisal." Bellow's "main reservation was that there was no objective voice anywhere *pointing out the meaning of the high esteem these people seemed to have for themselves, the real value of privilege.*" Bellow's criticism helped Salter tremendously.[20] They had a similar Jewish-urban background, and Salter both admired and envied Bellow, who could write several superb novels while Salter struggled to complete his own book. He felt uneasy with and inferior to the erudite and brilliant Bellow.

Bellow sold his time-share, but they remained friends and kept in touch. In a witty postcard of August 12, 2002, Bellow mocked his own fiction by parodying William Wordsworth's "A violet by a mossy stream": "Your birthday card made me happy. Yes, there was a story in the July *Esquire*. A columbine by the out house door. I assume you'll be in Aspen all winter. Shall

we meet in the East one of these days? All best, Saul."[21] On May 20, 1996
he wrote Salter, who was a lively and congenial guest among the wealthy
inhabitants of Long Island, "What a gift you have for filling your days with
good company. When your letters come to be collected, you'll be in a class
with Samuel Pepys," the popular 17th-century diarist.[22]

Bellow had been disillusioned and depressed by the French and postwar
Paris when he lived there in 1948, but Salter loved the city. He first visited the rather grim postwar France in 1950 while serving in the Air Force,
made many other journeys there and lived in Provence from 1967 to 1968.
Throughout his life he was obsessively and indiscriminately enchanted by
France. He told an interviewer: "I like France. I like the French and French
writers. I love the respect for writers and art. I like the bread, the food, the
regard they have for it, the way they eat it, and where. I like the French tem-
perament. I like the aroma of France." To him, Lawrence Durrell's "house
in the south of France seemed to sum up all the glamour of the literary,
foreign, independent life."[23]

Emphasizing the glamor rather than the hardships of travel, Salter
makes readers want to follow him through Europe and Asia and taste all
the pleasures on offer. He continued to glorify France in *Burning the Days*
and his essays in *Don't Save Anything*. In his travel book *There & Then* he
declares, like a besotted lover: "France was unalterably different, ancient,
stylish, beautiful, strange. . . . There was more than a hint of another life,
free of familiar inhibitions, a sacred life. . . . [In provincial France] you are
in a narrow world of passion, venality and style. . . . Paris is so legendary
that we have lived there as long as we can remember."

He never rhapsodizes about the more glamorous Riviera and Provence,
doesn't mention opera, theater, the Louvre and cultural sites. He even emphasizes the superficial aspects: "the thing I most admire in the French is
their concern for the appearance of things—shop windows, *mairies*, avenues, parks, railway stations, houses; it has a soothing effect." Salter's Paris
is mainly an attractive ambience for eating oysters in expensive restaurants.
He admits, "in the deepest sense Paris is closed to the foreigner."[24] His infatuation with France and Frenchness was more a nostalgic evocation of Hemingway's Paris in the 1920s than his own encounter with the unromantic
modern city. (Henry James remarked that Paris had already been ruined in
the 1870s.) Unlike Hemingway, the Francophile Salter did not speak fluent
French: his language was a rickety structure based on words for food and

drink. He did not know any French writers or artists, which enabled him to maintain his romantic fixation and soothing illusions.

Salter's attitude toward France was strongly influenced by the editor and his close friend Robert Phelps, and his favorite book was Phelps' edition of Colette's *Earthly Paradise: An Autobiography* (1966). Phelps did not translate or annotate this book and included one page by another critic in his brief and superficial three-page introduction. Phelps asserted, in a vague and meaningless comment, that Colette's book was her "personal myth, an emblematic image that merges the private life and the public art into a greater whole which then comes to incarnate some perennial tendency, or tactic, in human experience." In a self-serving puff, he equated Colette with the greatest French novelist and absurdly declared, "her place in twentieth-century fiction is very high, comparable among her countrymen only with that of Proust." [25]

Bellow had three children; Salter had four children with his first wife: Allan Conrad born in 1955, Nina Tobe in 1957, the twins James Owen and Claude Cray in 1962. Salter wanted to name James "Agamemnon," but settled for the middle name "Leander," which his son later changed. In 1967 the family sailed to France on the *France*, and all the children got seasick. The family took over an American-owned rented house from Robert Penn Warren and his wife Eleanor Clark in Magagnosc near Grasse, famous for perfume and thirteen miles north of Cannes on the Mediterranean. Warren's biographer Joseph Blotner noted, "La Moutonne was a large, three-story farmhouse on eight acres of untended gardens and terraces. It was built against a steep hillside, minimally modernized but commanding a sweeping view of the sea on three sides and the mountains on the other." [26] Salter worked on the script for *Downhill Racer*. Grasse had schools for the children, who played with and milked the goat Lily.

In letters to Phelps in the early seventies Salter, with gentle irony, described his teenaged daughter Allan as a flower child of the sixties: "She's a vegetarian, a gentle heart, she longs to move into some inarticulate young man's cabin, weave and read a little Hindu mythology." Mentioning a friend and neighbor he said, "My daughter has gone to Rome with Barbara Rosenthal—it's for the year if it works out and she can get into a school." Two years later he tolerantly added, "my daughter has decided to forget school for the present and perhaps longer." He also noted that his daughter Nina had profited from her years in Grasse: "She speaks French now with the ease, and much of the vocabulary of a Paris whore." [27]

A wartime aviator, Salter had always assumed that *his* life was in danger, and was used to dealing with crises and emergencies. The greatest tragedy of his life took place in Aspen on July 20, 1980. Five years after his divorce his eldest daughter, the 25-year-old Allan, died in a once-in-a-million accident when a nail in her shower hit a wire and electrocuted her. The current passed through the water to her body and caused a fatal heart attack. In a classical *apophasis*, Salter says he cannot write about it and then describes it in *Burning the Days* as if he were Orpheus trying to carry Eurydice out of Hell. In the saddest moment of the memoir, Salter writes with emotional and aesthetic control: "It was an electrical accident. It happened in the shower. I found her lying naked on the floor, the water running. I felt for her heartbeat and hurriedly carried her, legs across one arm, limp head along the other, outside. Thinking she had drowned, I gave her artificial respiration desperately, pressing down hard on her chest and then breathing into her mouth time after time. Nothing. I kept at it. An ambulance came. Someone pronounced her dead. I could not believe it." [28] He was not able to protect her or save her; his life-breath had failed to restore her to life.

Allan had been away and was using the shower for the first time. The local electrician, working on the cabin, had mistakenly connected a hot wire to the shower. Salter was writing, with windows open, in the nearby house. He heard her fall and cry out, pulled her away from the source of the electric current and lifted her naked out of the running water. He thought the fall had knocked her unconscious and she had drowned, and made frantic efforts to revive her. He must have felt tremendous guilt for either hiring the electrician or failing to save her, and wondered if this were some kind of punishment. It was a disaster for the younger children, especially Nina, who took it very hard. It also damaged his tenuous relations with his ex-wife, intensified their hostility and broke the last connection between them. They were too devastated to take legal action against the electrician.

When Gerald and Sara Murphy's 15-year-old son unexpectedly died of meningitis in 1935, Hemingway wrote a tender and moving letter that would have consoled Salter: "I can't be brave about it and in all my heart I am sick for you both. Very few people ever really are alive and those that are never die, no matter if they are gone. No one you love is ever dead." [29] In March 1974 Salter lamented, "the older children get, the more difficult and consuming they are." [30] But his surviving, good-looking children have turned out quite well. Nina had her own successful publishing firm in Paris.

James is a builder in Bozeman, Montana. Claude married a sculptor, lived near her mother in Aspen and sells real estate.

Salter's marriage had been troubled for many years. He left Ann soon after their wedding in 1951 for several dangerous years in Korean combat. When he called her from Travis Air Force base in California to say goodbye, she did not give him the emotional response he expected and a gulf opened up between them. She feared he would have many affairs and he thought she might already have a lover: "It was affectionate, but stiff. Perhaps my fault as much as hers. Perhaps she wasn't alone."[31] In 1957, when they had two small girls, he left the Air Force for an uncertain life as a writer.

Salter doesn't name his lovers in his books, but said he used to go to Billy's bar on First Avenue in New York when larking around in larking days.[32] He told me that he had a girlfriend in Paris named Frenia Stoker, who couldn't write but didn't need to. He loved, and perhaps invented, exotic names. Frenia had the same surname as Bram Stoker, the author of *Dracula*. He said his lover in Honolulu in 1948 was Doll Starker, an echo of Stoker and Jonathan Harker, who travels to Transylvania to meet the vampire Count Dracula. Doll liked to call herself Fred C. Dobbs, after the Bogart character in John Huston's *The Treasure of the Sierra Madre* (1948). Salter also wrote me that he'd had an affair with Huston's Italian mistress named Sonia, last name forgotten. Huston was a hard act to follow, and if she were an example of his cast-off women, Huston was a man to be envied.

Salter obsessively and bitterly returned to his failed marriage in essays, novels and interviews. He declared that people get married and then change their minds, and that his marriage had been a painful mistake right from the start. Referring to the ecstatic and then miserable marriage of the Berlands in *Light Years* and thinking of his own, he said their marriage had lasted too long, that there comes a time to be egoistic and put oneself first. He thought spending fifty or sixty years with the same person was too long. When there's nothing left to say in the protracted conversation, the endless dialogue informed by memory, it's all over. An attractive war hero, often alone in Japan, Europe and Hollywood, Salter had plenty of erotic opportunities and often succumbed to temptation. He told Phelps, "these demands for sexual exclusivity, of course, are not only made by women, but they are the most maddening thing on earth."[33] He could say with St. Augustine, "make me chaste, O Lord, but not yet."

In an interview he compared leaving the Air Force to getting divorced "when you really have put everything into it, then you say, 'It's over,' and you're going to have to start again." But he also asserted, "once you get married and have children, even if you get divorced, it's never really over."[34] In *The Art of Fiction* he digressed to note, "I was at odds with my wife, we were barely speaking; and I was thinking back to the days when we'd been happy."[35] He felt, as Dante wrote, "There is no greater sadness than remembering happiness in the midst of misery."

In September 1975, while living in Aspen, he suddenly told Phelps, "My wife and I are parting. There are two children still at home which pains me, but I won't be far off, just a few minutes' walk." In the next paragraph of the same letter he did not feel sad or regretful after finally making the fateful decision, but was exhilarated at the start of the ski season: "I love the fall. It's the time of year I have well-being, hope, even a kind of intoxication."[36] In his last novel, *All That Is* (2013), Salter explained, "I was blinded. I didn't know anything. Of course, neither did she. That was a long time ago. Then we got divorced. We were simply different kinds of people. She had the courage to say it. She wrote me a letter that said: *"We've each been going our own way without a lot in common. I really don't belong in your world and I don't think you belong in mine. I feel like probably I should be back where I fit in. We really weren't meant for each other."*[37]

Their problems were overwhelming and it's surprising that the marriage lasted for twenty-one years. He loved the captain's wife, who proposed Ann as a poor substitute for herself. Ann made the first sexual moves and he performed badly the first time in bed. Their backgrounds clashed. He was New York, military and Jewish; she was Virginia, horse-country and gentile. She was not intellectual and cared nothing for his writing. He left for the war right after their wedding, had affairs in the Air Force and suspected her fidelity. He was pressed for money and they had too many children; the twins might have been accidentally conceived. The marriage lasted too long, the dialogue ended and he had to protect himself and be selfish. She demanded sexual fidelity, he succumbed to temptation. Her farewell letter made clear that they came from different worlds and had nothing in common. Right from the start it had all been a terrible mistake. He forgot or denied that he had ever loved her.

Salter's son Jim explained that the marriage broke up because of his father's sexual behavior. His parents had different social needs and ideas. He didn't think a husband had to be faithful. She had a traditional upbringing, an old-fashioned idea of marriage, and couldn't accept his infidelities. He succumbed to many temptations in the movie business and felt guilty about them.[38]

Salter compensated emotionally for his divorce with editors, male friends and occasional lovers. In *Burning the Days* he confesses that he didn't at first know much about writing: "the making of notes, structure, selection, the most elementary aspects were a mystery to me."[39] So he was unusually dependent on and deferential to his editors for encouragement and advice: Joe Fox at Harper for *The Hunters* and *The Arm of Flesh*, George Plimpton at the *Paris Review* for *A Sport and a Pastime*, Rust Hills at *Esquire*, Ben Sonnenberg at *Grand Street*, Robert Ginna at Little, Brown.

His most important friendship—including affection, admiration and hero-worship—was with the best-selling writer Irwin Shaw. Both men had a lot in common. They were Jewish, grew up in New York—in Manhattan and in Brooklyn—and had changed their names. Salter had a well-educated West Point father and came from a wealthy background. Shaw had a Russian immigrant father who'd also made a lot of money in real estate. Both fathers were ruined and impoverished by the Depression. Salter and Shaw married gentile wives; both were divorced, though Shaw remarried his wife.

Salter devoted an entire chapter to Shaw in *Burning the Days*. Salter had been recalled to the Air Force in 1961 during the Berlin crisis when Russia had demanded the withdrawal of all armed forces in the city. The crisis ended with the partition of the city and the erection by East Germany of the Berlin Wall. Salter was stationed in Chaumont, 170 miles southeast of Paris. They first met for drinks in Paris that year, when Shaw was 48 and Salter was 36. Shaw had already done his best work, "The Girls in Their Summer Dresses" and *The Young Lions*. But Salter was in awe of Shaw, overwhelmed by him; he longed for and was gratified by an invitation to Shaw's elegant lunch. Shaw had the confidence of a leader, and Salter admired him as a father, great force and friend.

As Scott Fitzgerald said of himself in his *Notebooks*, Salter had the arrogance of failure, and feared Shaw's crushing wit. When a writer who had a great early success remarked to him, "Well, I've done it again," Shaw put him down with, "Don't say that, you didn't do it the first time." Salter thought Shaw was a writer of magnitude, sheathed in glamour like a movie star. He said, with considerable exaggeration, that Shaw's best-selling blockbuster *Lucy Crown* was translated into *every* language. Shaw poured out the words and was pleased with his own work. He boasted that he was better than Balzac, though he had all the faults and none of the virtues of the great French novelist. Though Shaw's reputation was inflated, Salter thought he deserved honors that he didn't get. When a short bespectacled man shrewdly told Shaw, "You're a good writer, why are you such a whore?" the huge Shaw answered him with a punch. When Salter heard that Shaw was dying he immediately flew from New York to Switzerland but arrived hours after his death.[40]

But no one now reads "Sailor Off the *Bremen*" and *Sons and Soldiers* is completely forgotten. Salter did not take Shaw as a model of how to write, but of how to live as a writer: "What I admired in him was he seemed to know how to behave. He embodied a lot of things that I respect."[41] But he also cast a cold eye on the impressive ruin, on the enormous difference between "what he did and what he might have done." In a moment of insight Salter "blamed him for the very thing I was afraid of doing myself: living in a world that was not truly mine"—in the Air Force, in his marriage and in Hollywood.[42]

Salter doesn't mention that in January 1965 he asked for the rights of Shaw's story "Then We Were Three" to make the movie that became *Three* in 1969. But the fabulously wealthy Shaw, in a shockingly rude *de haut en bas* reply, refused to give his close, struggling friend the rights to that minor work: "I'm afraid the terms you offer in your letter are rather unrealistic, as what you are asking me to do is to give you an option on the work for one year for $1,000. Even the slightest reflection on your part would prove to you that this is totally unacceptable. If you can work out something more reasonable on this, please let me know. Yours, Irwin." P.S. in the handwriting of his secretary: "That's a perfectly awful letter. I'm sorry that I had to type it. JTA."[43] Despite this insult, Salter wrote a Foreword to a reprint of Shaw's *The Young Lions* in 2000, and compared the battle scenes to Hemingway's description of the Italian retreat from Caporetto in *A Farewell to Arms*.

Despite his hero-worship, Salter was superior to Shaw in every way. Though better looking, he admired Shaw as a ladies' man. His West Point education was more demanding than Shaw's years in Brooklyn College. Salter was an officer who'd fought MIGs in Korea, Shaw was an enlisted man who'd made propaganda films in World War II. Salter, sometimes struggling for money, admired the successful and wealthy Shaw, who lived well and had the best of everything. Shaw turned out formulaic stories for the *New Yorker* and wrote a lot of mediocre work; Salter wrote much less but of a far higher quality. Salter's thin 284 pages of stories are worth far more than Shaw's bloated 756 pages of short fiction. Salter, long unrecognized, had a tremendous creative resurgence in his seventies and eighties; Shaw stopped writing in his last decades. Salter died quickly; Shaw had a long slow death.

I met Shaw on June 2, 1983 in Southampton, Long Island, to interview him for my biography of Hemingway and was not impressed. Drinking heavily, he was a physical wreck. He had a grand house with several servants and, feeling neglected and eager to prolong our talk, invited me to stay for lunch. His oppressive wife, who did not do the cooking, objected and told him that he couldn't have a guest unless he gave her advance notice. So we settled in late morning for a good bottle of Pouilly Fumé and another of Vouvray.

On Long Island, Salter befriended Peter Matthiessen, two years younger, a neighbor and tennis partner. A Yale graduate and cofounder of the *Paris Review*, he was a novelist, naturalist, expert on Africa and Zen priest. When Matthiessen was hard up, Salter offered to lend him money. He wrote a powerful recommendation, his "personal best," when Matthiessen was considered for a National Arts and Humanities Award. By contrast, Matthiessen sent a brief and unenthusiastic recommendation when Salter was nominated for a MacArthur Fellowship. He said more about Salter's need for money than about the excellence of his fiction: "Salter is surely one of our most gifted and dedicated writers, and it is a pity that financial considerations have turned so much of his energy toward screenplays and travel writing rather than to more lasting work." [44] Salter did not get the Fellowship.

In the early 1990s Salter wrote Matthiessen that Richard Pearce, Yale graduate and director of Salter's film *Threshold*, wanted to know if he was interested in writing a script for *Killing Mr. Watson*, which Pearce was going to direct. Matthiessen's novel, published in 1990 and based on a real story, was about a fugitive from justice who fled to the Florida Everglades and was mysteriously murdered. Salter wrote that it was being made for Turner television. The pay would not be wonderful. They were going to make the movie for what a leading actor earns on a theatrical film, so the writer will get what the second grip usually gets. But he thought he was done with all that work. "The waste, the waste," he said, echoing Joseph Conrad's "The horror! The horror!" [45]

On March 27, 2014, during Matthiessen's agonizing treatment for leukemia, Salter wrote an emotional and compassionate letter that tried to comfort his friend. He said that Peter was the most courageous man, and he had always admired him. He could not imagine what they've put him through during these past months, but he knew it was terrible and now it was even more difficult. He wanted Peter to know, because they never said these things, how much he esteemed and loved him.[46] Matthiessen died nine days later.

Though Salter had many friends, he did not dedicate most of his books. His parents, his first wife and his children, Robert Phelps and Robert Ginna, Bellow, Shaw and Matthiessen were not honored. He dedicated *The Hunters* and *Cassada* to Air Force pilots; *Burning the Days* to Kay, his second wife, and to William Benton, the editor of *Gods of Tin*; *Last Night* to George Plimpton; *All That Is* again to Kay.

Salter met Kay Eldredge—born in 1948, 23 years younger than Salter and only seven years older than his daughter Allan—when she worked on his television interview in 1971. She grew up in Denver, which he called "clean and juiceless as Queens, streets empty at six at night, dying people and cars."[47] She graduated from the University of Colorado and earned a Master's degree in journalism from Columbia. Unlike Ann, she adored and rejuvenated him, wanted to be a writer and to learn from him. The war hero could say, like Othello, "she loved me for the dangers I had passed, and I loved her that she did pity them." Salter kept his house in Aspen and found a new place for a new life in Bridgehampton. They "lived in painter's country, far out on Long Island, the flatness of the land, the incredible light."[48] He said it was about $400,000 from the ocean, remote enough to write but close enough to go into Manhattan.

In *Don't Save Anything* he observed, "there are few things more gratifying than being in the company of someone younger who admires you for your knowledge and is avid to have it shared."[49] Kay wrote scripts for Denver television, and a one-man play, *Yr. Obedient Servant*, performed in London in 1987; coauthored *Life Is Meals* with Salter; and wrote a preface to the posthumous *Don't Save Anything*. They lived together, right after his divorce, from 1976 until his death in 2015. She had a miscarriage; but later risked a trip to Paris when she was hugely pregnant. Their son Theo Shaw was born in 1985, 30 years after his first child, and named after Irwin who'd died the previous year. Following what he said was the birth ritual of French kings, Salter wet the baby's lips with a drop of Château Latour, an expensive red Bordeaux, so he would remember the taste all his life and love the grape. Salter finally married Kay, possibly to protect his estate, in Paris in 1998.

Though Salter was a close friend of Matthiessen, he did not ask him to read his unpublished work and, like Bellow, give an expert opinion: "I was afraid of his disapproval and too proud for advice."[50] But he let Kay read his manuscripts and said, "she's a writer and I value her opinion highly. It causes temporary hatred, but it goes away."[51] By contrast to their working together on *Life Is Meals*, Kay—like Salter commuting to Manhattan in the 1960s—often traveled to the city and used their *pied-à-terre* on West 45th Street to write and see plays. In an autobiographical story published five months after his death, she said she liked sex and was good at it, and indiscreetly added, "It's been years without it now—a long time before he died."[52]

Salter felt "you cannot teach someone to write any more than you can teach them to be interesting."[53] But he was often invited to lecture on writing, and taught courses at Alabama, Vassar, Iowa, Houston, Williams, Duke and Virginia. At Iowa he taught novels written in youth, though three of the nine writers he chose were in their mid-thirties and one in his late forties when they wrote these novels. The courses showed his taste in English, Russian and American fiction: Dickens' *The Pickwick Papers*, Gogol's *Dead Souls*, Melville's *Typee*, Tolstoy's *Childhood, Boyhood, Youth*, Kipling's *Plain Tales from the Hills*, Dreiser's *Sister Carrie*, Joyce's *A Portrait of the Artist as a Young Man*, Flannery O'Connor's *Wise Blood* and John O'Hara's *Appointment in Samarra*.

In April 2006 the writer-professor Reynolds Price invited Salter to Duke for a week. He taught five classes and gave two public readings, was treated royally and earned a lavish $20,000. At Virginia in the fall semester of 2014, Salter added several new books to those he had taught at Iowa: Isaac Babel's stories, Chekhov's "The Steppe," Maupassant's "Ball of Fat," Maugham's *Liza of Lambeth* and Frank O'Connor's "Guests of the Nation." He did not include Colette, and had a surprising admiration for the middlebrow O'Hara at both Iowa and Virginia. His revered masters were Gogol, Tolstoy, Kipling and Babel—the ones that really stand up.[54]

No student has written about Salter in the classroom, but he gave his own account of his teaching. His three public lectures at Virginia were published by the university press as *The Art of Fiction* (2016). Salter says writing is difficult and a few pages later contradicts himself by stating that writing is simple. He also confuses his student audience by remarking that you can't teach writing, then proceeds to give three brief, anecdotal talks on writers.

He praises the intellectual brilliance and ingenuity of Nabokov and Bellow, whom he didn't teach. He makes pointless references to Phelps' darling, the obscure French diarist Paul Léautaud. He emphasizes the need to visualize the scenes, and admires the opening of Hemingway's *A Farewell to Arms*, which makes style sexy and inspires "a kind of warning, an electricity running through you, the same as sex." He refers to his helpful editors, and mentions his own works without explaining how he wrote them: *The Hunters, Light Years, Burning the Days* and, without naming it, his story "Am Strand von Tanger." He concludes, "I'm listening to the words as I write them, to groups of words. I like to go again and again over their sound to lead me on to the next sentences. Sometimes I write down a little on what I intend to write, a few words to show the way." [55]

Salter was inundated with awards during the last thirty years of his life. He gave his acceptance speech for the Hadada Award on April 12, 2011. Hadada, enclosing Dada, was an African ibis, George Plimpton's favorite bird, and the black prize statue looks like a ruffled version of the Maltese Falcon. Salter said, "The *Paris Review* was always the pinnacle. You were thrilled if you were published there, and George Plimpton himself was practically mythical. He was a legendary figure." He recalled that *A Sport and a Pastime* was turned down by several editors, but Plimpton gave it a tremendous lift by publishing it in his imprint with Doubleday in 1967. Salter graciously concluded by saying, "This is my Stockholm." [56]

In 1993 Salter had hoped to go to Paris for a couple of years but, as the only child of an aged mother, was unwilling to put too great a distance between them. His mother died at the age of 96 in October 2000. She'd still been living more or less on her own, fell down and that was it. A phone call from New York summoned him back from Paris (he couldn't resist a short trip), and in a moving letter to Robert Ginna he described his response to her death. He hadn't wept for his mother, the last act was too long. He did sit with her at Campbell's, the funeral home where his father had been forty years earlier. He was alone with her for about half an hour and a wave of memory and emotions swept over him. He never became what she dreamed of. His real life was invisible to her, he was a kind of ne'er-do-well. Still, the journey had been so long. She disapproved of his first marriage and wasn't very keen on the second.[57] Kay, like Ann, was gentile; and his mother may have thought Kay was too young for him.

Apart from Salter's torrent of publications, his last decade was marked by travels and injuries. He took trips to Naxos and Mycenae in Greece; Madrid and Andalusia in Spain; St. Croix in the Virgin Islands. He went to St. Petersburg, Russia, in July 2007; to Upper Egypt in February 2010; to San Miguel de Allende in Mexico for several months in the winters of 2014 and 2015. He had back surgery in April 2013 with fair to good results; and in September 2013, at the age of 87, he broke his leg skiing. On his 90th birthday Peter Matthiessen's widow, Maria, gave a dinner party at her house in Sag Harbor, Long Island, for two dozen friends. He told his son James, "Don't come, it's no big deal." But it was a surprise party and he was delighted. Nine days later he died suddenly while exercising in a gym in Sag Harbor. At his memorial service in the Unitarian Church in Manhattan on July 28, 2016, the eloquent speakers included the novelist Richard Ford, Salter's Knopf editor Robin Dresser, Maria Matthiessen and his son Theo. The American and English obituaries were reverential, and he was universally recognized as a great writer.

TWO

FIGHTER PILOT AND NOVELIST

I

After graduating from prep school in New York, Salter planned to attend Stanford or MIT, but his father, who'd been first in his class at West Point in 1919, insisted that he enter the military academy. In essays in *Don't Save Anything* (2017) and *West Point* (2001), Salter recalled the extreme pressure placed on the new cadets, who were turned into obedient robots: "the first two months of cadet life is a period of intense physical and psychological stress and a rite of passage. There is shouting, heat, formation running, too much to be done in too little time, a nightmare of anxiety come to life."[1] "The rules to obey, procedures to follow, faces, names, responses—it comes in unending waves. This is the Honor Code. This is parade rest. That is Trophy Point. These are called trousers. Gradually, eating, running, dressing, drilling, you become part of it."[2] He also noted his intense intellectual training as a civil engineer: "West Point is unquestionably demanding. It requires more courses than Harvard—mathematics, physics, chemistry, history, economics, law."[3]

Edgar Allan Poe was the only major writer to enter West Point—though he went unwillingly and was soon expelled. The painter James McNeill Whistler also went there. After he failed his chemistry exam and was expelled, he declared, "if silicon had been a gas, I would have been a major general." (Hemingway echoed this in *Across the River and Into the Trees* when his embittered hero declares, "If I had lied as others lied, I would have been a three-star general.")[4] In 1945, during the war, Salter graduated early and was an impressive 49th in his class of 852: in the top 6 percent. The ceremony required full dress uniforms, and included regimental marching, brass bands, patriotic songs and hats thrown into the air (some not recovered). General Omar Bradley handed Salter his degree.

Still in his teens, Salter went to flight school immediately after graduation. While in training, he took off from a base in Newburgh, New York, about 40 minutes from West Point, got lost in a midnight fog and ran out of fuel. On Victory-over-Europe Day, May 8, 1945, he crashed his plane into a house in Great Barrington, near Pittsfield, in western Massachusetts. The two-story, black-shuttered, white house had steps leading up to the pillared front porch. A photo in the local newspaper (reproduced in *Gods of Tin*) shows the nose of the plane buried deep in the ground and the wingless fuselage, displaying the Air Force star, tilted at a 45-degree angle into the kitchen.

Salter's exciting account places the reader in the cockpit as the helpless plane seems to be torn apart by a giant monster. He emphasizes the swift passage of time with "moment" (twice) and "instant," and delays the impact as his light illuminates the stage of the disaster: "A moment later, at the far end, more trees. They were higher than I was, and without speed to climb I banked to get through them. I heard foliage slap the wings as just ahead, shielded, a second rank of trees rose up. There was no time to do anything. Something large struck a wing. It tore away. The plane careened up. It stood poised for an endless moment, one landing light flooding a house into which an instant later it crashed."[5] The Graham family, celebrating the return of their son from a prisoner-of-war camp and still awake late at night, were unharmed. Alerted by the increasingly loud noise, they had gone outside to see the plane. Out of gas, it did not explode or catch fire, and Salter luckily survived with a broken tooth.

In his last novel *All That Is*, Salter wrote there was no time to reflect in a crash and he acted instinctively: "I don't think you have to be afraid of crashing. It's quick. It's all over in a second. It's what happens before that, when you know you're about to crash."[6] In his essay "Lost in the Air," on the disappearance of the Malaysian Airlines flight in 2014, he recalled his feelings during his own catastrophe: "I've known the anxiety of being completely lost, flying, at night. It can be extreme. You're traveling at close to five hundred miles an hour, and every minute that goes by takes you further into being lost unless you get help from ground radar somewhere or somehow figure out the error. If you maintain altitude, is it a safe altitude or should you climb? How long have you been lost?"[7] The crash almost destroyed his military career. He had to fly transport planes for the next six years in Hawaii, the Philippines, Okinawa and Japan.

Salter had not foreseen the Korean War, but it was great good fortune for him and revived his career. He noted, "it was operatic, saying goodbye to your family, and carrying the fear that you wouldn't come back—never confessing it," and he needed luck as well as ability.[8] In October 1949 Mao had defeated the Nationalists, and it was essential to stop the communists from conquering Korea. The American pilots, flying daily missions to the silent and muddy Yalu River, half an hour away on the Chinese border, dominated the sky and intercepted MIGs on their way back to their bases in the north. They supported the ground troops, protected photo-reconnaissance planes and escorted fighter-bombers en route to their targets: bridges, railroads and the North Korean Officers' Academy.

Max Hastings' *The Korean War* gives the essential history of this aerial combat. He shows what Salter was up against (and leaves out of his novels) and is worth quoting in full: "The air war over Korea gave birth to a new concept—combat between jet aircraft—and revived all the traditional arguments about air support for ground operations. . . . The first MIG-15 jet fighters appeared in the skies over Korea in November 1950, sending a shockwave through the West. Some fifty MIGs, flown by Chinese and Soviet pilots, were initially deployed. The Communists revealed their advance to the frontiers of technology. Within six months there were 445 MIGs operating from the political sanctuary of air bases beyond the Yalu."

The Americans retaliated with their latest plane: "Then came the Sabre, the F-86 which became the principal weapon of the U.N. The first wing was deployed in December 1950, reinforced by a second a year later. Sabres were in chronically short supply to maintain U.S. air strength worldwide, and there were never more than 150 deployed in Korea, against the much greater number of MIGs. But the West, and the United States in particular, has always produced pilots of exceptional quality. From beginning to end, they proved able to maintain air superiority over North Korea, despite all that the Communist air forces could throw against them."[9]

The *Encyclopedia Britannica* gives a precise account of Salter's F-86 Sabre, a fiercely armed, single-seat, single-engine jet fighter with swept-back wings: "Though inferior to the MIG-15 in weight of armament, turn radius and maximum speed at combat altitude, the F-86 quickly established supremacy over its Soviet adversary, in part because of its superior handling characteristics. It had a top speed of almost 700 miles per hour in level flight and a maximum service altitude approaching 50,000 feet. Besides missiles, its armament included .50-inch machine guns or 20-millimetre cannon in the fuselage and rockets or bombs under the wings." Salter noted, with ironic understatement, their vulnerability: "jet engines are simple in design and extremely reliable although subject to damage if anything reasonably substantial comes into the intake."[10]

Three squadrons of Sabres were based on the huge airfield at Kimpo, a few miles west of Seoul and 200 miles from the Yalu River. It was a dreary place, surrounded by rice paddies, with little to do when off duty except drink, play cards or visit the nurses' compound. Hastings describes the plan of attack: "They took off one by one at three-second intervals, then climbed into formation, spreading out across the sky to cross the bomb line above the confronting armies. They patrolled at around 40,000 feet, or as low as 20,000 if they were escorting fighter bombers. At those heights the Communist flak presented a negligible threat. A careful pilot could extend his patrol endurance to as much as ninety minutes. Senior American airmen became exasperated by the manner in which the military took the Sabres for granted and thought they could conduct ground operations without the slightest threat of enemy interference in the air."[11]

In *War on the Rocks*, the military historian Mike Benitez explains the combat formations: "The planes formed a 'fighter wall' that was meant to cover more area while preventing the enemy from getting around the fighter and attacking the aircraft performing air-to-ground missions." The pilots would take great risks to stay in the air until their planes lost power and they had to make a forced landing: "Hoping to have more time to find and kill a MIG, F-86 pilots became accustomed to flying past the minimum fuel needed to safely make it home. To get home, they would climb to altitude, shut off the engine and glide back to base and then restart the engine once close to the field for landing. When the engine failed to restart, pilots performing dead-stick landings were celebrated rather than reprimanded for their dangerous behavior."[12]

Hastings writes that Air Force commanders incessantly protested "about the political limitations on their operations around and beyond the Yalu.... It was a source of constant irritation to the aircrew that they could approach targets close to the Chinese border only on an east-west course to avoid the risk of infringing Chinese air space." America did not want to provoke China into a full-scale invasion of Korea. "Despite the strict rules against crossing into enemy territory, many Sabres in hot pursuit flew forty miles into China. . . . The optimum range was around 200 yards, and to gain an accurate shot a man might be flying as slow as 200 knots. The MIGs' cannon could be deadlier killers than the six .5-caliber machine guns in the nose of the Sabres. . . . But they remained unchallenged as the outstanding aircraft of the Korean War. Of 900 enemy aircraft claimed destroyed by the U.S.A.F. pilots, 792 were MIG-15s destroyed by Sabres."

The bail-out choice and rate of survival depended on the weather: "If an American aircraft was hit, in winter the pilot would try to bail out overland, for the sea was too cold to offer much prospect of survival. A pilot who ditched in the winter months could last three minutes in the water before reaching his dinghy, and seven minutes thereafter before his saturated fly-ing suit froze. But in summer he would always opt for the sea if he could, where the huge and efficient rescue organization might reach him, even under the Communist guns."

Hastings concludes: "'Operation Strangle' was a systematic attempt to cut off the Communist ground forces in the front line from their supplies by the sustained exercise of air power. Pyongyang and other major cities had been flattened, hundreds of thousands of North Korean civilians killed. Yet there remained no evidence of the predicted collapse in the Communist will to win."[13] The war settled into bloody stalemate along the original line of demarcation until the armistice in July 1953. The peace treaty has never been signed.

The fighter pilots had courage, nerves of steel, quick minds, mastery of powerful machines, ability to face any emergency and to survive if shot down in North Korea. Lifted as if on angels' wings, they each flew two or even three missions a day. They were constantly torn between the impulse to shoot down MIGs before completing their tour and the desire to survive 100 sorties and go safely home. When pursued by the Sabre jets the MIGs, named for the designers Mikoyan and Gurevich, fled across the Yalu River and into China.

On March 14, 1952 Salter lost control of his plane and almost fell out of the sky. He took a series of emergency moves, managed to solve the problem and made a safe but scary landing. He described the desperate maneuvers in *Gods of Tin*: "Almost got killed. The stick froze. Used both hands and couldn't move it. I knew I was going to die. . . . Still going down, at no more than

300 feet. No effect. I punched off my fuel tanks, pulled up the landing gear, flaps, speed brakes. Suddenly the stick gave, began to move. I declared an emergency and made a long, straight-in, landed with gear down, flaps, and stick absolutely frozen. When I parked my hands were still shaking."

Two days later Salter just missed a kill when he unintentionally hit the flap lever and reduced speed at the crucial moment: "Just as I was about to fire, he began pulling away. I fired as he went, discovered my flaps were down. Terrible, stupid feeling. Missed a big chance. Knew there would be others but not like this. I could have had a kill, everything."

On April 30, Salter almost wrecked another plane: "A lurch as a tire blew. The end of the runway was coming up. I suddenly thought I'll just turn at the end, onto the taxiway, but as I did, almost relieved, the right landing gear folded under the strain. The wing hit and buckled." Fortunately, he was saved by an indulgent colonel: "They wrote it off as a combat loss, the low fuel, a damaged plane just behind me, plus the high idle of the engine. I wasn't charged with an accident," which would have damaged his career as well as the plane.

Three months later, on July 4 and near the end of his tour, Salter got his first kill. He describes the enemy plane in cinematic terms, its slow descent that ends with an image of death in a pastoral setting: "I get a solid burst into his fuselage. Intense, bright flashes. We watch the MIG spin down from 30,000 feet, very leisurely, until finally in some wooded hills its shadow rises to meet it and it hits and explodes."[14]

Though 2,714 planes were lost (at $178,000 each) in the Korean War and 1,180 Air Force personnel were killed, Salter risked his life 100 times and was never shot down. In an interview he casually observed, "I never saw a dead body. In fact, the whole time I was in the air force lots of people got killed, heaps of them, but the only thing I ever saw was a helmet with some brains in it."[15] He may have been thinking of Randall Jarrell's poem "The Death of the Ball Turret Gunner," in which "washed out" means both failed out of flight school and flushed out of a plane: "When I died they washed me out of the turret with a hose."

In letters to me in 2006–07, Salter vividly recalled the war. He mentioned carrier-based fighters on the Pacific island during the fierce battle in August 1942. He woke up with fingers feeling swollen, the way pilots did on Guadalcanal. He sometimes thought of the men they called Pappy, who were 27 or 28 years old. After reading about coal miners in D. H. Lawrence's

Sons and Lovers, he said their faces reminded him of fighter pilots' faces, not black coal dust but the marks of the oxygen mask and a dirtiness of the bare skin that was not covered by it.

He did not want postwar reconciliations with his old Russian enemies, who inflated their number of kills and claimed false victories. He told me that he refused to meet any Russian MIG pilots. American fighter pilots were boring enough and he'd read articles about the MIG pilots based on recently released material. "They were full of shit." He knew how many of our pilots were shot down. Like Walt Whitman he could say, "I am the man, I suffered, I was there."

In his autobiography *Burning the Days,* Salter recalled an illuminating moment that would lead to a radical change in his life: "At many parties I was among the loudest and most disheveled—the drinking and singing, the shouting of nicknames. One night a classmate I knew only slightly, standing beside me, asked in a quiet voice, 'What are you doing this for?' 'Doing what?' 'This isn't really the person you are.'"[16] This remark made him wonder why he was living so far from the people who interested him, and he longed for a different and superior existence.

In July 1957 Salter left his promising career as a lieutenant colonel (destined perhaps to become a high-flying general) after twelve years in the Air Force. He had two small daughters, born in 1955 and 1957, and discussed this crucial decision—the most important in his life—with his wife, whom he'd married in 1951. She didn't fully understand what was involved, but did not try to change his mind. He thought there would be some strong reaction in the Pentagon when he resigned his commission, that "someone would shake his head with regret at the departure of a regular officer, but there was none."[17]

Salter loved the Air Force and left it reluctantly. Nothing in the future could equal the excitement of fighting the Russian MIGs. In his *Paris Review* interview he declared, "Everything that meant anything to me . . . everything I had done in life up to that point, I was throwing away. I felt absolutely miserable—miserable and a failure."[18] He failed because he left the service before realizing his own full potential and compensating for his father's mediocre military career. He was "abandoning my capital, my country. My life. My destiny."[19] It felt precisely like divorce, but even more emotionally searing than the eventual breakup of his marriage. Asked if he regretted leaving the Air Force, he replied: "Yes. Every day. For a long time, every day. I wasn't really a writer yet.[20] . . . As a pilot you're nobility from the very beginning. As a writer you aren't anybody until you become somebody."[21]

Though destined for the high ranks of the Air Force, he threw away the security, power and prestige of the service, and had to start his chosen career as a writer at the bottom. He had done things in combat that no other writer could do, but that didn't count in the literary world. He admired serious authors but they rarely noticed him. Failure in war was death; failure in fiction was merely disgrace. But writing freed him from the rigid discipline and philistine values of military life, and the Korean War gave him his first and most valuable subject.

Many modern writers—including Joseph Conrad, Isak Dinesen, Rebecca West, Nathanael West, Irwin Shaw and John le Carré—had adopted pseudonyms. Unwilling to join the prevailing Jewish literary trio of Saul Bellow, Bernard Malamud and Philip Roth, he changed his name from Horowitz to Salter to mark the transition from combatant to civilian life, from destruction to creation. He explained why he chose Salter (Wilfred Owen's middle name) and said, "I had a whole list of last names that used the same A and E vowels as James. I wanted two syllables for the rhythm. James Salter had a faintly biblical sound to it, so I impulsively took it."[22]

There are several other explanations. The French expression *reculer pour mieux sauter* contains the near homonym *sauter*, which suggests a strategic withdrawal from military duties and drawing back to make a better jump into writing. He also thought of Psalter, the volume containing the Book of Psalms, though (unlike P. G. Wodehouse's Psmith) he dropped the "P." "Salty" is tough and aggressive, salt is essential to life and a metaphor for faith. In Matthew 5:13 Christ tells His followers: "Ye are the salt of the earth: but if the salt have lost his savour, wherewith shall it be salted?"

II

The title of Salter's *The Hunters* (1956) suggests how fighter-pilots were driven by man's primitive urge to kill animals. The explorer and traveler Wilfred Thesiger, who dispatched hundreds of wild beasts in Africa, expressed the major theme in Salter's book: "most men have an inborn desire to hunt and kill. . . . The sound of the bullet striking home and a clean kill, with the animal dropping where it stood, was the climax of the hunt."[23] In the novel, the pilots ruthlessly compete for glory while hunting the enemy.

Salter has always been praised for the style that enhances his theme. The first paragraph of *The Hunters*, which sets the contemplative scene before the fighting takes place, echoes the superb last paragraph of James Joyce's story "The Dead" (1914):

> [Snow] was falling on every part of the dark central plain, on the treeless hills, falling softly upon the Bog of Allen and, farther westward, softly falling into the dark mutinous Shannon waves.[24]

Salter varies this with similar participles and geographical direction, winter weather, rough water and distant places from cities to streets, all getting smaller and more sharply focused. He rhythmically repeats Joyce's "on . . . on . . . upon" with "over . . . over . . . over":

> A winter night, black and frozen, was moving over Japan, over the choppy waters to the east, over the rugged floating islands, all the cities and towns, the small houses, the bitter streets.[25]

Salter was also inspired by the Bible, Stephen Crane, Joseph Conrad and two classic books by daring aviators. He echoes Ecclesiastes 3:2: "A time to be born, and a time to die" in "A way to live and a way to die," and recalls Philippians 4:7: "The peace of God which passeth all understanding" in "that gift of silence that surpasses speech." Crane's *The Red Badge of Courage* refers anonymously to "the youth" and "the tall soldier"; Salter refers to "the lean man." In *Heart of Darkness* Conrad mournfully declares, "We live, as we dream—alone." Salter reaffirms the fighter pilot's solitude with "You lived and died alone."

Most important, *The Hunters* and its successors *Arm of Flesh* (1961) and *Cassada* (2000) were influenced by Antoine de Saint-Exupéry's *Wind, Sand and Stars* (1939). The French flyer portrayed in lyrical prose the conflict between duty and freedom, the pilot's excitement and danger, knowledge and exploits. Salter's accounts of aerial combat were influenced by Saint-Exupéry's description of threatening atmospheric turbulence: "As every pilot knows, there are secret little quiverings that foretell your real storm. No rolling, no pitching. No swing to speak of. The flight continues horizontal and rectilinear. But you have felt a warning drum on the wings of your plane, little intermittent rappings scarcely audible and infinitely brief, little cracklings from time to time as if there were traces of gunpowder in the air. And then everything round me blew up"—as if he had been hit by an enemy plane.[26]

Salter was also influenced by Richard Hillary's *The Last Enemy* (1942) which, like Saint-Exupéry's book, was both romantic and stoical. Hillary compared single air fights to the jousting of medieval knights: "it was individual combat between two people, in which one either kills or is killed. It's exciting, it's individual and it's disinterested. . . . To be up there alone, confident that the machine would answer the least touch on the controls, to be isolated, entirely responsible for one's own return to earth—this was every man's ambition."[27] He described being horribly burned when trapped in his airplane cockpit in September 1940 and the series of ghastly operations on his charred face. After his book was published and praised, and while he was still an invalid with stiff fingers, the reckless Hillary was allowed to fly again. In January 1943 he lost control of his plane and died (like Saint-Exupéry) in a crash. In "An Irish Airman Foresees His Death," W. B. Yeats imagines the pilot reflecting on his past and future, weighing his life and death, seeking glory and submitting to his predestined fate:

A lonely impulse of delight
Drove to this tumult in the clouds;
I balanced all, brought all to mind,
The years to come seemed waste of breath,
A waste of breath the years behind
In balance with this life, this death.[28]

Salter's Preface to the revised 1997 edition of *The Hunters* describes the opposing planes and their mode of combat: "The Russian planes were swept-wing MIG-15s, well-designed and armed with rapid-firing cannon. There were many of them, flying out of airfields in China that for political reasons were never bombed. The F-86 could not fly quite as high—to about 45,000 as against 48,000 feet—and its performance at high altitude was not as good, but lower down it was slightly superior." Their battles, nine miles high, were fought at close quarters and lasted for only a few moments: "Fighters don't fight, as Saint-Exupéry wrote, they murder, and the act was usually done by getting on the tail of the other plane, as close as possible, even point blank, and firing." The planes had ammunition for "only eleven seconds of firing, but a burst of two or three seconds in a fight could be quite sufficient." During the Korean War there were only thirty-nine American air aces with five or more kills.

Salter gives his characters unusual, allusive names. Cleve Connéll suggests clever, meat cleaver and cleavage from his comrades. His rhyming-name adversary Ed Pell—hell and pell-mell—sows confusion and disorder. Colonel Imil is egoistic and military. Colonel Moncavage is an odd mix of monk and savage. "Casey Jones," with his distinctive black-striped MIG, is the most dangerous Russian ace. He is nicknamed after an American locomotive driver, known for his speed, who was killed in a train collision in 1900 and became the subject of a popular ballad.

Like Salter, Captain Connell has a military father who did not see action in World War I. He also had been to a military academy and was on the elite aerobatics team that practiced in North Africa. One of 100 American pilots on the Korean air base, he's the leader, alone in his cockpit, with a protective wingman. On his ecstatic first kill, "He fired again. A solid burst in the fuselage. The silver lit up in great flashes of white. . . . Suddenly he saw something fly off the MIG. It was the canopy, tumbling away. A second later the compact bundle of a man shot out." His enemy is dead, his plane destroyed.

The self-seeking ace-pilot Lieutenant Pell, like the mountain climbers in Salter's novel *Solo Faces*, is a fanatic with a visceral compulsion to risk his life. Pell was based on the handsome Lieutenant James Low (1925–2017), born the same year as Salter in Sausalito, California. Low served in the Navy in 1943–46 and in Korea in 1951–52. He soon got a reputation for leaving his formation to pursue MIGs. He had six kills in two months early in 1952 and three more kills in October. He flew Phantom jets in Vietnam, was shot down and captured in December 1967 and was released in July 1968. Brave but unreliable, Low was not promoted beyond the rank of major.

Aged twenty-five and six years younger than Cleve, Pell endangers the other pilots by refusing to follow orders. He abandons his leader DeLeo in order to get his kill, and shoots down a spectacular seven enemy planes. The Russians seem willing to fight only when he's in the air. Pell's antithesis is Abbott, who'd shot down six German planes in World War II, but has lost his nerve, is burnt-out and afraid of everything. He claims mechanical failures and aborts his missions, but after landing states that his plane is all right. Quite useless in combat, he's soon transferred to a harmless staff job.

As in his skiing film *Downhill Racer*, Salter contrasts the scenes of talk and waiting with those of silence and action. Halfway through *The Hunters*,

Cleve and DeLeo go on leave to Japan for nonstop drinking and plentiful sex. In the bath, "The water was clear and scalding. Everything was washed away. He floated in a dream of disconnected languor. The girl was in it, too, with her flawless skin and sturdy body sensuously distorted beneath the surface. . . . She had abandoned the virtuous reserve of upstairs. She caressed him beneath the water. She presented herself to him deliberately."

By contrast, and only six years after Hiroshima, Cleve visits the famous artist Miyata, who'd lost decades of work in the 1944 incendiary raid on Tokyo. Instead of feeling devastated and suicidal, he surprises Cleve by explaining, "It was finally like being born again, I decided. I started life for a second time." Aldous Huxley had the same response in 1961 when his house in Los Angeles burned down. He lost everything but said, "It does make one feel extraordinarily *clean*." [29] Cleve also has an unexpected idyll with Miyata's teenaged, English-speaking daughter, who makes him dream of a more peaceful and creative life. A great contrast to the high-priced prostitutes in the bath, "She had that gift of silence that surpasses speech, the elusiveness that allows itself to be endowed" with meaning.

After this peaceful interlude, the novel speeds to its fatal conclusion. While in Japan, Cleve had missed a big battle. The Americans lost three planes, but shot down eight MIGs. In the next fight he gives up his precious kill to help Pell, who's in trouble but gets another MIG. Pell repays Cleve by insulting him and shouting, "You're always off somewhere when there's a fight, in Tokyo or someplace." Cleve punches him and friends break up their fight. Cleve then rightly declares that the egomaniacal Pell did not protect his leader, Lieutenant Daughters, and was responsible for his death.

Cleve tells Colonel Imil that Pell must be grounded. Protecting his star fighter, Imil insults Cleve by repeating Pell's unjust charge: "You never seem to be on the missions that get into fights." When Cleve argues with him, Imil compounds the insult by exclaiming, "I don't have to be told by some captain how to run my wing or who to ground. . . . You listen to me. I don't listen to you." He also humiliates Cleve by placing Pell in the lead firing position, and putting Cleve in the last plane to take off. His wingman Hunter laments, "What a place to be on a mission like this. It'll all be over by the time we get there."

The Joint Chiefs in Washington finally give permission to bomb enemy territory, and in the last big battle the fighters attack the heavily defended Chinese hydroelectric dam on the Yalu River. Sounding like a football coach giving a pep talk, Imil tells his men: "our job is to get those fighters-bombers in and out, and that's what we're going to do." (Their assaults destroyed 90 percent of the power in North Korea.) This time, Cleve kills his prime target, Casey Jones. "He fired again. . . . Solid strikes along the fuselage. There was a burst of white flame and a sudden flood of smoke. The MIG pulled up sharply, climbing. It was slipping away from him, but as it did, he laced it with hits. Finally, trailing a curtain of fire, it rolled over on one wing and started down"—like a wounded animal.

Cleve runs out of fuel in the hunt and, in the greatest scene in the novel, must glide back to the base without power: "He knew he could make it. The last thousand feet, coming easily down the path of the final approach he knew so well, was overwhelmingly fulfilling. Dead sticking it in, he landed a little long but smoothly in the stillness. He felt an emptying relief as his wheels touched the runway. He cracked the canopy open. The fair wind came in to cool him." He was safe.

Cleve then discovers that his wingman Hunter has not returned. The movie camera in Cleve's plane got stuck and didn't work, and without film or Hunter he has no way to confirm his kill. In a supreme, ironic sacrifice, another form of heroism, Cleve confirms that his own kill was made by the dead Hunter, who's posthumously honored. Just after Pell gets his last kill, he sees—in the final victory over his adversary—the destruction of Cleve's plane: "One wing had been shot off it. He had watched it going down in a long, shallow trajectory near the river, spinning over and over all the way."

The fierce rivalry between Pell and Cleve has ended with a series of sacrificial and tragic events. Pell abandons DeLeo to get another kill, then fails to protect Daughters who is shot down. Cleve gives up a kill to help Pell, and credits Hunter with his own unconfirmed destruction of Casey Jones. Salter's lyrical account of Cleve's death concludes the novel with a repetition of the predatory title: "They had overcome him in the end, tenaciously, scissoring past him, taking him down. Their heavy shots had splashed into him, and they had followed all the way, firing as they did, with that contagious passion peculiar to hunters."

When *The Hunters* was published under a pseudonym and Salter was still in the Air Force, he liked to hear the pilots trying to guess the identity of the author. He sold the film rights, got $52,000 after commissions and asked Paramount to pay $13,000 in four yearly installments. There had been several classic flying movies from *Wings* (1929) to *Twelve O'Clock*

High (1949). In the best of these films, *Dawn Patrol* (1938), the squadron commander, played by Basil Rathbone, emphasizes the danger of death and daring personal courage: "It's a slaughter house, that's what it is, and I'm the executioner. You send men up to die. They don't argue or revolt. They just say 'Righto' and go out and do it. Listen to them pretending that death doesn't mean anything, trying to live just for the minute—the hour, pretending they don't care if they go up tomorrow and never come back"—before they've even had a chance to live.

The film of *The Hunters* (1958), starring Robert Mitchum and Robert Wagner, and lifelessly directed by the actor Dick Powell, was disappointing. It portrayed fighter pilots in Korea—one of them reckless, the other frightened—dedicated to shooting down Russian MIGs and becoming an admired ace. But it had little to do with Salter's novel. The dialogue is flat and filled with clichés. Mitchum's love triangle with a pilot's wife lacks passion. The Swedish actress May Britt is a stuffed dummy. Robert Wagner is unconvincing as the swaggering hero. The Japanese background is fake. The screenwriter Wendell Mayes defensively said, "While we used the title, what I wrote was from start to finish an original screenplay. There wasn't anything else to do, because the novel could not be adapted. It was too internal. They do make mistakes in Hollywood in buying material."[30] Salter declared, despite the highly praised aerial footage, "the movie was a disaster: it did not even have the right aircraft."[31]

Salter used his precious flying experience throughout his career. In a series of rescue missions, he revised *The Hunters* in 1997, completely rewrote *The Arm of Flesh* as *Cassada*, and added his unpublished journal to passages from these two novels in *Gods of Tin* (2004). Salter told Ginna that the Air Force had just ordered 2,300 copies of *Gods* to give to all the officers. Two phrases from *Cassada*, "the friezes of heaven" and "the aura of instruments," would have been more poetic and suggestive than the dull and misleading title, which leads to two dead ends: "casada" means "married" in Spanish, though Cassada is a bachelor. The pilots in the novel ask Cassada if he's related to the controversial and charismatic Air Force lieutenant-general Pete Quesada (1904–1993), but since there's no connection the question seems pointless. Salter, mentioning Quesada, wrote me that he served under him at the end of his career, and that he had the Kennedy élan. In *Across the River*, Hemingway praises the general whose planes protected the soldiers: "for ground support give me a man like Pete Quesada. There is a man who will boot them in."[32] Another real-life model for Cassada was George Cortada: "He was from Puerto Rico, small, excitable and supremely confident. Not everyone shared his opinion of his ability—his flight commander was certain he would kill himself."[33]

Salter brilliantly sketches the settings in *Cassada*. One base is near Munich in Bavaria. In the spring the Isar River "was racing under the bridges, rushing pale green, bringing the city to life." Trier, in the Rhineland, "was an old town of dark red brick, a town dating back to Roman times. There were remains of a large amphitheater, some Roman baths, and vineyards up in the hills." The pilots fly over Rome, crossing the Mediterranean and the islands, to Libya on the North African shore. Libya also has Roman ruins at Leptis Magna and Sabratha, and evokes memories of Montgomery's Eighth Army fighting Rommel's Afrika Korps in their sun-baked armor.

The style of the novel is both spare and poetic. Plane wheels "fold birdlike beneath as they rose from the runway." Pilots make a "tight, fetal turn." The needles on the instrument panel "suddenly, ominous as serpents, raised their heads." The top of the canopy "becomes white with little stars of frost, as exact as if they had been etched in the glass." Speeding at eight miles a minute, the plane "seemed incredibly heavy against the sky." "Spending the last of his fuel is like diving, with lungs bursting and no breath left." The pilot is "connected to the plane ahead by a single filament finer than silk and no stronger." He is also inextricably joined to his own plane: "the ship seemed firm under his hand, obedient to the last moment. . . . The sound of the engine, closer to him than breathing, is more familiar than his heart." The power surges through the pilot's body and propels him to the kill.

Salter said the rewritten and improved *Cassada* "is meant to be the book the other might have been."[34] Pilots in *The Hunters* fought MIGs. Pilots in *Cassada* don't fight wars and merely fly "as if they were returning from an actual mission." Stationed in 1955 in West Germany, which was divided like Korea into democratic and communist sectors, the pilots have to remain alert in case the cold war with Russia suddenly turns hot. In the east, "the enemy lay, sometimes inactive, sometimes flying themselves on a parallel course waiting for the slightest violation of the invisible border, or lurking below the contrails, unseen." Some daredevils, lured by dense rain and fog, take risks to achieve fame in peacetime. Meanwhile, the pilots try to pick up women in German bars, compete with other squadrons to log the highest number of flying hours, and fly to the clear blue skies of Libya, in light planes with no external drop tanks, for gunnery competitions. Salter explains the complex procedure: "The first tow ship took off early at eight, climbing at a steep angle with the target, a long, fabric panel, trailing behind. A few minutes later the first flight of firing ships, trim as hornets, followed."

The main characters in the novel are the squadron commander Major Dunning, who "had led fighter-bomber missions in Korea, rail cuts far to the north." Captain Isbell, his operations officer, "experienced, confident, untiring, He had seven hundred hours in the airplane and two thousand besides, a hundred and sixty of them flying against the Russians and Chinese in Korea, fierce fights along the Yalu." The third hero is Grace, "a pilot everyone respected, who had flown in combat and been shot at, who'd been hit by ground fire and brought the airplane back somehow, a man you could count on."

Robert Cassada, the new pilot, is unfairly compared to these heroic men, and subjected to a series of disastrous tests and public humiliations. He's mocked when he doesn't drink manly coffee and told, "Maybe you need some tea." After following his instructor's crazy rolls, the novice vomits onto his flying suit and into the plane, and emerges in front of everyone smelling of puke. Dunning, echoing "throw up," rubs it in by stating, "I like to see my pilots eat a good breakfast before they go up. But in your case I don't know." Cassada carelessly opens a bottle of champagne and soaks the dress of Dunning's wife, who calls him an idiot. He throws his shoe and breaks a light bulb, and angers his commander by getting glass all over the barracks floor. He boasts about his hits before the gunnery scores are calculated, fails his test, can't pay his debt when he loses a bet and is told, "let's face it. You're not about to hit anything."

Cassada seems to be a complete failure. He admits, "I don't know what I'm doing here," and desperately wants a senior officer to have confidence in him. But Wicked Wickenden, his commander, persecutes him as Claggart persecutes Melville's Billy Budd, and calls him a fool. Cassada asks for a transfer to another flight, but Isbell refuses to make the change. When Wickenden predicts that Cassada (like the real George Cortada) is going to kill himself, Isbell orders him to take care of Cassada. Instead, Wickenden continues to undermine his fragile confidence.

The novel is written in brief, unconnected and deliberately unfinished episodes, leaving readers eager for more sharp dialogue and longer descriptions of the two unhappy marriages and an adulterous affair. Before leaving on a trip Isbell summons his wife to bed, but she fails to respond:

"It's getting late," Isbell finally remarked.

"I guess so."

"How much longer are you going to read?"

"Oh, a little while," she said.

"Come on."

"What do you mean ?"

"You know what I mean. You can read all the time I'm gone. You've got five weeks." . . .

She simply didn't feel that way. It was a cold act, there was something selfish at the heart of it. Why was it that important? It wasn't; just some kind of male itch.

Cassada also has bad luck with women. He meets an attractive, responsive, English-speaking German who seems to like him. Suddenly, the married Isbell appears, embraces her and claims her. Cassada pleads, "This is not on duty. . . . You can't pull rank." Isbell tells him, "I don't have to," and takes her away.

Dunning's wife aggressively taunts her husband about wearing his well-earned medals and about the priest's sanctimonious memorial service for a dead flyer:

"Why doesn't somebody clue them in?" she says.

"Fine. Why don't you?"

"I'm hardly the one to do that."

"You can say that again," Dunning says.

"You bastard."

"Watch yourself. Enough's enough, you know what I mean?"

Isbell and Dunning can command men but cannot control their wives, who resemble the bitchy, castrating, adulterous Margot Macomber in Hemingway's African story: "They are the hardest in the world; the hardest, the cruelest, the most predatory and the most attractive and their men have softened or gone to pieces nervously as they have hardened." [35]

In Trier the pilot Godchaux (hot god) accidentally meets the bored and dissatisfied Mrs. Dunning, who's attracted to him and seductively asks, "Where'd you get your eyelashes?" They have lunch and drink white Moselle wine as she flirts with and flatters him, and confesses that she's had an abortion. They find a comfortable hotel near the Roman gate, have sex and meet again later on. Still bitter after his divorce, Salter adds a personal note: "You choose your wife yourself, that was the thing, but of course you didn't know what you were choosing. He had known after the first week, the deadness that lay between them, but he believed it might be overcome."

In the climactic episode, Isbell loses radio contact during a storm and Cassada, low on fuel, misses three landings. But he makes a last attempt to find Isbell, his tormentor and nemesis, and guide him into the base. Isbell manages to eject: "with a shock, a hunching jolt, he is gone, through the darkness, into the black air." A search party finds Cassada's plane debris and his dead body. Despite all his failures, he has sacrificed himself, like Cleve in *The Hunters*, and achieved moral greatness. Pleased with his prophecy and indifferent to Cassada's death, Wickenden praises himself: "He was right all along. He feels only the satisfaction of it, of having been redeemed." By contrast, Isbell ruefully concludes: "Now that it is too late he is certain that Cassada bore something unique, something they had missed, the sum of their destinies."

Salter announces the theme in his Foreword. Like the best *matadors*, the pilots who take the greatest risks achieve the greatest fame: "the best along with the worst pilots got killed." In a fine passage at the beginning, Isbell sees a deer—hunted, wounded and pursued—which foreshadows Cassada's fate and resembles William Cowper's "A Stricken Deer" (1785):

> I was a stricken deer, that left the herd
> Long since; with many an arrow deep infixed
> My panting side was charged, when I withdrew
> To seek a tranquil death in distant shades.[36]

Salter describes the fatal wound as the animal feels it: "The *hirsch* was stepping slim-legged through [the woods], unsteadily but with a matchless grace, stopping every couple of yards while his stomach filled with blood. . . . The *hirsch*, feeling for the one time ever a terrible dizziness, begins to move faster, in panic. The twigs are exploding."

Going through Cassada's possessions after his death, the pilots find an unidentified vow or prophecy that links him to the dying deer. The passage

slightly misquotes Revelation 19:17 and describes the cannibalistic destruction of armies and of Cassada himself: *"Come gather for the great supper of
God, to eat the flesh of kings, the flesh of captains, the flesh of mighty men."*

In 2006, forty-four years after his last flight, Salter was pleased to be
invited by a general, who admired *The Hunters*, to fly an F-16. It was ten
times more powerful than the F-86 and took off from an air base in Fort
Worth. Salter hadn't lost his touch—like swimming, he never forgot—and
did turns, loops and other tricks. The young airmen were impressed that the
81-year-old relic had known the astronauts and the famous fighter pilots,
and told him to keep the flying suit.

THREE

THE FATE
OF PLEASURE

A Sport and a Pastime and *Light Years*

I

In his early masterpieces, *A Sport and a Pastime* (1967) and *Light Years* (1975), Salter writes with sophistication, style and skill about the search for an ideal way of life. The earlier novel explores a purely sensual existence; the second portrays a life centered on family and work. In both novels his characters try to fix their privileged moments in time, hold on to precious pleasures and keep the best of them forever, but inevitably suffer the ennui, decay and loss that make such a quest impossible.

Sport was written with the coldly erotic eye of Henry Miller and the precise observation of Henry James. "My ambition," Salter noted in his introduction to the Modern Library edition of 1995, "was to write a book every page of which could seduce, a book that was flagrant but assured, of imperishable images and obsessions."[1] In a subtle, cunning fashion, Salter creates a narrator, a romantic way of life and a purely physical liaison—and then undercuts all three.

The title of *A Sport and a Pastime* is ambiguous and allusive. Baseball is the American sport and pastime, but the novel is not about sport—though some of the sexual encounters are quite athletic. "Sport" means "sex" in Ben Jonson's "To Celia": "Come, my Celia, let us prove, / While we can, the sports of love," and in John Milton's "Lycidas": "To sport with Amaryllis in the shade." The epigraph from the Koran supplies and explains the ironic title: "Remember that the life of this world is but a sport and a pastime." It echoes Ecclesiastes 1:2, "Vanity of vanities; all is vanity," and suggests that sex, like other mundane amusements, must not be taken seriously. Worldly things are essentially ephemeral; only the spiritual life has permanent value. Sex in the novel is not merely a pastime, but a full-time occupation and obsession.

The novel is set in Autun, a provincial town 185 miles southeast of Paris. Named after the Emperor Augustus, it has Roman walls, gates, temple and amphitheater, and a Romanesque cathedral. The population in 1962, when the novel takes place, was 15,300. The young American hero Phillip Dean drives his lover Anne-Marie around France in a rare and luxurious Delage D-6, a symbolic extension of himself. The convertible has a tilted windshield, long sleek hood, wavy front fenders, high chrome grill, soft leather seats and huge yellow headlights, and can speed up to 100 miles an hour.

In the opening scene the unnamed thirty-four-year-old narrator leaves Paris by train for Autun (just as, toward the end of the novel, his friend Phillip Dean leaves Autun by train for Paris) and observes the French landscape. His fellow passengers "are staring, as drained, as quiet as invalids . . . waiting to see the doctor." As they travel through the countryside, he sees "people on the *quai* standing still as cows." "Still," meaning quiet, immobile and continuous, is a key word in the novel. As Dean and Anne-Marie drive around the countryside in his Delage, they pass through tranquil villages where men pedal slowly on bicycles. As the narrator penetrates into *La France profonde*, "the details of a whole new world are being opened to him." He plans "to walk these village roads, follow these brilliant streams" and encounter "those small epiphanies of which the town is comprised."[2]

The year is 1962 and Algeria, in its final agony after eight years of armed rebellion, is about to declare independence. The novel is not set in colorful Provence or on the Riviera, but in a dull town in central France, during a full year that moves from early autumn to late summer. The narrator observes, with his keen photographer's eye, precise details of French life that might escape him in a glamorous, sun-drenched resort. In the silent back alleys of Autun the "cats know the way." The bodies of oysters, in their deep irregular shells, lie "pure and glistening." A woman's "false teeth, white as buttons, belonged to her husband." Beneath the hood of the racing car lies a complex "distillery of ducts and hoses." In a menacing slaughterhouse "the skin magically parts, the warm insides pour out . . . while their eyes were still fluttering, the huge, eloquent eyes of young calves." Salter can be amusing about the provinces. In boring Bagnoles in Normandy, where the lovers can't find a decent hotel, Anne-Marie, consulting the guidebook, irrelevantly remarks that "there's a hospital for the insane." When they seek diversion in a movie theater, "there are a few people already inside—that's something, at least."

Salter's style features closely observed details, sentence fragments, suddenly shifting viewpoints and striking similes. A character unrolls exotic "names like a splendid carpet"; fields are "as pale as bread"; girls have "ankles white as soap"; an Algerian's body is as "bony as feet"; Anne-Marie's shower-soaped breasts "glisten like seals"; and old church walls have "cracks wide enough for birds to nest in." Literary allusions, sometimes in iambic pentameter, illuminate the meaning and enhance the interest of the novel. "Great lovers lie in hell, the poet says": Dante placed the adulterous lovers Paolo and Francesca in the *Inferno.* "A grave crisis of the soul": "dark night of the soul" in St. John of the Cross. "A dome of stained fragments": "a dome of many coloured glass" in Shelley's "Adonais." "Burst upwards on creaking wings": "Downward to darkness, on extended wings" in Wallace Stevens' "Sunday Morning." "Life is measured out in mean proportions": "I have measured out my life with coffee spoons" in T. S. Eliot's "The Love Song of J. Alfred Prufrock."

Salter's style, widely admired by other writers, combines Hemingway's short, incisive yet metaphorical and richly suggestive sentences with Fitzgerald's chromatic and impressionistic nuances of mood and feeling. Ford Madox Ford's description of Hemingway's prose also applies to Salter's: his "words strike you, each one, as if they were pebbles fetched fresh from a brook. They live and shine, each in its place. So one of his pages has the effect of a brook-bottom into which you look down through the flowing water. The words form a tessellation, each in order beside the other."[3]

Like Hemingway, Salter refrains from moral judgments and coercive interpretation in his fiction, and his objectivity can both tease and seduce the reader. Hemingway nicknamed his oldest son "Bumby"; Cristina Wheatland is called "Bummy." "We stop at the Foy. It's nice to enter, to be inside. The wood of the floor feels good" echoes Hemingway's simple yet sensual style. Streets "curving down like a woman" recalls Brett Ashley "built with curves like the hull of a racing yacht" in *The Sun Also Rises.* Phillip Dean is named after a character in Fitzgerald's "May Day." In Salter's portrayal of fashionable Parisian society "one meets a certain kind of people, people with money and taste," like the characters in Fitzgerald's novels. Salter writes of the glamorous Cristina, "this is the extent of her power, this intimation of sexual wealth. [Her husband] Billy always talks about how beautiful she is. It's almost as if he's protesting: but she *is* beautiful. And she is. Their life is arranged to exhibit this beauty," just as Fitzgerald's life displayed his beautiful, sexy and seductive wife Zelda.

Love, carnal and fated, fills these pages. In *Don't Save Anything*, Salter quotes Gabriele D'Annunzio's *The Triumph of Death*: "There is but one intoxication on earth, the certainty, the absolute unshakable certainty of possessing another human being."[4] In his introduction to Donald Sultan's art catalog, Salter takes this a step further and connects sex to art: "Rilke once wrote that the artistic experience was very close to that of sex in its ecstasy and pain, a different form of the same longing and joy."[5]

The novel focuses on Phillip Dean, aged twenty-four, a schoolboy hero and Yale dropout from a wealthy family, whose mother drowned herself when he was six years old. His French girlfriend, Anne-Marie Costallat, born in Nancy in October 1944, was deserted by her father and is now aged eighteen. An ordinary provincial typist, who surrenders to and is utterly possessed by Dean, she has an insatiable appetite and loves sex even more than he does. She refuses him nothing, offers everything and devotes herself to pleasing him. She gives him attention and affection, moans and cries out with pleasure, and fulfills all his desires. She vainly hopes to marry him and go to America; he plans ways to escape from her. Their sexual encounters are seen from his point of view, though she sometimes flatters him by exclaiming that it's the best sex she's ever had.

Dean believes, with William Blake, that the female body is holy, that "the nakedness of woman is the work of God," and obsessively explores her body as if it were the sacred precincts of a forbidden city. "Her nakedness compels him," the narrator writes. "No matter what he does, he cannot commit it to memory. It seems to be given to him in a series of revelations that are like flashes." As they have sex while the symbolic hands of the town clock jerk in unison to new positions and the freight cars clash against each other in a nearby terminus, she realizes the fragility of their affair and says she wants to hurt him, to force him to remember her. Later, as they engage in more extreme acts, she's afraid that he will hurt her physically. Though he's madly attracted to Anne-Marie, Dean keeps his relationship with her separate from the rest of his life. He is ashamed of her cheap clothes and won't introduce her to his family and friends.

Two other, thinly sketched couples contrast with these sexually consumed lovers. The unnamed narrator longs for women and is frustrated by them. He courts a divorcée, Claude Piquet (named for a tricky card game), and is shocked to discover that "she's been in love with someone else the whole time" and plans to marry that man. The narrator is also attracted to Alix, a sophisticated American girl. He says that she's "completely unaffected by my presence. At first, in fact, she ignored me, but her attention is worse" when she interrogates him. He takes her home at dawn, hoping to seduce her, but she dismisses him with a tired smile and disappears behind a locked door. His own existence "suddenly seems nothing" and he surrenders his identity. He begins to live a vicarious life, and becomes the mirror image and alter ego of his intimate friend Phillip Dean.

Billy and Cristina Wheatland, the affluent and apparently happy Parisian expatriates, have lent the narrator their house in Autun. They also have sexual problems. Cristina casually remarks that they slept together before they married but rarely have had sex since then. After they quarrel she expresses her anger by insulting him with an obscene gesture. He responds, with dialogue that recalls Hemingway's Francis Macomber: "'Keep it up,' he warns. 'What's that, sweetheart?' she asks. 'You're going to get it,' he says." Dean enjoys the infinite pleasures of love; the narrator longs for sexual connection; the Wheatlands' sexual life is almost extinguished.

In his *Paris Review* interview Salter said that he had to choose between three ways of narrating the story: "This book would have been difficult to write in the first person—that is to say if it were Dean's voice. It would be quite interesting written from Anne-Marie's voice, but I wouldn't know how to attempt that. . . . Having a third person describe it, somebody who is really not an important part of the book but merely serving as an intermediary between the book and the reader, was perhaps the thing that was going to make it possible."[6] Even Marcel Proust, struggling to make his first-person narrator aware of events he hadn't witnessed, has him peer through windows, overhear conversations and discover letters. Salter's narrator presents a similar technical problem. He seems to be modeled on Nick Carraway in *The Great Gatsby*, a servant, not an actor, in life. He carefully observes but does not directly participate in the main action. He cannot know, much less vividly recall, all these intimate details, even if Dean had rather caddishly told him—and there is a great deal that could never be told.

The ever-so-subtle narrator constantly casts doubt on his own powers of observation. He frequently warns the reader that he is unreliable, that he is not telling the truth about Dean and cannot possibly know about what he describes in such vivid detail. He says the lovers "vanish into hotel rooms—one cannot follow. There are long silences filled with things I ache to know." He characterizes himself as "a double agent, first on one side—that of truth—and then on the other." He specifically says, "I am not telling the truth about Dean, I am inventing him. . . . I have invented it all." Dean enjoys the sex life that the narrator lacks; and the narrator, carried away by the sexual encounters he describes, takes more pleasure in recounting Dean's sex life than in having his own.

When asked about this discrepancy, Salter evaded it by saying: "The question of the novel's narrator is often posed, and how much of what he relates is invented or imagined. Very little, in my opinion. I am impressed by his powers of observation and tend to trust his description of scenes."[7] The narrator is both a first-person character who expresses his own feelings and describes his relations with Dean, as well as a third-person authorial voice who vividly relates the sexual encounters between Dean and Anne-Marie.

Despite his denials, the problematical narrator has many ways of finding out about his hedonistic hero. He talks to Anne-Marie and reads the entries in Dean's secret notebook. Dean tells him about his enviable love life; and the narrator watches, discovers, remembers, dreams and fantasizes about what William Blake called "the lineaments of gratified desire." He also imagines what happened and invents new erotic scenes. "To believe," he affirms, "is to make real." It's even possible that Dean's story never really occurred, that the narrator made it all up for his own delight and amusement. Like Leopold Bloom in Joyce's *Ulysses*, he gets more pleasure from imagining than from participating in Dean's melancholy eroticism. Bloom excites himself by fantasizing about Blazes Boylan, his wife's lover, who urges him to "apply your eye to the keyhole and play with yourself while I just go through her a few times."[8]

Alluding to D. H. Lawrence's *Lady Chatterley's Lover* in his introduction to *Sport*, Salter recalls the "once-infamous book in a locked case in the library which I opened with almost trembling hands."[9] Lawrence wrote that his anal sex scenes in *Lady Chatterley's Lover* wanted to recapture "the warm blood-sex that establishes the living and revitalizing connection between man and woman."[10] In that novel, Connie and Mellors reached "the core of the physical jungle, the last and deepest recess of organic shame.

The phallus alone could explore it. And how he had pressed in on her! . . .
Now suddenly there it was, and a man was sharing her last and final nakedness, she was shameless."[11] In Lawrence's ideological novel, sex banishes
the inhibitions between the aristocratic lady and the earthy gamekeeper
on her husband's estate. Like Lawrence, Salter wants to break down all
physical barriers and reach the final transcendent moment. Though Dean
and Anne-Marie come from different social classes and countries, they have
few inhibitions to break down. With no social context, they pursue sex for
purely sensual reasons.

Salter describes with ingenious virtuosity the theme and variations of
more than forty carnal duets. Their love-making is lyrical: "His hands float
on to her. The sum of small acts begins to unite them, the pure calculus of
love. He feels himself enter. Her last breath—it is almost a sigh—leaves her.
Her white throat appears." They also engage in Lawrencean anal intercourse:
"Suddenly he feels her flesh give way and then, deliciously, the muscle close
about him. He tries not to press against anything, to go in straight. She is
breathing quickly, and as he withdraws on the first stroke he can feel her
jerking with pleasure. It's the short movements she likes. She thrusts herself
against him. Moans escape her. Dean comes—it's like a hemorrhage—and
afterwards she clasps him tightly." Finally, they are "united by a bloodstream
which carries the same sensations," by a physical rather than emotional
connection. The purity, the essence, the highest good in life (Salter suggests)
is sensation, being acutely and pleasurably alive in the moment—all the
rest is dross. The novel, he explained in the *Paris Review* interview, was
intended "more or less as a guide to what life might be, an ideal."[12]

In an important passage, Dean tells his younger sister, Amy, about his
attempt to achieve a superior kind of existence, a Rilkean egoistic and aesthetic pursuit of perfection:

> "Life is composed of certain basic elements," he says. "Of course,
> there are lots of impurities, that's what's misleading. . . . In all of us
> there's the desire to find those elements somehow. . . . Why can't each
> of us, properly directed, build a life, I mean a happy life?"
> "If you could achieve that [she says], you'd have everything."
> "And without it you have . . ." he shrugs, "a life. . . . Just like every-
> body's," he says. "I don't want that."

But Dean's ideal life, built on a rather refined and precious form of pleasure, assumes inherited wealth and precludes work.

Salter's lovers are undeveloped characters, portrayed in a deliberately external way. Far apart culturally and intellectually, they have a limited knowledge of each other's language. They have little or nothing to say to each other and tend to speak "only of banal things: shoes, her work at the office." There's no sign of the brilliant mind Dean displayed before leaving Yale. He was an exceptional student and found the work too easy. The pair exist entirely in a sensual world, and spend most of their time driving around the countryside (once, all the way across France from Nancy to Brittany), eating in restaurants and having sex in hotels.

Though the lovers achieve sexual ecstasy and have their transcendent moments, they're beset by practical problems. They're alone most of the time, cut off from the real world and absorbed in each other's bodies as they explore her country. Living without company in isolated places, they inevitably begin to get on each other's nerves. There's an emptiness at the center of the lovers' transient existence and the basic elements do not, finally, burn out the impurities and cohere into a happy life. The unreality of it all is emphasized by their narcissistic habit, especially toward the end of the affair, of looking into mirrors. They pose naked before a mirror; their eyes meet for a moment in the mirror; the narrator can no longer identify with Dean's personal power and without it his friend "is empty, a body without breath, as ordinary as my own reflection in the mirror." When Shakespeare's Prince Hal grows tired of pleasures, he remarks that "If all the year were playing holidays, / To sport would be as tedious as to work." Dean's persistent pleasures eventually become a burden.

Anne-Marie is careless about taking precautions and Dean worries that she will get pregnant. She wants to marry him, but he doesn't want to marry her: "All of Anne-Marie's joy proceeds from the hope that they are only beginning. . . . For Dean, every hour is piercing because it is closer to the end." He invests too much meaning in erotic experience, which eventually bores him. Ostensibly romantic, the book also has shocking anti-romantic elements that clash with its lyrical sensitivity. They suggest that the lovers are, in the midst of happiness, indeed approaching the end. As the female body ceases to be holy the lovers are consumed by the sex that nourished them.

Dean constantly undermines his strong attraction to Anne-Marie and prevents himself from falling in love with her by emphasizing her physical defects. He notes that her face is pretty but cheap. She has pimples on her back, odorous hairy armpits, discolored and neglected teeth, pale nipples and different-size breasts. He mentions her rotten breath three times, but doesn't remedy this problem with mouthwash. The narrator even notes Anne-Marie's farts and vomit, menstrual blood and tampon string; Dean's sperm in her mouth and dripping out of her parts. All this suggests that her animal self, for all its exquisite attraction, has become repellent.

Lord Byron—echoing the words: so, roving, night, heart, loving, moon, wears and still (a favorite Salter word)—brilliantly expressed the limits of sensual satisfaction in one of the saddest and most poignant lyrics in our language:

> So we'll go no more a-roving
>   So late into the night,
> Though the heart be still as loving,
>   And the moon be still as bright.
>
> For the sword outwears its sheath,
>   And the soul wears out the breast,
> And the heart must pause to breathe,
>   And Love itself have rest.
>
> Though the night was made for loving,
>   And the day returns too soon,
> Yet we'll go no more a-roving
>   By the light of the moon.[13]

Byron acknowledges that though the heart is "still as loving," as we grow older we need "rest." The passionate love that once kept us awake all night cannot last forever, though the memory of it endures. Byron accepts the inevitable decline of passion; Dean and Anne-Marie struggle to sustain it.

Always short of cash, Dean has sold his plane ticket home. After his wealthy father, who disapproves of his idle life, refuses to give him money, he borrows his return plane fare from his sister, from her friend and from the narrator. He and the narrator then seal their friendship with a symbolic communion: "He offers me some segments of orange. We sit eating them. The cool juice fills our mouths. The seeds are heavy and very white."

Nevertheless, Dean falsely claims that he owns the Delage and offers it as collateral for the narrator's loan. He also falsely swears on the head of his mother that he will return to Anne-Marie, who doesn't know that his mother has killed herself. So Dean gives up the sexual life that the narrator can't have and the Wheatlands don't have.

The narrator wants the reader "to be as resigned" as he is. Yet when Dean tells him that he's abandoning Anne-Marie and returning to America, the narrator becomes upset, angry and filled with a "delicate hatred." Dean has destroyed his voyeuristic world. The narrator hints throughout the novel that Dean is a doomed Byronic hero and sees in him "the eyes of Lorca, someone who is to be taken out of life and destroyed, we will never find the reason."

In a superb passage that recalls Salter's flying days, he describes Dean's escape as his plane takes off from Orly airport. He conveys the airborne sensation by appealing to the reader's sense of sight, sound, movement, speed and height: "All the perfect machinery of flight is beginning its motion. The huge, graceful wings are quivering. The engines roar. And now, at the last moment, it begins to move, slowly, with a majesty I cannot bear, for a long time seeming to go no faster until suddenly it is racing past, raising, clearing the ground. It climbs steeply. The soft darkness of the summer sky receives it," as Anne-Marie had once sexually received Dean.

Dean's fatal motor accident in America is foreshadowed when he sees the result of a car crash while driving the Delage: skid marks, broken glass, car turned upside down, motorbike crushed beneath it, corpse laid out on the side of the road, dark splash of blood. But it's possible to find the reasons for Dean's death. Unfit for ordinary married life, "just like everybody's," he is fated to live intensely, burn out and die young. The lovely Delage (not really his), which helped define his romantic existence and which he left behind in France, is personified as "a very old man fading, it has already begun to crumble before one's eyes." Dean has dominated Anne-Marie, but succumbs to his death wish as his passive French lover survives. She mourns his death, but fears she too would have died in the crash if she'd returned with him to America. The narrator had once wondered if, "by any rearrangement of events, by any accident could she, I dream, become mine?" But after Dean's death, when this dream comes true, he can't drive his car or inherit his girl and doesn't want to possess Anne-Marie, whose reality cannot possibly match his idealized conception of her.

Salter had a deep distrust of marriage, and in 1967 was miserably entangled with his wife and heading for a divorce. He gave the unhappy Anne-Marie his wife's name, and gave Claude Piquet the first name of his daughter. Dean had practiced and rejected a kind of stultifying, meaningless married life on the beach at Brittany. But Anne-Marie's talk was banal, they had little to say and he was terribly bored: "Years of marriage. After breakfast it is quite a long time until lunch, and after lunch, the whole afternoon." This bourgeois life would merely degrade and destroy the exquisitely erotic existence he had once enjoyed with Anne-Marie. The novel ends with an ironic passage—echoing *Hamlet*'s "consummation devoutly to be wished"—about the kind of constrained existence that Dean had feared: "She is married. I suppose there are children. They walk together on Sundays, the sunlight falling upon them. They visit friends, talk, go home in the evening, deep in the life we all agree is so greatly to be desired." *Calme*, perhaps, but sadly lacking the Baudelairean *luxe et volupté*. Like Lolita at the end of Vladimir Nabokov's novel, the nymphomaniac renounces her sensational sexual past and settles down to a dull domestic life.

A Sport and a Pastime was rejected by four or five publishers, who said the sexual scenes were too repetitive and the characters too unsympathetic. It was finally published by George Plimpton's Paris Review editions, but sold less than 3,000 copies. Considered shocking in 1967, it was well received in the 1985 North Point reprint (sixth printing in 1997), in the 1995 Modern Library edition, and in the 2006 Farrar, Straus and Giroux and Picador editions with an introduction by the novelist Reynolds Price. In my inscribed copy of the novel Salter wrote that *Sport* "Represents, I think, the *apogee*." It is now treasured as a literary masterpiece for its lyrical style, French setting, insight into sexual obsession and bitter ending.

II

Salter described his rather chaotic method of composing *Light Years* (1975) in letters to Robert Phelps: "I have character notes written on menus, *Paris Tribunes*, envelopes. . . . I already have one [outline] twenty pages long plus fifty pages of microscopic notes, but now I must combine and improve these."[14] Farrar, Straus rejected the novel; Viking and Holt-Rinehart did not offer a decent advance when he showed them the first 185 pages. When Joe Fox at Random House accepted the book Salter hoped to get $15,000. This once seemed to be a lot of money, but after agents' fees and taxes it would only stretch for six or seven months. In the end he got only a disappointing advance of $7,500. Graham Greene, whom Salter had interviewed for *People* magazine in 1975, arranged for his firm Bodley Head to publish the English edition in 1976.

Like Phillip Dean in *A Sport and a Pastime*, Nedra Berland in *Light Years* (1975) is afraid of leading an "ordinary life." The later novel—denser in texture, deeper in characterization, more ambitious in themes—portrays the ideal existence that is never quite realized in *Sport*. Salter said it was "probably my best book." He listed 36 possible titles for the novel, and his excellent choice suggests vast astronomical distances in trillions of miles as well as careless, light-hearted years illuminated by radiance.[15] The different kinds of light convey the shifting moods of the novel. Salter is constantly aware of the changing seasons, the variable weather; of the clash of light and dark, of day and night, sea and sky, city and country, theaters and fires. Viri and Nedra, the husband and wife, have carefully created a harmonious setting for their domestic happiness. But as Viri observes, "There are really two kinds of life. There is the one people believe you are living, and there is the other." When they deliberately destroy it their lives become dark and chaotic, and the glorious glow is finally extinguished.

The characters' names are exotic and suggestive. Berland, the surname of Viri and Nedra, hints at European capitals, Berlin and Berne. The sharp-tongued architect Viri echoes virile and *vara*, the picador's spear in a bull-fight. In real life, the critic Rosa *Berland* wrote an article on Remedios *Varo*, a Mexican surrealist artist. The actual models for the Berlands were Salter's friends and neighbors, the Rosenthals. Barbara took the teenaged Allan Salter to Italy; Laurence was a successful composer of movie music.

The luxurious, almost perfumed ambiance of *Light Years* resembles an elegant James Ivory film. Salter's characters, like those in Fitzgerald's fiction, "are tasteful, educated, cultured. Their sensibilities are delicate, their clothes and houses are stylish. They are often beautiful. Their lives are, superficially, enviable."[16] As W. B. Yeats wrote in "A Prayer for My Daughter," everything is comfortable, courteous and civilized: "a house / Where all's accustomed, ceremonious."[17] In the beginning, the Berlands seem to be an ideal couple. Viri owns a successful architectural firm and has a Gatsby-like obsession with custom-made shirts. They have an attractive country house on the Hudson River, with a pony stable and a conservatory; two beautiful little girls; congenial and sophisticated friends who admire their life. They have wit, charm and elegance; good taste in décor and clothing, food and wine; and sufficient money to buy the best of everything.

Salter portrays their mutual understanding through amusing dialogue. When Nedra, describing the sexual life of eels, explains, "at depths of uncounted feet they mate and die," Viri alludes to the *Liebestod* in *Tristan and Isolde* and remarks, "it sounds like Wagner." When she encourages him by declaring that he's as talented as the great architect Philip Johnson, whom he's just spotted in an elevator, he ironically says, "it didn't seem to worry him." Salter describes their porcelain life in a sensual style that replicates the dreamlike perfection of their fragile world: "The small cup in her hand, the clearness of her voice, the white of her clothing—it was she who was central to the room, her movements, her smiles. Beneath their brilliance women have a power as stars have gravity. In the bottom of her cup lay the warm, rich silt."[18]

The novel opens in the autumn of 1958 when Vladimir (called Viri), Jewish and educated at Exeter and Yale, is thirty; the beautiful Nedra (her exotic name hinting at a longing for Europe) is twenty-eight; their children, Franca and Diane (called Danny), are seven and five. It ends twenty years later—their aging dog Hadji, moving from puppyhood to senescence, marks the passage of time—in the spring of 1978 (a date beyond the time of writing). The magic and security of their life, suffused with well-being, is broken first by Viri's infidelity and then (independently) by Nedra's—though neither of the affairs lasts very long. Their fragile fortress cannot withstand the siege of betrayal. Both kill, with their secrets and deceptions, something sacred and inviolable: good faith.

Viri falls in love with his exotic secretary, Kaya Doutreau (whose surname suggests doubt, de trop and Cointreau). Salter, as always, is superb when portraying their passion. As Kaya moves toward her bath, "she passed by him, naked, her skin grazing his. He was overwhelmed by this vision of her, he could not memorize it, he could not have enough. She was indifferent to his presence. Her nudity was dense, unchildish; her buttocks gleamed like a boy's." Like Phillip Dean, he can't remember, no matter how riveted his gaze, her nakedness. It's impossible to hold on to the fleeting moment of pleasure. Like Anne-Marie, "she would permit anything." But when Viri impulsively visits Kaya's apartment on the way to work, she's intimate with another man and can't (in both senses) let him in. Devastated by her betrayal, he waits till they've left and then, in a childish rage, cuts the heart out of her most precious dress. Later, when he sees her by chance in a restaurant, he's ashamed of himself for losing her.

Nedra's a more complex character. We learn much more about her background: first when her crude traveling-salesman father visits them, then when she returns to her shabby background in Altoona, Pennsylvania—a railroad town in industrial decline—to be with him when he's dying of lung cancer. "It took a long time," Salter observes, "it took forever; days and nights, the smell of antiseptic, the hush of rubber wheels. This frail engine, we think, and yet what murder is needed to take it down." The dying man, like a loose tooth that seems about to fall out, needs forceful wrenching before he's torn from life. The point of these morbid scenes is to show how deeply Nedra hates the swamp of her origins and dreads the possibility of regression: "it was desolation to her, ruin. What failure to someday crawl back; it would erase everything in a single day. . . . She had turned her back on it forever." Everything she had done since leaving Altoona and marrying Viri was meant to refine a life that would obliterate every trace of her past. She thinks she deserves the very best without earning it, and her expectations and demands destroy her.

Nedra is "subtle, penetrating and sometimes mischievous, strongly inclined to love and not overdelicate in the ways that must be taken." She's extravagant and selfish, has no real friends, does as she pleases but cannot be pleased. Viri, despite everything they have, cannot give her what she needs (whatever that is); she wants a new life, but doesn't know how to find it. So she takes a lover, Jivan, of vaguely Levantine origin, who looks like a wastrel boy lounging in a Mexican square and owns a moving and storage company. He's Viri's friend, a frequent visitor to the house, intimate and treacherous with their children.

One of the great moments of the novel is reminiscent of both the contrapuntal technique in *Madame Bovary*, when Rodolphe tries to seduce Emma in the coarse surroundings of the agricultural fair, and of the montage technique in a movie. To show the effect of her betrayal, Salter subtly shifts from Jivan's sexual encounter with Nedra to his serpentine insinuation into the household. With his characteristically hypnotic pronouns, "her . . . her; her . . . her," Salter writes: "At noon, twice a week, sometimes more, she lay in his bed in the quiet room in back. On the table near her head were two empty glasses, her bracelets, her rings. She wore nothing; her hands were naked, her wrists." His sexual performance, though physically satisfying, is mechanical, egotistical, joyless: "He was doing it in the same, steady rhythm, like a monologue, like the creaking of oars. Her cries were unending, her breasts hard. . . . Her hair was spilled about her. He did not alter his pace." Then, unobtrusively, we slide from her body into her house: "Viri, light the fire, would you?" "Let me do it," Jivan offered." Then, back to their sex: "She saw him far above her. Her hands were clutching the sheets."

As Franca watches the symbolic fire crackle and burn, she intuits the truth about her mother's infidelity before her father does. Franca "knew already, as a cat knows, as any beast; it was beating in her blood." Later on, again in Nedra's home, Jivan watches her, as Viri reads to the children, and thinks: "His mistress was untouchable. She was in the midst of ritual and duty. He was jealous, but he did not show it. They were precious to her, these things; they were her essence. It was because of them she was worthy of stealing." Viri begins to sense that Jivan is hiding something that he doesn't yet understand, and suggests that they have something "strangely in common." Nedra cruelly agrees and, alluding to the fact that she's sleeping with both of them, emphasizes their similarity by saying, "I think you do." Jivan's treachery contaminates their life and is profoundly disgusting. As Leo Tolstoy wrote in *Anna Karenina*, "All happy families are alike; every unhappy family is unhappy in its own way."

Nedra takes another lover, the so-called poet André Orlosky. Unlike Jivan, he "did not yet leave telephone messages or sit at their table," though he may soon do so. Viri, though weak, finally confronts her. Nedra, trying to disguise her true feelings as Viri expresses his outrage, calmly replies that she finds André interesting:

"Just how interesting?"
"Oh, Viri, you know."
"As interesting as Jivan?"
"No," she said. "To be honest, no."
"I wish I didn't find it so disturbing."
"It's not that important," she said.

Then, without begging her, or ordering her, to stop, Viri changes his tack and mentions their daughters. Like the little girl in Henry James' *What Maisie Knew*, they have been polluted by adult evil:

"These things . . . I'm sure you realize these things, done openly . . ."

"Yes?"

". . . can have a profound effect upon children."

"Well, I've thought about that," she admitted.

"You certainly haven't done anything about it."

"I've done quite a lot." . . .

"I'm afraid it makes me ill."

Beneath the tranquil surface of their ironic conversation—"To be honest. . . . I've done quite a lot"—there's a volcano of bitterness and despair, rage and revulsion, her selfishness, his pain.

Attempting to distract her and repair their marriage, Viri takes her to England. But Nedra's happiness on that journey with Viri reveals, ironically, how unhappy she's been with him in New York. Her marriage, she feels, is dead and turned to dust. Like Henrik Ibsen's Nora, she wants to break out of her doll's house and to "live." She wants to be free, gets divorced, but is "bound to be unhappy." She loves her daughters, but abandons them and returns to Europe, to Davos, a ski resort in Switzerland. Broken loose from Viri's anchor, she drifts aimlessly. She returns to America, fails an acting audition, works as a part-time florist and takes another transient lover, the actor Richard Brom. She fears loneliness and old age, becomes fatally ill. It's significant that the glamorous but superficial Nedra drifts into fashionable mysticism. She dabbles in tarot cards, astrology and palmistry, takes yoga lessons and repeats the pseudo-profundities of her hairy-eared Indian teacher.

As characters briefly appear, suggest different marital unions and then fade out of the story, scenes from the past gracefully enter and illuminate the present. The mood begins bright, then turns dark, as *Light Years* elegizes the evanescent beauty of domestic life. When Salter was writing this self-reflective novel, his own marriage was irretrievably breaking down. At the end of the book, as Salter noted in *The Art of Fiction*, "The animals die, the house is sold, the children are grown, even the couple themselves have vanished."[19] The Berlands have a perverse desire to destroy their own happiness, and the corruption of their too-perfect marriage is like that of Maggie Verver and Prince Amerigo in Henry James' *The Golden Bowl* (1904) and of Nicole and Dick Diver in *Tender Is the Night* (1934).

Victims of their flawed characters and of the inexorable passing of time, Viri and Nedra are also threatened by the accidents and violence, the disease and death of their friends, which put their own plight into tragic perspective. Their daughters' friend Monica has cancer, suffers an amputation and dies. Another girl, Leslie Dahlander, is thrown from a horse and turned into a broken doll. In the last days of summer, their cultured friend Arnaud Roth lies on the grass and leans on his elbow, "posed like a Manet" (a fine allusion to *Déjeuner sur l'herbe*). Later on, he lies in the gutter. Alone at night and unable to find a cab in a dangerous part of the city, Arnaud is savagely beaten by two robbers and loses an eye: "Whatever they were hitting him with sounded like a wet rag. It was the beginning of one thing, the end of another. He was staggering forth, like a flagellant, from the ease of uninjured life. . . . He lay for more than an hour, the cars swerving past, never slowing." Like the editor Ben Sonnenberg, Viri's closest friend, the art dealer Peter Daro, dies slowly and painfully of a sclerotic disease that hardens his flesh into wood: "At his funeral, in the coffin, was a face colored with cosmetics, like an invincible old woman or some kind of clown."

Viri's love for his children reflects Salter's paternal tenderness and affection. In Danny's painful rite of passage, Viri discovers that his daughter has a lover whom she cares for more than she loves him. Danny's sexual awakening and first seduction run parallel to her mother's affairs, and make Nedra even more eager for pleasure and desperate to seize it. Danny falls in love with a worthless would-be sculptor, Juan Prisant. He lives in a squalid studio (attractively bohemian to a well-bred girl) and assembles pieces of wood. He leads her to his high bed, mounted on four columns, and in a brilliant scene takes her as if by right. Her passive eagerness for sexual experience is touchingly contrasted to his laid-back lechery:

> He knelt beside her and stroked her hair. She trembled beneath his kisses. . . . Every part of her consciousness was willing, compelled. . . . As he lifted the dress from her raised arms, they wilted as if powerless. . . . His hands were slipping gently inside the elastic of her panties. . . . The marvelous, dumb mound, hair pressed flat, is revealed to the light. He touches her; it's as if she is killed, she cannot move. . . . He was naked, his body was scalding her. She was helpless, he was parting her knees.

Her body, which used to belong entirely to her, now belongs to him.

After Nedra divorces him, Viri sells the house and goes to Europe, to Rome. He works in an architect's office and has an affair with the attractive Lia Cavalieri. She loves him, and introduces him to the language and culture of Italy, but (unlike the selfish Nedra) she's too devoted and self-effacing, too clinging and devouring. Like Phillip Dean with Anne-Marie, Viri resents her emotional needs and becomes dissatisfied with their sexual life: "The act was somehow shameful, an act of boredom and desperation; entered into because everything else had failed. It ended quickly. He lay by her side and put his arm beneath her head, drawing the robe over her at the same time as if she were a shop and he were closing her for the night—a shop one had to talk to." Viri marries her for the same reason that he sleeps with her—because everything else has failed. Again like Phillip with Anne-Marie, he leaves her behind, with unconvincing promises to return, and goes back to America.

Viri walks in the woods near his old house, amidst the Chekhovian dead trees and ruined memories. There he finds the family's long-lost ancient pet tortoise, elemental, a lone survivor, a symbol of continuity. The reptile's quiet perseverance gives Viri the courage to pick up the broken pieces of his existence. On the bank of the river, where the novel began, he thinks, "I am ready, I have always been ready, I am ready at last." Having shed his house and Roman flat, his two wives and two jobs, and stripped down to his essential self, he's now prepared either to live the life he'd always hoped to have or face impending death.

This poignant contemporary novel embraces serious themes: the shocking difference between apparent and hidden lives, the life other people believe you're living and the real one; Nedra's quintessentially American idea that "everything is possible," undermined by the crushing discovery that "you can't have everything"; the vain hope that it's also possible "to feel safe with someone who will never betray you"; the unavailing belief that the innocence of children can provide absolution for their parents; and, most importantly, the inevitable "pang of bitterness and loss"—a dominant theme in modern literature.

Like *Sport*, *Light Years* provoked some contemptuous reviews, and Salter was wounded more by the negative notices than pleased by the favorable ones. "You don't just shrug reviews like those off," he bitterly recalled. "They are blows."[20] Again like *Sport*, the novel was rapturously received when reprinted. In a retrospective review of 2006, James Meek wrote, "In

Light Years, Salter's mastery of time, his themes of nobility, ruthlessness and failure in the quest for love and glory, his interest in the erotic and the aesthetics of pleasure, achieve their richest realisation."[21]

Most significantly, Richard Ford's introduction to the Penguin edition of 2007 alerted readers to the achievement of the novel. Noting the menacing undercurrent, he wrote that the Berlands were "a golden couple living a gilded, countrified life of late-lasting, candle-lit dinner parties, interesting friends, beautiful children—all with a river view. Only just beneath the afflu-ence's shiny surfaces there are also frustrated ambitions, enervated passions and a nagging fretfulness that life should be richer still, though neither of the Berlands possesses the clear-sightedness to make that life happen." It is "an immensely readable, luminous novel that radiates gravity, great in-telligence and verbal virtuosity."[22]

FOUR

SOPHISTICATED STYLE

Salter was frequently praised for his elegant style. Michael Dirda said "he can break your heart with a sentence."[1] Richard Ford spoke for many admirers when he proclaimed, "It is an article of faith among readers of fiction that James Salter writes American sentences better than anyone writing today. Sentence for sentence Salter is the master."[2] He achieves his intriguing effects by distilling and refining two different styles: the lush romanticism of Scott Fitzgerald and the stoic realism of Ernest Hemingway. Fitzgerald described the sophisticated but destructive social life of the upper class on the French Riviera and Long Island, where people "smashed up things and creatures and then retreated back into their money or their vast carelessness."[3] In a terse, precise, austere prose, Hemingway portrayed the violent initiations and ordeals of big-game hunting, bullfighting and war. Salter had so thoroughly absorbed their work that his echoes came spontaneously and naturally. He imaginatively transformed the essence of two great American novelists into his own pure, exquisite, lyrical-masculine style.

Like Ford Madox Ford, Salter was "mad about writing." The French naturalist Georges Buffon had observed, "Style is the man himself," and Salter emphatically agreed, "Style is the entire writer."[4] He also admired the lucid prose of A. J. Liebling, and described his own style as well as Liebling's in his introduction to the 1986 reprint of *Between Meals*: "It was a very idiosyncratic style, one of precision, ease and richness of detail. . . . It stimulates the senses, assists in clarity of view, and provides a feeling of approval towards life."[5]

Salter's innovative style is succinct and compressed, elliptical and elusive, with short sentences and fragmentary phrases, sudden switches in point of view, subtle glides between the past and present. His letters can be witty about building a cabin: "[My daughter] is helping me in a sort of sunbathing way"; offer a disconcerting simile about a woman who lacks *savoir faire*: "[She has] a beautiful ass, but it's like a beautiful car the owner doesn't know how to drive"; be aphoristic about Robert Redford: "Like all great rulers, he sleeps badly"; and evoke watery moods: "That hour when, by the sea, the sun seems to burn without heat, the wind rises, and the noise too." Salter has been called "a writer's writer," but not a popular one. He dismissed this double-edged compliment and told an interviewer: "I've complained about that enough and let it go. But it implies writing too good for your own good."[6]

Salter remarked, "I want to learn new words: that is one of the most thrilling things on earth."[7] For him, as for the Roman poet Plautus, *nomen est numen*: the name defines the essential spirit of what it signifies. Some vowel-filled names cast spells for him: Paavo Nurmi, the Finnish runner (and name of Salter's dog); Jean Genet, the French writer; Lamont Pry, the American artist; Adrian Arcaud, a small-time fascist; Zane Amell, an Air Force pilot who drank ten martinis in ten minutes. The unusual names of Salter's first three children have strange associations. His oldest daughter, Allan Conrad, recalled Air Force friends; his second daughter, Nina Tobe, echoed Toby jug and Tobe Hooper, a horror-film director; his third daughter, Claude Cray, suggests crayfish and the Kray twins, notorious British gangsters. He even liked the two middle "u's" in the French town of Autun (but not, presumably, the same placement of vowels in Duluth).

Salter was also influenced by Lawrence Durrell, who set his characters in Egypt and gave them exotic names: Nessim, an Arabic flower; Justine from De Sade; Balthazar and Mountolive from the Bible. Salter recalled in 1995, "it's been a long time since *The Alexandria Quartet* [1957–60]. I remember being knocked out by it, its sophistication, the intensity of that physical world and not only physical, the feeling of a knowledge of living."[8] Salter also indulged in rather obscure and pretentious story and chapter titles: "My Lord You" from an old Chinese poem in *Last Night* (2005); "Pronaos," the vestibule in a classical temple, and "Ukiyo," the floating world of Japanese art, in his autobiography *Burning the Days*. Edgar Allan Poe declared in his story "Ligeia": "There is no exquisite beauty . . . without some *strangeness* in the proportion."[9] Salter, who loved strangeness, agreed: "There is no real beauty without some slight imperfection."[10]

I

Salter and his style-master Fitzgerald had some personal traits in common. They were commissioned at the end of the First, and the Second, World Wars, but were not sent overseas in time to see action in Europe. Salter lived modestly but, like Fitzgerald, had a weakness for the wealth and luxury he'd tasted while working in Hollywood, and was pleased to associate with rich people. The Malibu beach house of Robert Redford, who'd starred in the film version of Fitzgerald's novel, was (Salter said) "redolent of '20s life with *Gatsby*."[11] Fitzgerald portrayed glamour and romance, beautiful girls, dreams squandered and doomed lovers. Salter wrote me that he was drawn to failures and romantic figures.

Henry James' story "The Middle Years" (1893) first expressed one of Fitzgerald's crucial ideas: "A second chance—*that's* the delusion. There never was to be but one."[12] Thinking of his alcoholic failures at the end of his career, Fitzgerald declared in *The Crack-Up*: "There were no second acts in American lives."[13] But Salter, a great performer, disagreed. He had a second act after his plane crash in Massachusetts and a third act in Hollywood.

Salter read Fitzgerald's stories and novels early on, *The Crack-Up* when it appeared posthumously in 1945, and was inspired by Fitzgerald's magical glorification of New York. In *The Great Gatsby* (1925) Nick Carraway, driving from Long Island into Manhattan, has great expectations: "The city seen from the Queensboro Bridge is always the city seen for the first time, in its first wild promise of all the mystery and the beauty in the world."[14] Salter began his prose poem *Still Such* (1992) with visual images: "Down Fifth Avenue with the tail-lights, dark, the wet streets gleaming. . . . Dawn near, the whole city for your happiness."[15] In his last novel *All That Is* (2013) New York, wealthy and shining, promises beauty and sex: "the brilliant theater of the great store windows, mansions of plenty, the prosperous-looking people. . . . The city was brilliant and vast. The shops were lit along the avenues as they passed. In the room he took her in his arms. He whispered to her and kissed her."[16]

In a joyous and colorful, bitter and tearful passage in *The Crack-Up*, Fitzgerald wrote: "I remember riding in a taxi one afternoon between very tall buildings under a mauve and rosy sky; I began to bawl because I had everything I wanted and knew I would never be so happy again."[17] In his story "Bangkok," Salter expresses a similar exaltation—before the inevitably shattered illusions: "That morning on Hudson Street, sitting there in the sunlight, feet up, fulfilled and knowing it, talking, in love with one another—I knew I had everything life would ever offer."[18] In a travel essay in *There & Then* (2005), Paris has the same seductive thrills. As in *Gatsby*, the car is a vehicle for sex as both automobile and bountiful girls have their "top down": "driving through the streets with six girls and the top down, a couple of them sitting on it, or beside us, a couple on our laps."[19]

The last page of *Gatsby* describes the fading light and flowing water around Long Island, where Salter lived for the last thirty-five years of his life:

Most of the big shore places were closed now and there were hardly any lights except the shadowy moving glow of a ferryboat across the Sound. And as the moon rose higher the inessential houses began to melt away until gradually I became aware of the old island here that flowered once for Dutch sailors' eyes—a fresh, green breast of the new world.[20]

The first, striking paragraph of *Light Years* (1975) describes the scene in the same lyrical prose, and with the poetic alliteration of water, wind, wide, wheel; broken, brackish, blue, beneath, blurring, birds; disappear and dream. On the Hudson River, site of West Point and the villages where Salter lived for decades before moving to Long Island, the wind and birds replace Fitzgerald's ferry and moon, the season is late autumn, and both writers evoke a vivid memory of the past:

The water lies broken, cracked from the wind. This great estuary is wide, endless. The river is brackish, blue with the cold. It passes beneath us blurring. The sea birds hang above it, they wheel, disappear. We flash the wide river, a dream of the past.[21]

Salter also absorbed Fitzgerald's social themes, his nostalgia and lyrical regret. There was always the threat of boredom, of disenchantment. In *Gatsby*, the heroine who has everything, including two men in love with her, asks: "What'll we do with ourselves this afternoon . . . and the day after that, and the next thirty years?"[22] In *A Sport and a Pastime*, Phillip Dean, on the beach in Brittany, fears endless ennui: "Years of marriage. After breakfast it is quite a long time until lunch, and after lunch, the whole afternoon."[23]

While still a teenaged cadet at West Point, Salter was attracted to Fitzgerald and published in the college magazine (October 1944) a story that evoked the title of Fitzgerald's novel: "Empty is the Night." Salter recreated Fitzgerald's portrayal of the enchanting but tragic marriage of Gerald and Sara Murphy, the models for Dick and Nicole Diver in *Tender Is the Night* (1934), in the elegant but doomed marriage of Viri and Nedra Berland in *Light Years*.

II

Hemingway glorified Paris in the same way that Fitzgerald glorified New York, and both taught Salter how to live as well as how to write. His infatuation with Paris began as early as 1939, when he was fourteen and saw the World's Fair in New York: "Everything French was very stylish, very glamorous. That was the Paris of that time. Also, Hemingway. But it wasn't about his books. It was about stories about him. *The Sun Also Rises*. I wanted to go there. I wanted to live that kind of life."[24] In his letters and travel essays Salter often expresses his longing for Hemingway's Paris, his *recherche du temps perdu*: "How I would have liked to have lived in France in the 20s and 30s. That was my true period and place." Alcoholic pleasures inevitably recalled his hero: "icy gin in the late afternoon is as beautiful to me as Hemingway's days in Paris."[25]

Referring to the café and restaurant enclosed by lilacs and with a "Hemingway Bar," and to the title of one of Hemingway's best stories, he wrote in *There & Then*: "There is a Paris of Hemingway, its resonance still strong, the light at the Closerie des Lilas, rooms at the American Hospital dedicated to women named Macomber."[26] Salter was stationed in Chaumont, in Lorraine, when recalled to active duty in 1961; and lived with his family in Grasse, in Provence, in from 1967 to 1968.

When explaining how Hemingway described sex, Salter used the Master's repetition and alliteration to define what he himself aimed for in *A Sport and a Pastime*: "Hemingway wrote a startlingly sensual English, very male and very sensual, alive to the senses, and sex, sensationally alive, both in the flesh and/or in the mind."[27] In the *Washington Post* he praised the style, speech and vivid descriptions of Hemingway's posthumous novel, *The Garden of Eden*, which had been patched together by an editor: "What is marvelous about the book is the dialogue and pace—the hard, oblique, unreal lines that Hemingway's people often speak. . . . What he does offer and abundantly is an almost physical excitement and pleasure. His lines, unspoiled by ornament, are beautiful to see and hear, and the Europe and Africa that he discovered and brought to us are still remarkably fresh. Europe in particular remains his Europe, the Paris and Spain, the towers of northern Italy, the rivers, forests, waiters and hotels." The theme of the novel, Hemingway said, is "the happiness of the Garden that a man must lose." Hemingway clearly inspired Salter, who remarked, "there are very few people who make you feel like writing and make you envy the writer as much as he does." [28]

In *Across the River and Into the Trees*, Hemingway described the Italian author and warrior Gabriele D'Annunzio—the subject of Salter's essay in *Don't Save Anything*—as "writer, poet, national hero . . . macabre egotist, aviator, commander, or rider, in the first of the fast torpedo attack boats . . . the great, lovely writer of *Notturno* whom we respect, and jerk." [29] In a letter to me Salter acknowledged his envy, and described Hemingway with the same mixture of negative and mostly positive qualities. He had an aversion to Hemingway, writer's envy and life envy, but he didn't like bigger than life, dominating, hunting and fishing, greatly talented, egoistic, charming, hugely admired men.

Salter wildly overrates Paul Hendrickson's gimmicky and mediocre *Hemingway's Boat*: "It is a book written with the virtuosity of a novelist, hagiographic in the right way, sympathetic, assiduous and imaginative." He claims that Hendrickson is a deeply informed and inspired guide who has researched exhaustively and never loses the power to amaze. But there's no original material, apart from endless repetitions about Hemingway's boat, in this derivative and familiar book. Hendrickson's main informant, Walter Houk, merely reported a swim in Hemingway's pool and a day trip on the *Pilar* with familiar drinks and fishing, and did not record Hemingway's conversation.

Despite Salter's lifelong absorption in Hemingway, he repeated many errors from Hendrickson's book. Hemingway had been to five (not three) wars. He hunted in East (not West) Africa. His style was not influenced—as the old chestnut has it—by Sherwood Anderson, Gertrude Stein and Ezra Pound, but by Leo Tolstoy, Rudyard Kipling, Stephen Crane and T. E. Lawrence. Salter says "none of his novels is set" in America, though *To Have and Have Not* is set in the Florida Keys. *The Old Man and the Sea* is not one of his most "enduring works," but a simple-minded account with obvious religious symbolism for the middlebrow readers of *Life* magazine.

But Salter does pay tribute to Hemingway's style: "He pared things down. He left out all that could be readily understood or taken for granted and the rest he delivered with savage exactness." Salter's description of Hemingway's deep-sea fishing recalls his own experience as a wartime fighter pilot when he struck down enemy planes and heard their screaming engines crash. The battles were "long, were savage, almost prehistoric, with the heart-stopping thrill of the strike and the line screaming from the big reel." He calls Hemingway's suicide "not a failure of courage but a last display of it." [30] Later on, Salter condemned *Papa Hemingway*, by the loathsome parasite A. E. Hotchner, as "the most odious, self-serving book ever." [31]

Salter wrote an incisive essay on the Russian Isaac Babel, one of his favorite authors. In his *Paris Review* interview, he said: "Babel has the three essentials of greatness: style, structure and authority. There are other writers who have that—Hemingway, in fact, had those three things." [32] Babel and Hemingway both had an obsessive concern with compression and explosion, ferocious control and eagerness to twist language in order to gain nervous immediacy. Their tales of cruelty are defined by concision, intensity, violence and resolution. Both writers note the weather and describe the natural landscape—the rivers and the stars. They employ effective repetition; emphasize lingering pain, gratuitous cruelty and morbid details; adopt an ironic viewpoint, stoical attitude and poetic rhythm; and exalt personal courage. Salter quotes Babel's famous but exaggerated remark, "No steel could pierce the human heart as deeply as a period in exactly the right place," to emphasize the importance of the perfectly placed and punctuated sentence. [33]

Hemingway and Salter had similar descriptions of the seasons, snow and skiing. The inscription on the statue of Hemingway next to his house in Ketchum, Idaho, alludes to the hunting season: "Most of all he loved the fall." In a letter Salter wrote, "I love the fall. It's the time of year I have well-being, hope." [34] When living in Paris in the 1920s, Hemingway often spent the winters in Alpine ski resorts. In "Christmas at the Top of the World," a dispatch for the Toronto *Star* (December 22, 1923), he portrayed the excitement of high-altitude skiing in Switzerland: "At the top we could look out over the whole world, white, glistening in the powder snow, and ranges of mountains stretching off in every direction." (This sentence foreshadows his superb description of the snow-covered mountain in Tanganyika: "as wide as all the world, great, high, and unbelievably white in the sun, was the square top of Kilimanjaro.") "Then in one long, dropping, swooping, heart-plucking rush, we were off. A seven-mile run down and no sensation in the world that can compare with it." [35]

Salter's description of weather, winter landscape and the protective reaction of animals in *All That Is* recalls the best of Hemingway: "It had snowed before Christmas but then turned cold. The sky was pale. The country lay silent, the fields dusted white with the hard furrows showing where they had been plowed. All was still. The foxes were in their dens, the deer bedded down." [36] Salter's exact description suggests maximum meaning. Christmas was cold, pale, white, still, and silent as the snow absorbed the sound. The foxes and deer were hidden and safe until the next hunting season.

Salter's best screenplay, *Downhill Racer* (1969), dramatized skiing. The critic John Simon, who went to Horace Mann prep school with Salter, said the skiers in his novel *Solo Faces* (1979) "spoke in a kind of Hemingway of the slopes." [37] In a striking passage in "The Skiing Life," Salter wrote, "a train went past us in the dusk with lighted windows, the swift, slender cars. In town the streets were snow covered and there were barns mixed in with the houses and hotels." [38] The dusk contrasts with the light in the windows, the narrow railroad cars thin out as they speed by and the mountain towns have been transformed into ski resorts.

In another essay, "Classic Tyrol," Salter pays vivid tribute to the Master who inspired him: "Very few writers can appeal to the senses so, and of course Hemingway is one of them. It was he who introduced me, I think, to the idea of long, secluded winters and the mountain villages in which, during the 1920s, he spent them. . . . [He would] go to a place where the rain would become snow, coming down through the pines and creaking beneath their feet as they walked home at night in the cold. . . . He worked on *The Sun Also Rises* in Schruns [Austria]. He made me like skiing although I never dreamed I would ski." [39] Salter spent his winters skiing, like Hemingway, after he bought a house in the Rocky Mountain town of Aspen, Colorado, in 1969.

Hemingway's powerful stylistic and thematic influence shows up in specific scenes. *The Sun Also Rises* ends with poignant irony as the alcoholic, promiscuous Brett Ashley alludes to the war that has destroyed her lovers, and the stoical Jake Barnes says it's foolish to think they could have been happy: "'Oh, Jake,' Brett said, 'we could have had such a damned good time.' 'Yes. Isn't it pretty to think so?'" In the last line of *All That Is*, the hero Philip Bowman suggests, more positively, an out-of-season trip to Venice: "Yes. Let's go in November. We'll have a great time." In *Light Years*, when Viri Berland says, "greatness, like virtue, need not be spoken about in order to exist," his friend Reinhart replies, like Jake, "It would be nice to believe."[40]

In *Death in the Afternoon* (1932), Hemingway explained how an author can be more effective by leaving out details: "If a writer of prose knows enough about what he is writing about he may omit things that he knows and the reader . . . will have a feeling of those things as strongly as though the writer had stated them. The dignity of movement of an ice-berg is due to only one-eighth of it being above water." Salter specifically refers to Hemingway's theory in his story "Cinema" when the tip of the iceberg represents the fear beneath it: "Only occasionally, like the head of an iceberg ominously rising from nowhere and then dropping from sight did the terror come into view."[41]

Interchapter XIV in *In Our Time* (1924) describes the bullfighter's fade-out perception of his own impending death: "Maera felt everything getting larger and larger and then smaller and smaller. . . . Then he was dead." In "Cinema" again, the ecstatic author, his talent finally recognized, fades into sleep and out of the story: "he lay there becoming small, smaller, vanishing."[42] Salter recreates the death of the matador in the lost consciousness of sleep.

The unhappy wife in Hemingway's "Cat in the Rain" childishly repeats "I want" six times when demanding trivial possessions and an impossible change of seasons: "And I want to eat at a table with my own silver and I want candles. And I want it to be spring and I want to brush my hair out in front of a mirror and I want a kitty and I want some new clothes." In *Light Years*, the arty Nedra Berland also insists and repeats: "I want to go to Europe. I want to go on a tour. I want to see Wren's cathedrals, the great buildings, the squares. I want to see France."[43]

In Hemingway's "Hills Like White Elephants," set in Spain, the young man tries to persuade his girlfriend to have an abortion, never mentioned but made clear in the context. Alienated from her, he's too literal-minded to understand her fears or share her imaginative world view:

The girl was looking off at the line of hills. They were white in the sun and the country was brown and dry.

"They look like white elephants," she said.

"I've never seen one," the man drank his beer.

"No, you wouldn't have."

Salter uses the same laconic dialogue in "Comet" when Philip points out the rare comet and Adele cannot see it:

—The comet, he said. . . .

—I don't see any comet, she said.

—You don't?

—Where is it?

—It's right up there, he gestured,

and reveals the emotional and perceptive distance between them.[44]

Hemingway's novels made an equally strong impact on Salter. The first paragraph of *A Farewell to Arms* (1929) vividly evokes the Italian setting: "In the bed of the river there were pebbles and boulders, dry and white in the sun, and the water was clear and swiftly moving and blue in the channels." Salter's description of Yosemite also includes the flowing river, translucent water and clear pebbles: "In the late afternoon the trees seemed rich and green, the Merced River clear enough to see every pebble in its bed."[45]

In Robert Jordan's sexual encounter with Maria in *For Whom the Bell Tolls* (1940), Hemingway employs bold repetition and compound present participles to convey the movement and feelings of the lovers: "closely holding, closely held, lonely, hollow-making with contours, happy-making, young and loving . . . with a hollowing, chest-aching, tight-held loneliness." Salter also uses kinetic present participles in *All That Is* to describe Bowman having sex with a German woman: "This time he went in easily. The morning with its stillness. He stayed unmoving, waiting, imagining unhurriedly everything that was to follow. He was making it known to her."[46]

Salter's short-lived play *Death Star* (only two performances in 1970), like Hemingway's *Across the River and Into the Trees*, "dealt with the dying days of a great military commander, a repentant one." Hemingway wrote that his hero Richard Cantwell "only loved people, he thought, who had fought and been mutilated." Salter similarly said, "I want to write about people who cannot modify themselves to reality" and have been hurt.[47]

Like Cantwell with the young Renata in *Across the River*, Bowman in *All That Is* spends a lot of time instructing his women. He gives his girl a tutorial on Hemingway's "The Killers" (which inspired decades of gangster movies) and, imitating the style of the story, locates it in New Jersey:

> It's in the evening. Nobody's in the place, there are no customers, it's empty, and two men in tight black overcoats come in and sit down at the counter. They look at the menu and order, and one of them says to the counterman, This is some town, what's the name of this place? And the counterman, who's frightened of course, says, Summit. It's right there in the story, Summit, and when the food comes they eat with their gloves on. They're there to kill a Swede, they tell the counterman. They know the Swede always comes there. He's an ex-fighter named Ole Andreson who doubled-crossed the mob somehow. One of them takes a sawed-off shotgun from beneath his coat and goes into the kitchen to hide and wait.

Andreson, who's failed to throw a fight for the gamblers, passively awaits his execution. Bowman then continues his enthusiastic lecture: "It's marvelous. Fabulously written. If you never read another word of his, you'd know right away what a great writer he is. . . . I'd like to meet Hemingway. Go down to Cuba and meet him." Later on, Bowman corrects himself: "It was not even the diner that Hemingway wrote about, he now knew. That was another place called Summit, near Chicago."[48]

Salter had Fitzgerald and Hemingway, and their great themes of loss in love and war, in his literary bloodstream. His magical absorption and stylistic variations of these authors both stimulated and nourished his style. As T. S. Eliot observed in "Tradition and the Individual Talent," we "often find that not only the best, but the most individual parts of [an author's] work may be those in which his ancestors assert their immortality most vigorously."[49]

FIVE

UNICORN
IN THE STABLE

Hollywood

When Salter sold the film rights of *The Hunters* for $60,000, enough to live on for three years, he left a promising military career to become a full-time writer. But his second novel *A Sport and a Pastime* (1967) had a cruel and discouraging reception. To support his wife and four children, he turned to lucrative screenwriting. He made a tremendous change from the military to the literary world, and then from literary life to Hollywood.

Salter was dazzled and inspired by the European New Wave of films in the early 1960s, and said Antonioni's *L'Avventura*, Godard's *Vivre sa vie*, Resnais' *Last Year at Marienbad* "cast a new light on the whole idea of movies." These directors abandoned conventional plots in favor of innovative narration and troubled mood, long takes and slow pace. Their ambiguous and elusive characters, suffering from ennui and desperation, expressed the alienation of modern man. Salter recalled, "To think that I would be involved in the making of a film was enough to give me the energy and the courage to do all kinds of writing." He wrote for the movies through the 1960s and mid-1970s, and later regretted that "one often becomes committed to a completely worthless thing but pursues it with just as much ardor as if it were something good."[1] Four of his sixteen film scripts were made and three of them appeared in 1969—an extremely high rate of success. But except for his ski movie *Downhill Racer*, the others—despite good actors—were flops. Deeply disillusioned, Salter came to feel movies were a waste of time and effort, but the money he made enabled him to return to serious fiction.

Salter got his start, by chance, when he met the writer-producer Lane Slate (a near anagram for Salter). Slate owned a Delage car, like Phillip Dean in *Sport*, and Salter called him "a man of taste who lived in a kind of indulgent squalor, an expert on painting, automobiles and Joyce [*sic*]. . . . He was irreverent and well-read, with a handsome face and a mouth that never opened in a smile, so bad were his teeth." As Slate declined, Salter "felt his confidence in me began to slip." After Salter had left the table, he'd seen Slate "mechanically pouring what remained in other glasses into his own." [2]

Their first effort (August–September 1962) was a documentary, *Team, Team, Team*, about a West Point football squad preparing for the Army-Navy game. It was twelve minutes long, and when they showed it to a film distributor he said, "it would be better if it were shorter." Salter claimed that it won first prize at the 1962 Venice Film Festival, but he does not specify the category and there is no record of this award.

Another ill-conceived and unfinished project, *Daily Life in Ancient Rome*, with satiric narration from the Roman historians Sallust and Livy, contrasted their ancient descriptions of decay with the glittering surface of contemporary New York. Salter and Slate had more luck in 1963–64, despite the strict budget of $7,500 for each episode, with a ten-part series on the American circus for PBS. They also made a film about three little-known and now-famous painters. Fifty years later in March 2012, the New York Armory exhibited Salter's photographs in "American Masters Seen Through the Lens of James Salter." The catalogue described how

> he shot the artists in their studios, at work on pictures that are now considered masterpieces of the era. Andy Warhol, fresh-faced and boyish, before fright wigs, shades and downtown cool; Robert Rauschenberg, handsome, serious and intent, with a glass of vodka not far away; Larry Rivers, the famous profile, glamorous as a movie-star himself. . . . These photographs have been paired with paintings of each of the artist-subjects, providing a narrative view of process and product, keeping, as Rauschenberg said, "history and love alive." [3]

Salter began his first feature film *The Appointment* (1969) with Peter Glenville, the English actor and director of *Becket*. Glenville (1913–1996) came from a theatrical family and had studied law at Christ Church, Oxford. While planning *The Appointment* he was directing *Hotel Paradiso* (1966), a British comedy based on a stage play, with Alec Guinness. The producer Martin Poll considered many different actors: Brigitte Bardot, Virna Lisi, Julie Christie and Kim Novak; Marcello Mastroianni, Oskar Werner and Charles Aznavour. Simone de Beauvoir, and Suso D'Amico who scripted *The Bicycle Thieves*, were possible writers. The MGM budget was $2,250,000 for a twelve-week shooting in Rome and four weeks in a studio.

Salter got the writing job, perhaps *faute de mieux*, which paid well: $3,000 for twelve weeks' expenses, $10,000 for the first draft, $3,000 for rewrites and another $10,000 when the movie was made. In a letter to Poll from France on June 14, 1965, Glenville analyzed Salter's character and limitations: "Salter came here and we had a very long, interesting and productive discussion. I suggested that he should have a further meeting or meetings should he so desire but he seemed quite happy to go off to Italy and get on with the job. He certainly is intelligent and keen and extremely cinema-conscious. It remains to be seen if his Americanism will be a help or a hindrance."

Poll, the boss, was critical and condescending, treated Salter as a novice and made him do several rewrites. In August and October 1965, Poll wrote Glenville: "I told Salter that I was surprised that it took him all this time to write forty pages and the changes were minor details. . . . I think Jim has captured the flavor and written a very interesting first draft. You have discovered a fine writer. It is exceptionally edifying, since his first 12 weeks resulted in a sketchy treatment." The film was about a marriage that became a nightmare through the husband's suspicion of sexual betrayal.[4]

Sidney Lumet—the director of *Twelve Angry Men*, *The Pawnbroker* and *Fail Safe*—eventually took over from Glenville. He later said: "I once did a picture called *The Appointment*. It had fine dialogue by James Salter, but a dreadful story line that had been handed to him by an Italian producer. I presume Jim needed the money. The picture had to be shot in Rome."[5] In his autobiography *Burning the Days* Salter lamented, "the film was badly miscast and had the wrong director. Because of his ability and reputation he had the unquestioning confidence of everyone, though he later told me he had agreed to make the movie mainly because he wanted the chance to learn something about color from the experienced Italian cameraman."[6]

Based on a story by Antonio Leonviola, the movie had well-known actors: the Egyptian Omar Sharif, after his triumphant appearance in *Lawrence of Arabia* and *Doctor Zhivago*; the French Anouk Aimée who'd been in Fellini's *La Dolce Vita*; and the Austrian singer Lotte Lenya, in a cameo role as antique dealer and upmarket procuress. The Sharif character, love-struck by Aimée, his law partner's fiancée, steals her away and marries her. But he suspects that she may secretly be Rome's highest-paid prostitute. He attempts to entrap her by posing as a potential client and, as the film's advertising poster says, "He has to keep his appointment even if the woman turns out to be his wife." But he never catches her in the act. When the un-stable wife commits suicide, the husband realizes that she was innocent and that he was responsible for her death. The themes of romantic obsession and destructive jealousy are not effectively dramatized, and the movie is merely a weak imitation of Luis Buñuel's *Belle de Jour* (1967). In that bril-liant, tragic film a beautiful married housewife with masochistic fantasies (Catherine Deneuve) secretly works in a high-class brothel under the name of Belle de Jour.

After Salter's initial enthusiasm had subsided, he took a more jaded view of moviemaking and criticized the "really arty stuff by auteur directors who make beautiful films that critics talk about but that nobody ever sees and that certainly don't make any money." He bitterly noted, "I experienced a lot with this film, most of it sorrowful. . . . The best script I had done at that time became the worst film I have ever been connected with."[7] "Lumet sim-ply butchered it. He didn't even have the slightest idea. The film was a disas-ter. It was ridiculous."[8] Though nominated for the Palme d'Or at the Cannes Film Festival, it was booed by the spectators: "The audience, at a moment when they should have felt fulfillment, broke into loud laughter" and he felt humiliated.[9] The attempt to capture the static solemnity, enigmatic ennui and melancholy mood of a European art film in *The Appointment* wasted a lot of talent in a dud movie. It was never distributed in America and has disappeared. As Samuel Johnson said after the failure of his play *Irene*: "I had thought it had been better."[10]

Salter's "Cinema" (1970), in his story collection *Dusk*, expresses his anger about making *The Appointment*. The leading actor, with a telltale space between his front teeth and a passion for bridge, is clearly based on Sharif. The disillusioned director plays a losing card, knows the film is going badly but pretends that all is well. The autobiographical writer has changed his name (as Salter had done when he became a novelist) to Lang, after the German director Fritz Lang. An outsider confined to an inferior hotel and placed at a distant restaurant table, he mentions Buñuel and is satiric about the picture. He has written a superb script that's been mutilated: "Its power came from its chasteness, the discipline of its images. It was a film of indirection, the surface was calm with the calm of daily life. Beneath the visible were emotions more potent for their concealment."[11] In a prosaic parallel to the glamorous affair of the two leading actors, Lang has sex with the rather sad Italian publicist. She then phones to tell him about a lonely astronomer who discovered a new planet during royal festivities in Milan in 1868. Her call proves that she believes in his talent, that he must persevere like the astronomer, and makes him feel ecstatic.

Salter wrote and directed his second film, which also failed as he tried to imitate the slow and moody movies of the arty Europeans. Like *L'Avventura*, *Three* (1969) has several shots of waves breaking on rocks to suggest a tumultuous atmosphere, which doesn't exist in the film. He also tried many close-ups of ordinary people and places to suggest the tone and background. *Three* was based on a short story "Then We Were Three" by Irwin Shaw. Salter would later explore the theme of *Three* in "The Captain's Wife" chapter in *Burning the Days*. He writes in that book, at first "we lived as three." After his marriage, "there were three of us again, and it was still she and I who were intimates."[12]

The film's budget was $260,000. Shaw got $32,000 for the rights; Salter was paid much less: $6,750 for his script, pre-production expenses, plane fare to Europe and additional expenses in Italy. In several long letters in August–September 1964, the old pro Shaw was eager to help and talk about Salter's script. He made many shrewd, detailed and useful suggestions about the structure, characters, dialogue and locales. In one six-page letter Shaw said he was afraid his frank criticism would offend Salter. He answered Shaw with an eleven-page letter that agreed with most of Shaw's ideas.

To preserve his artistic independence, Salter defended his script and claimed that he could make it work. He maintained that the life of the young middle-class characters begins with an agony of sexual deprivation, and that the underlying ominous tone is barely felt. But they have experienced a unique beauty and joy at the end of that unforgettable summer, and want to prolong their precious hedonism. He insisted that he still found the script good, and promised that its thrilling camera work would make it a marvelous film to *see*. After getting Salter's letter and rereading the script, Shaw crushingly concluded that he was dropping out of the project. The script didn't work, and it was not a picture that he and Salter could make together.[13] The tremendous amount of thought, advice and labor by two skilled professionals could not make a successful movie.

In *Three* two American college friends—one idealistic, played by Sam Waterston, the other bold, played by Robie Porter—on a summer vacation in Europe, fall for a charming and rather mysterious English girl, Charlotte Rampling. In order to preserve their friendship they agree, while traveling together in Italy and France, to maintain purely platonic relations with her. The plot goes all the way back to Shakespeare's early comedy *Love's Labour's Lost* in the mid-1590s. In the play the King of Navarre and his three companions agree to a life of study and self-improvement, and to banish all thoughts of women and love. When three women from France unexpectedly appear, the young men forget their vows and submit to their charms.

The supposedly poor students drive an old Peugeot, but stay in expensive hotels, have a full breakfast and eat in fine restaurants. They sit in cafés, visit museums, dance with girls and go to the beach—though the women are not (as was common) topless. Rampling wins money at a casino, and they inspect an empty bullring when they mistake the date of the *corrida*. Content to drift with her two admirers, Rampling has a sullen mouth and elusive character. Though worldly wise she confesses, "I don't know anything about anything." She's hurt but pretends to be indifferent when Porter seduces an Italian girl. Rampling calls Waterston "poor boy"; and when she says, "You're nice," he defensively replies, "I try not to be." She invites him to her room but, though deeply attracted to her, he remains faithful to his pact. Though a weak swimmer, he tries to rescue a drowning man while his friends merely look on. That evening, too exhausted to go out, he immediately falls asleep and wakes to discover that Porter has spent the night with Rampling. Porter gets the girl, Waterston gets the car. Abandoning his high-minded beliefs, he drives away to get the ship home and return to the reality of law school and a conventional life. There may be a homosexual subtext in which Waterston and Porter are actually in love with each other and suppress their feelings through their obsession with Rampling.

Salter said the behavior of the actors was, as usual, detestable. He declared that the rebellious young actress "chewed wads of gum, had dirty hair and wore clothes that smelled. She was frequently late, never apologized, and was short-tempered and mean. . . . Midway through shooting, she refused to continue unless her salary was doubled and, equally important, her boyfriend took over as director. She got the money but the producer refused to back the mutiny and to set me adrift. When I heard what had happened I found it hard to suppress my loathing."[14] It's amazing that Salter could publish this description in the *New Yorker* and in *Burning the Days* (1997) while Rampling was still alive.

It's also surprising that Salter, with so little experience, directed the picture. But he was trained at West Point to prepare for anything, assume command and have his orders obeyed. He worked hard for long hours on the picture, mostly with people he didn't like. He said a director "must create an atmosphere in which people can work,"[15] and admitted that he "was too restrained in both the scenes he wrote and the direction he gave to the actors."[16] In his *Paris Review* interview he recalled: "I now see I was somewhat inadequate as a director. I should have spent considerably more time with the actors and understood the psychology of what was going on."[17] But he was satisfied with the film at the time and, unlike *The Appointment*, it had considerable success at Cannes.

Salter was ambitious and wanted to make an extraordinary movie. But he needed the genius of an Antonioni to sustain an audience's interest in a film that had very little action, minimal dialogue, long silent passages and characters who were too preppy to be decadent. Molly Haskell, a prominent critic in the *Village Voice* (January 1, 1970), emphasized its weaknesses. She complained that the story was slight, the characters uninteresting and the direction sluggish, and concluded: "Salter is allergic to conversation the way people in real life are allergic to silences. He thrives on pregnant pauses . . . that don't conceal anything" beneath the surface. After the painful experience of *Three*, Salter never wanted to direct another film.

Robert Redford, the star of Salter's third film, had read and (unlike Shaw) liked his screenplay for *Three*. The making of *Downhill Racer* (1969) began in 1963 when Redford was acting in Neil Simon's play *Barefoot in the Park* and they met in New York. He impressed Redford by holding up a transparent leaf and asking, "See how the veins appear? I want to write about the vital veins, without the leaf, and create the very essence of meaning."[18]

At first Roman Polanski, a keen skier like Redford, was going to direct *Downhill Racer*, and Salter and Redford had meetings with him. Polanski then became interested in *Rosemary's Baby* and Redford refused the role of the satanic husband. When Polanski left, Redford remained committed to *Downhill*. A big star after *Butch Cassidy and the Sundance Kid* (1969), he raised $20,000 to make a fourteen-minute promotion short that featured many ski crashes. He took the Alpine project to the Austrian-born Charles Bluhdorn, head of Gulf and Western in New York, which owned Paramount Pictures. Bluhdorn said, "Write the script. We'll make it."

Salter and Redford went to the 1968 winter Olympics in Grenoble, stayed in cheap French hotels and even slept in corridors when all the rooms were occupied. They watched the members of the American ski team, and learned how they ate, talked, trained and prepared to race. The real-life ski models for the characters in the movie were Billy Kidd, a quiet young man from Vermont, and "Spider" Sabich, a more outgoing man from California.

Salter wrote the script and walked around his room reciting the lines to hear how they would sound, but his characteristic style and dialogue did not come through on the screen. The dismissive Gulf and Western officials did not respect his creative efforts and, like all writers, he wanted to protect his own words. The producer Richard Gregson was on the scene with his new wife, Natalie Wood, a friend of Redford who'd costarred in two films with him. Redford hired Michael Ritchie, a television director, for a lower-than-usual fee. The son of a Berkeley psychology professor, Ritchie had graduated from Harvard. He was impatient with camera setups, wanted to speed up the action and make a documentary-style picture.

Downhill was filmed in Kitzbühel and St. Anton, Austria; Wengen, Switzerland; and Megève, France, and the European settings—streets, hotel, restaurants—were authentic. They had filmed during the Olympics when there were plenty of spectators and didn't have to pay extras to form the crowd. When they changed scenes they had to smooth out the snow, as the desert sands had been smoothed out for new scenes in *Lawrence of Arabia*. Redford, the main character, had hurt his tendon just before arriving and they had to disguise his limp for a week with long shots.

The fast pace of the movie slows down for Salter's best scene: Redford's encounter with his father when he returns home to Idaho Springs, Colorado. His father asks why Redford is skiing if he doesn't earn any money. Seeking glory, he says, "I'll be famous. I'll be a champion," to which the sardonic old man replies, "World's full of 'em." The actual film was mistakenly left out of the camera when this scene was shot. They didn't discover the problem until they had moved to Los Angeles and had to reconstruct the cabin on the Paramount lot.

Downhill Racer is essentially a ski movie with conventional scenes linking the races, which reached a speed of eighty miles an hour and were praised by experts for their accuracy and truthfulness. The real American team had trained for four years for their run in the Olympics, the winner often decided by 100ths of a second. The sudden liftoffs and plunging flights recall Salter's fighter-pilot missions in Korea. The plane battles and ski runs both last only two to three minutes, and often end in crashes that destroy both lives and careers. The ski crashes also recall riders falling off their horses during battle scenes in a western.

The producers didn't want to get a restricted rating that would exclude the potentially large teenage audience. So Redford's kissing and bedroom encounters with two women are tame and unexciting. When he returns to Idaho Springs he meets an old girlfriend for discreet sex in his car. In Europe he has another subdued liaison with a Swiss-German woman, played by the wooden Swedish actress Camilla Sparv, the ex-wife of Robert Evans, head of Paramount. When she breaks a date with Redford to attend her family Christmas and then chatters about it, he leans on the car horn to shut her up.

Like the competitive, reckless air ace Pell in *The Hunters*, Salter portrayed Redford as "supremely talented and untouched by humility, cocky, selfish and outspoken in guarding his own interests."[19] He's a loner who doesn't connect with his coach, teammates, girlfriends or father, whose severe character explains Redford's aggressive personality. Salter said Redford's character "had neither compunction nor regret. He was a prick." In his original script the coach had sought a gold-medal winner for years and "finally found the chance but with an individual he disliked, even despised, a crude, self-centered Redford."[20] It was daring to make Redford's character unsympathetic, but he's not nasty enough to be really interesting.

When an American skier complains, "he's not for the team and never will be," Redford says, "Well, it's not exactly a team sport." Redford gets late numbers in the starting lineup, 88 and 77, and refuses to participate in his first run because his speed would be decreased by the ruts from previous skiers. He tells his coach, played by Gene Hackman, "I could have won if I had a lower starting number." "No." "Why not?" To suppress his ego and encourage him to try harder, Hackman tells him, "You weren't good enough." Redford then wins the race, as he predicted, with the more advantageous number 15. Salter's touch appears when the Swiss woman reads aloud a German newspaper article about Redford. He doesn't understand the language, but egoistically asks her to read it to him again.

George Orwell's ideas about international competition in "The Sporting Spirit" (1945) apply to downhill racing, although skiers compete individually against their own team as well as against the clock. Orwell observed that instead of bringing nations together in Olympic harmony, "Serious sport has nothing to do with fair play. It is bound up with hatred, jealousy, boastfulness, disregard of all rules and sadistic pleasure in witnessing violence: it is war minus the shooting."[21] Salter's themes, like Orwell's, are the brutal nature of competition and the high cost of success.

At the end of the film Redford, defying strict orders and arousing the wrath of coach Hackman, skis simultaneously and dangerously with his main American competitor, who crashes and leaves the way open for his victory. When his German competitor also falls, Redford wins the gold medal. All the attention is focused on him, and we don't see the ceremony awarding the silver and bronze medals. In *The Natural*, based on Bernard Malamud's baseball novel, the main character strikes out. In Redford's film of the book he hits a home run. Redford explained that you can't disappoint the audience who have sat in the theater for two hours. In contrast to Salter's original ending, Redford has to win the downhill race.

Pauline Kael's influential review in the *New Yorker* (November 15, 1969) repeated Molly Haskell's criticism of Salter's limited dialogue: "The techniques of *Downhill Racer* deserve a better script. The scenarist, James Salter, tries for the spare, taut, 'masculine' style of Ernest Hemingway. Maybe the script had to be tacked together to fit the ski footage, which is the true excitement of the film; still, crucial scenes are so laconic they sound as if they'd been written by Calvin Coolidge, and they get unintended laughs."[22] The producers and Redford mauled Salter's script and he took the bullet for its failure.

Writing from his home in Aspen, Colorado, in the early 1970s, Salter told a friend, "Redford's been here, visiting. What a lovely life success brings. . . . Like all great rulers, he sleeps badly. He lives in a haughty, casual style. Yesterday he was reading his journals from *Gatsby* to me. I was depressed— he's not a bad writer, he observes with great shrewdness, even wit." Praising Redford's successful film festival in Utah, Salter added, "He's a remarkable guy. Even if he weren't an actor and an idol, Sundance would be a great achievement."[23]

As with *Downhill Racer*, in April 1975 Salter left for Europe to do background work for his film script *Solo Faces*. The title suggests the face of the isolated climber confronted with the unyielding face of the mountain. He loved Europe and wrote, "The work here will be easy for me: listening to taciturn mountaineers talk about their climbs, looking at some of their films." A year later, he said it is "the best film I've ever written. I'll be crushingly disappointed if it's not cherished." But his friendly relations with Redford and confident mood had dramatically changed. He now became a humiliated suppliant: "I have not heard a peep for these two months and more. I tried to call Redford twenty times. Nothing. I even hung around Los Angeles for a week hoping to hear from him. No. So when you think of the glamour and ease of film writing, think of this. Unspeakable business. No wonder everyone is corrupted by it. I had hoped to sit down and start a book."[24] Like Axel Heyst in Joseph Conrad's *Victory*, he felt "the germ of corruption had entered his soul."[25] After Redford finally rejected the cherished script, Salter rewrote it and published it as a novel in 1979. Changing *Solo Faces* from screenplay to fiction marked his long-sought transition to serious work.

Years later the slightly contrite Redford called Salter, said he wanted to keep in touch and invited him to meet at a posh New York hotel. Salter was still resentful about having to change the script of *Downhill Racer* to make Redford look more heroic, and about Redford's rudeness and rejection of *Solo Faces*. Salter contrasted the performance of Meryl Streep, who had mastered the Danish accent in *Out of Africa*, to Redford, who didn't even try to play an Englishman and was terrible in that film. He thought Redford was not a great actor, but embodied the image that's required on screen. Redford testified to their friendship by giving the keynote speech when Salter received a lifetime achievement award at the annual *Paris Review* ceremony in April 2011.

Salter made extreme changes in script, mood and pace from the slow settings of *The Appointment* and *Three*, to the ski action of *Downhill Racer*, to the serious medical drama of *Threshold* (1983). In the last two films the linking scenes between the main action are not dramatically effective; but skiing is visually exciting in *Downhill* and surgery in *Threshold* is not. Salter had to acquire much more knowledge about medicine than he had to learn about Europe for his previous films. In December 1967 Dr. Christiaan Barnard, the South African cardiac surgeon, made the first successful human heart transplant. In December 1982, the month before *Threshold* opened, Dr. William DeVries installed the first artificial heart. This should have provided excellent publicity, but didn't really help the film.

The producers asked the medical engineer Robert Jarvik to design an indestructible heart to be used in the movie. Salter noted that Jarvik's heart "is nuclear powered, and the moment when the natural heart of the young woman who receives it is removed forever is a chilling one." He added that Dr. Denton Cooley, the famous American cardiac surgeon, instructed the Canadian actor Donald Sutherland "in surgical matters and even made a brief appearance in the film."[26] In April 1977, when the project seemed to be going well, Salter was suddenly told to rewrite his script for the third time—without pay.

The title of *Threshold* suggests the sharp contrast between death and life, human and artificial heart, failure and success. The film recalled the mad scientist and creation of Dr. Frankenstein's monster, and was mistakenly called science fiction, but it is more sci than fi. In the movie, filmed in Ottawa General Hospital, a famous heart surgeon collaborates with an egomaniacal scientist-inventor, Jeff Goldblum. A patient tells the gentle, skillful and brainy Dr. Vrain (Sutherland): "People come here because you are the best. People come here when they've been given up for dead. They come here expecting miracles."

The goats in the hospital laboratory have had experimental transplants, but must have their television channels frequently changed so they won't get bored by watching the same program. One man dies after the failure of a human heart transplant. Another hopeless, near-death, seventeen-year-old patient has a childlike face and wears little girl's clothes to make her seem more vulnerable and tragic. She agrees to accept the artificial heart; and when she's on the operating table an unusual shot from above looks down from her head to her toes and briefly exposes her breasts and pubic hair. She survives the surgery and—echoing Arthur Rimbaud's famous phrase "I is another"—asks "Is this me? Am I the same person? Will I live?" In the film's sly dig at egoistic auteur directors, Salter has Jeff Goldblum appear on television and take all credit for Sutherland's success by claiming that surgeons (like screenwriters) are merely technicians and have no creative imagination.

Salter called *The Appointment* "so awful" and *Three* "poorly written"—by him. *Threshold* was "pretty good," even though "the writing was imperfect, the budget was too small and the actors were not all the ones we wanted. Some of the best scenes were dropped or awkwardly played."[27] Though the audience did not want to watch the repetitive and bloody surgical scenes, Vincent Canby in the *New York Times* (January 2, 1983) called the film "a rigorously unhackneyed medical drama . . . a neat, modest movie about the professional life of a good doctor, played with unexpected warmth, wit and restraint by Mr. Sutherland." The script and direction "are full of right decisions that are difficult to describe since they are so perfectly functional."

Salter left tantalizing hints about some of his promising scripts that did not reach the screen. He said in an interview, "I had written books no one had published, stories that nobody accepted, so I wasn't too astonished to find that a film I had written was not made." [28] *The Lighthouse* was merely a title. His play *Poisonous Soil* was never produced. *The Raincoat*, perhaps inspired by Gogol's "The Overcoat," was a project for the producer Chris Mankiewicz. *Traps* was based on the Swiss-German novel by Friedrich Dürrenmatt. *Goodbye, Bear* portrayed an irresistibly cynical New York girl who has an unhappy love affair and disappears into the currents of Manhattan. Two ill-fated projects were to be produced by Salter's friend Robert Ginna. *The Blue Clown* had a sinister and tyrannical political background and was supposed to star Paul Scofield and be directed by Maximilian Schell. Salter, describing a prematurely buried project, lamented that "clods of earth have been tumbling onto *Warsaw*. No one will put up the money. We hold a mirror before its mouth to see if it is still breathing." [29]

Salter's play *The Death Star* was actually staged in the Theatre at St. Clement's in New York on November 12 and 13, 1973, with Kevin McCarthy in the leading role and a large supporting cast. Salter confessed: "[It] was too ambitious, with some startling moments but weak in structure. It focused on the vain belief that the death of a legendary military figure, a repentant one, could still the human urge for war. Those days will return, it said, that chaos. There were more than thirty roles, played by twenty actors. . . . From the earliest moments, when the curtain was raised, I saw it was wrong." Ben Sonnenberg caustically told Salter, "I didn't like it, not at all. All the directorial choices were wrong, casting, staging, everything." Like Shaw's condemnation of *Three*—"That was a lousy movie you made"—friends he respected poured salt into his wound. [30]

Salter had no better luck with the movies that were made by others from his work. *The Hunters* (1958) was a disappointment. It portrayed a group of fighter pilots in Korea, competitively and ruthlessly dedicated to shooting down Russian MIGs and becoming a greatly admired "ace." *Boys* (1996), with the young Winona Ryder, was supposedly based on Salter's story "Twenty Minutes" but had almost nothing to do with it. In the movie a girl is thrown from a horse and knocked out. Instead of recalling her past life before dying in twenty minutes, as in the story, students from a nearby boarding school smuggle her into their room while the police search for her. There was also a short-lived twenty-two-minute movie, "Last Night," with Frances McDormand, vaguely based on Salter's story.

Most well-known writers who worked for the movies—William Faulkner, John Steinbeck, Truman Capote and Vladimir Nabokov—hated Hollywood, took the money and escaped. Gore Vidal, contrasting the collaborative method of movies with the individual writer, wondered if "such a collective activity as a movie can be regarded as an art at all." Aldous Huxley fiercely agreed: "I shall stick to an art in which I can do all the work by myself, sitting alone, without having to entrust my soul to a crowd of swindlers, vulgarians and mountebanks." Joseph Mankiewicz, who collaborated with Scott Fitzgerald on his only screen credit, *Three Comrades* (1938), observed that Fitzgerald, like Salter, "had simply wandered away from the field where he was a master and was sludging around in an area for which he had no training or instinct."[31]

S. J. Perelman was amusing about his degrading submission to Hollywood. In response to an offer he remarked: "Considering the Kanchanjunga of unpaid bills I have, the appalling heat of N.Y. and the even more appalling sparsity of subjects for *New Yorker* pieces, I was aboard the plane and practicing yesmanship before he'd hardly finished talking." Working on *Around the World in 80 Days* was "all pretty much what I anticipated, hysteria and money being spent like water, ten-million-dollar deals, Mike Todd talking into three phones at once and flying to Mexico and returning from Mexico and Christ-all knows what."[32] A contemporary novelist, who also worked on several successful films, told me:

> Salter's four films made out of sixteen screenplays would be regarded in Hollywood as astonishingly successful. Scriptwriting is a highly technical and unliterary craft. The awful aspects are always the discussions, the rewrites, the idiotic suggestions. A movie script is regarded as a farrago of changes, and the scriptwriter is just a hack who has surrendered his power, independence and integrity for a big payday. It was sheer drudgery. I hated myself afterwards for being involved and taking direction. I would never do it again.[33]

In the 1970s Salter enjoyed the generous perks, but felt seduced and corrupted by the luxury of first-class planes, expensive hotels and fine restaurants, all lavishly funded for script conferences and "research trips." In 1970 Salter went to Corsica with the director Stanley Donen. Salter and his friend Lorenzo Semple rewrote *Avalanche Express*, about the CIA chasing Russian spies. The studio liked their script and flew them to London for consultations, but the director Mark Robson rejected it: a great waste of time but good money. In 1978 Semple, who knew how to work the system, took Salter on a luxurious trip to Tahiti for research on *Hurricane* (1979), an adventure movie based on a novel by Nordhoff and Hall. Unlike the delayed payments and royalties when he was writing a novel, Salter earned instant money for movies that were never made. Nevertheless, he followed the miserable trajectory of serious writers in Hollywood. As late as November 1972, after three of his movies had appeared in 1969, he still lived hand-to-film and had to take a six-week assignment to see him through the winter and spring. Torn between films and fiction, he complained, "I am living two lives. I must abandon one, but I'm afraid if I put myself entirely in one it won't support me, it will give way."[34]

He dreamed of spending his life in the theater and never seeing a movie again. In a late interview he blamed himself: "Hollywood didn't work out for me, really. I don't think about it that much but it's probably my fault as a screenwriter. I mean, the movies kept being bad. That can't all be somebody else's fault."[35] He repeatedly ignored his success, emphasized the waste and angrily noted: "The balance between what I wrote and what was made was low, about four scripts written for each one shot, with the best work often ending in the trash. The waste was depressing. . . . You write a lot, and only a limited amount, if you're lucky, ever reaches the stage of being filmed or on the screen itself. I think that's a very high price to pay."[36] He thought, as Shakespeare wrote in Sonnet 129, that Hollywood was "The expense of spirit in a waste of shame."

Like the earlier screenwriters, Salter recalled the false promises, the forced rewrites and the humiliating rejections, and stressed his self-contempt when he worked for the movies. It's a great pity that he didn't channel his anger and disgust into a satiric Hollywood novel like Nathanael West's *The Day of the Locust* (1939) and Fitzgerald's *The Last Tycoon* (1941), both made into good films. In 1980, after *Solo Faces* was published, Salter bid farewell to Hollywood with a printed refusal card that imitated the one his intellectual hero Edmund Wilson had sent out in 1944. Wilson said he "regrets that it is impossible for him to: Read manuscripts. Write articles or books to order. Make statements for publicity purposes. Judge literary contests. Give interviews." Salter's card said that he "regrets he is far too occupied to: Write a movie script. Polish a movie script. Read a movie script. Take a meeting."[37] Finally, he wittily remarked that leaving movies "wasn't abrupt. I just said I would like to do less of this. I would like to do much less. I would like to do none of it."[38]

SIX

DANGER AND DISILLUSION

Solo Faces and *Dusk*

I

The Romantic poets praised the beauty, majesty and awesome power of the Alps. In *The Prelude* (1805), William Wordsworth described the tremendous force of the torrents that poured down from the mountains and through Chamonix in southeast France:

> the wondrous Vale
> Of Chamouny had, on the following dawn,
> With its dumb cataracts and streams of ice,
> A motionless array of mighty waves,
> Five rivers, broad and vast.[1]

A decade later Percy Shelley described the towering and dangerous snow, ice and rocks in a poem about Mont Blanc (1816), the highest peak in Europe:

> Mont Blanc appears—still, snowy, and serene—
> Its subject mountains their unearthly forms
> Pile around it, ice and rock; broad vales between
> Of frozen floods, unfathomable deeps,
> Blue as the overhanging heaven, that spread
> And wind among the accumulated steeps.[2]

In *Modern Painters* (1843) the keen climber John Ruskin had a religious response to the mountains that stretched toward heaven and were "the centres not only of imaginative energy, but of purity."[3] He was a great admirer of J.M.W. Turner, who painted the swirling colors and vertiginous heights of the Alps. Caspar David Friedrich's *Wanderer Above the Sea of Fog* (1818) portrays the hero triumphantly standing on a mountaintop and surveying the peaks that jut through the clouds below him. Turner's and Friedrich's pictures were matched in modern times by Ansel Adams' photographs of Yosemite: towering, austere, jagged black-and-white images of cloud-swept skies, glistening lakes and dangerous ascents on steep surfaces.

Most of the action of *Solo Faces* (1979) takes place in Chamonix and its hero Vernon Rand makes his most perilous ascents on Mont Blanc, but his attitude to the Alps is completely modern. He feels a sense of inarticulate wonder but is not content with hiking on the lower slopes. He values expertise, skill, risk-taking and the reward of personal validation. Obsessed with his own achievement, he wants to conquer nature, not just admire it.

Salter based his hero, Vernon Rand, on the American mountaineer Gary Hemming (1934–1969), the embodiment of extreme audacity. Hemming's diary lists the perils that Rand also faced, from exhaustion at high altitudes to threatening weather and extreme cold: "You are just never safe. Every single step is dangerous. From the time you leave the valley till you return the mental pressure alone is exhausting enough. You're almost always between 10,000 and 15,000 feet, almost always carrying packs of 30 to 40 lbs. on your back, almost always in a hurry because of the weather or the approaching darkness, always cold or damp or hungry, or all three." Hemming became famous in August 1966 when he rescued two Germans stranded on the Dru far above Chamonix. After his last diary entry, "An aesthetic death. The only thing that can compensate for a ruined life," Hemming killed himself.[4] Rand's death-wish in the novel echoes Hemming's suicide.

W. H. Auden and Christopher Isherwood's play *The Ascent of F6* (1937)—about leadership and ambition, power and tragedy—also illuminates the themes of Salter's novel. Michael Ransom, a famous climber, leads an expedition to reach the top of the fictional Himalayan mountain F6 (named after the Karakoram mountain K2). Ransom asks, "Supposing I abandon the mountain. What shall I do? Return to England and become a farm labourer or a factory hand?" He paraphrases *Henry IV, Part II* to explain his obsession with risks: "Is Death so busy / That we must still kick our heels / And wait for his obsequious secretaries / To page Mankind at last and lead him / To the distinguished Presence?"[5] Racing to defeat his rival climbers, Ransom helps destroy his own companions, reaches the peak and dies.

Solo Faces began as a screenplay that Robert Redford rejected and Salter turned into a novel. Robert Ginna, who'd commissioned Salter's interviews for *People* magazine, had become an editor at Little, Brown, and paid a handsome and unexpected advance of $50,000. The title suggests Rand's solitude and isolation when he faces the forbidding faces of the mountains. The novel, which describes how to climb and the kind of men who accept the challenge, returns to the heroic characters and lean style of *The Hunters*. Mountain climbing, like military campaigns, includes wounds and deaths, failures and retreats, conquests and transcendence. The mountaineer, like the airman and the hawk, looks down from up high. Both pilots and climbers must be fearless, and have expert knowledge, speed and judgment.

The novel begins when Rand is 25 or 26 years old. Born in Indianapolis, he grew up in California, quit college, was drafted into the army and deserted. He moves to Chamonix but never learns much French. Utterly alone, despite male friends and many lovers, he's a rebel, outlaw, noble savage and overreacher. Like Nietzsche's Zarathustra, he yearns to rise above ordinary humanity and stride from mountain peak to peak. When fame suddenly comes, he rejects it. He's fatally flawed and longs for death.

In *Solo Faces*, as in *Downhill Racer*, the focus remains on the mountains and the love interest is transient. Though not a considerate lover, the wild and reckless Rand is catnip to women but can't commit to any of them. His affairs between ascents are brief, and he tentatively returns to women only when his climbing career is finished. In California he first lives with Louise: "She was sardonic, pale. She wanted to be happy, but could not be."[6] He climbs gently with her 12-year-old son Lane, named for Salter's film partner Lane Slate. Like Phillip Dean and Viri Berland, Rand promises to return.

Rand's most important love affair is with Catherin, a French bank teller in Chamonix. Like Aspen, the once unspoiled town has become built up and crowded. She undresses and apologizes for her flat chest; he seems urgent and overpowering to her. Like the fictional Anne-Marie and Lia in *Light Years*, Catherin is sexually available and self-effacing: "She had no desires of her own. She had abandoned them, she accepted his. His intensity almost frightened her, his abruptness. A soon as it was over he fell asleep." Like the real Gary Hemming, Rand doesn't want to be a tied-down father, and when his lover gets pregnant he rejects her. She leaves for Grenoble and returns to her old lover who takes responsibility for her child. In a touching scene Rand, still searching for a vital connection, returns to see his newborn son and perhaps recapture Catherin. She forbids him to enter her house, shows the baby from an upstairs window, then closes the shutters and banishes him from her life. Rejected by her, he suffers from vague longing and momentary regret.

Other women make only cameo appearances. In Paris he lives in the apartment of Colette, sleeps with her, loses interest and immediately falls asleep. She looks after him and advises him; he resents her attentions. They go to Belle Isle off the coast of Brittany with her friend Simone. The latter is nervous and high-strung, grinds her teeth in sleep and has wiry pubic hair. Still, she's a woman; despite her imperfections he sleeps with her. Colette, referring to herself in the third person, furiously screams: "you turn your back for a minute and he sleeps with your friend. It's disgusting. . . . When someone trusts you, you mean you don't feel any regret if you betray them?" He doesn't feel anything. *C'est dommage.*

At a party in Paris he meets the American Susan de Camp, blonde, clean-faced, sun-tanned, wealthy, divorced. Eager for sex like all the others, she pulls up her skirt and seductively shows her panties. But the encounter is not much fun: "That night he lay beside her brooding, more and more discontent, for half an hour, trying to make pleasure finally open its wings." Grateful for his attention, she reassures him by ignoring his poor performance, "That's all right. Really, I'm used to it." But he's filled with a sense of disgust. He returns to California and calls Louise. She wants to see him but he keeps on moving along. Paula, a divorced teacher in California, gets only half a page. She has dark hair and a carefree smile, is sloppy, tells outrageous drunken stories and swears that they are true. He drives away as usual but tentatively returns to her at the end of the novel. All the women lack some essential quality; Rand is incapable of love and fidelity. He feels that lovers will drain the vital energy he needs to confront the perilous mountains and pull him away from his death-defying ascents.

The Alps are both inspiring and associated with death. Rand sees the mountains as a feared and formidable enemy that has to be conquered. The paradoxically fixed and tempestuous "rock is like the surface of the sea, constant yet never the same. One should always climb as if the rope were not there. . . . A great mountain is serious. It demands everything of a climber, absolutely all. It must be difficult and also beautiful" to be worth the risk. Modern techniques and equipment have made it possible to conquer the highest peaks. Salter enhances the atmosphere by lacing the text with technical words: abseiled, *aiguilles*, belaying, *bloc coincé*, carabiners, *couloir*, crampons, *éperon*, *étrier*, jumar, *rognon* and (with a pun): "never trust a piton you don't put in yourself."

The dominant theme in *Solo Faces* is the conflict between courage and fear, holding on and falling off, often expressed in terms of light and dark. Thomas Mann's *Death in Venice* portrays the emotional implications of this theme. The main character's "favorite motto was 'hold fast': indeed, in his novel on the life of Frederick the Great he envisaged nothing else than the apotheosis of the old hero's word of command, '*Durchhalten*,' which seemed to him the epitome of fortitude under suffering."[7] In "A Litany in Time of Plague" the Renaissance poet Thomas Nashe mourned beautiful youths who metaphorically fell to their deaths: "Brightness falls from the air; / Queens have died young and fair." At the end of "The Dead," one of Salter's favorite stories, James Joyce uses the poetic "falling" to suggest death: "snow falling faintly through the universe and faintly falling."

Solo Faces is structured by a series of six crises that match Rand's six women: Neil Love slipping, Jack Cabot injured, John Bray dead, Rand stranded, Italians rescued and Rand's final failure. In each crisis, the greater the risk, the greater the achievement: *ad astra per aspera* (through hardships to the stars). In the first foreshadowing chapter, while Rand works as a laborer outside Los Angeles, he saves a coworker named Gary from falling off a church roof. Japanese amateurs are frequently seen "falling off—it was not unusual to see one in midair." All the crises are associated with slipping or falling. While ascending Pointe Lachenal with the agility of a lizard or squirrel, Rand senses imminent danger: "a terrible event, some suspension of physical law, might take place and everything he knew, was sure of, hoped to be, in one anarchic moment would dissolve. He saw himself falling." Neil Love then slips, fails to self-arrest, bounces down as if he would come apart and is saved by the soft snow.

When Rand climbs with his closest friend, Cabot "performed a sacred act—he began to fall. . . . Cabot's head had fallen forward, his legs dangled." Rand "half-expected the wet gleam of brains as he removed the helmet. The blood rushed forth. It was dripping from the jaw." They spend the night on a narrow ledge and lightning strikes nearby: "Suddenly the dusk went white with a deafening explosion. Blue-white snakes of voltage came writhing down the cracks," threatening to unleash an avalanche. Rand manages to save the injured Cabot and bring him down to base camp.

As Rand makes his way up an ice-filled crack, Bray's foot slips, he tries to get a grip and is afraid that he cannot hang on. As they descend, Bray's worn rope is cut against a sharp rock. He seems to float down the face as Rand witnesses the fatal accident and cries out, "Someone's fallen!" Still in Chamonix, Rand hears that Cabot fell in the Wyoming Tetons and asks, "How far did he fall?" but doesn't know till later on what actually happened. In the final thematic chord at the end of the novel, Rand "had gone as far as he could, had climbed as high. He could go no farther. . . . At that moment he did not want to slip, still grasping desperately for a hold, but instead to suddenly jump clear, to fall like a saint, arms outstretched, face to the sky. He thought of dying. He longed for it."

Salter quotes but does not identify the rousing St. Crispin's Day speech from Shakespeare's *Henry V* to set the stage for Rand's two courageous triumphs: "And gentlemen in England now a-bed will think themselves accurs'd they were not here." When Bray gets sick and fails to turn up, Rand recklessly decides to climb Frêney alone. It was "a buttress, inaccessible and huge, on the side of Mont Blanc. There had been famous tragedies on it." His rope is frozen, hands are numb, and he's afraid he will drop the end and be doomed. When the weather suddenly changes he's stranded overnight and the next day. Reported missing and thought to be dead, he somehow manages to get down and is received like a hero.

Rand speeds into action when he learns that an Italian man and a woman, one badly injured in a fall, have been trapped for nine days on the Dru. The forbidding mountain is "Dark, with black lines weeping down it, a Babylonian temple smashed by centuries, its pillars and passages sheared away, the huge fragments floating through thousands of feet of air to explode on the lower slabs, legendary, unclimbable for decades." A massive rescue operation of 200 people, including guides, gendarmes and mountain troops using lowered cables and helicopters, have failed to get up the North Face. In a daring feat Rand decides to go straight up the West Face, packed with solid ice. He does not let the vastness affect him, clings to the side of the monster and "had his teeth in the great beast," the evil and destructive Antichrist in Revelation 13. Rand rescues them, claims them as his own and brings them safely down. Like Lord Byron after publishing *Childe Harold's Pilgrimage*, Rand wakes to find himself famous throughout Europe. But he hates the sudden publicity: the admiration and photos, interviews and articles. Always the loner, he tries to hide from them.

Weakened by fame, Rand is defeated on the Walker, his last challenge. There was nothing to hold on to: "He was not going to be able to do this. He knew it. The will was draining from him. He had the resignation of one condemned. He knew the outcome, he no longer cared, he merely wanted it to end. The wind had killed his fingers." He's lost his courage and has failed. No longer a hero, he abandons mountain climbing, his *raison d'être*, and continues to drift through a meaningless life.

When Rand returns to California, he learns that Cabot, who fell in Wyoming, had been in a coma for a week. Salter writes with bitter irony, "At first they thought he would never come out of it and only half of him did." He is now paralyzed from the waist down and confined to a wheelchair. On their earlier climb Cabot said he brought his wife Carol along "to milk her" for sexual pleasure. In a subtle moment she tells Rand that Cabot is sexually incapacitated and he resists the temptation to betray his friend and sleep with her.

When Cabot fell and smashed his face on the Dru, Rand had urged him to hold on, told him he could make it and saved him. Like a faith healer, he now attempts the impossible task of forcing Cabot to get out of the wheelchair and walk. He falsely insists, "there's nothing physically wrong with you. Something is keeping you in that chair." Rand pulls him out of the chair and Cabot collapses onto the floor. To test their courage to walk and to die, Rand threatens to kill himself by playing Russian roulette. He pulls the trigger six times and survives. Without telling Cabot, Rand has secretly removed the bullets from the chamber, and forces his friend to watch Rand try to kill himself.

After completing the circle to California and leaving Cabot, Rand ends up working in a Florida wrecking yard that symbolizes his wretched condition. He's lost his courage and interest in climbing, and exclaims, "It is finished." He also winds up very tentatively with Paula, who tells him: "I want to trust someone. I want to feel something. With you, though, it's like somehow it goes into empty air"—like a man falling or a bird that's just been hit. Voicing the recurrent theme, he tells her, three times, to hold on. The novel ends with Rand, now 34, unable to accept love and trust, and with an indeterminate clash between his own darkness and the promise of Paula's lighted room.

Solo Faces was well received and sold a respectable 12,000 copies. The American novelist Vance Bourjaily, in the *New York Times* of August 15, 1979, called it "a beautifully fashioned and satisfying novel . . . an adventurous and exciting book." The English novelist Francis King, born in a Swiss ski resort and writing in the *Spectator* of February 16, 1980, observed, "I can think of no novel that comes closer to explaining the nature of mountain climbing's mystique. The single mindedness with which Rand sets out on his lonely conquests is a potent metaphor of the artistic vocation. Climbing and the highest artistic achievement demand a similar ruthlessness both with self and with others; and in each the aspirant may suffer an inexplicable loss of nerve or of inspiration, so that in a moment he plunges from the airiest heights to the darkest depths."

II

The title of Salter's story collection *Dusk* (1988) suggests the fading daylight and the waning of the characters' lives. The men are often aspiring or failed writers who regret their unfulfilled potential and envy rivals' success. They feel sexual frustration and have sad affairs. The women may be beautiful and in their prime, but must find a lover before they decline: their "lives were ready to be capsized, a vague feeling of unseen fracture. It was exciting."[8] Salter always describes the setting and the weather, the atmosphere of both city and countryside in America and Europe. His people are self-consciously foreigners, out of place wherever they are, at odds with each other and with themselves. His dominant theme is loss, especially loss of hope.

Through cultural allusions, vivid details and simple sentences, Salter hints at the intense feelings of lonely people. He writes that he aimed to create a mood that illuminates the meaning: "Beneath the visible were emotions more potent for their concealment."[9] He uses literary associations to add color and interest to the stories. "Five in the afternoon, the vanishing light," evokes Lorca's poem on Sánchez Mejías, the matador alone in the bullring, to convey the essential isolation of his characters, "*a las cinco de la tarde.*"

Salter brilliantly compresses two great lines of modern poetry— "Downward to darkness, on extended wings" from Wallace Stevens' "Sunday Morning" and "A sudden blow: the great wings beating still" from W. B. Yeats' "Leda and the Swan"—into a phrase about a dying goose: "graceful neck still extended, great wings striving to beat." Salter also draws inspiration from one of his favorite stories, "My First Goose," in Isaac Babel's *Red Cavalry* (1926). Babel described how a goose's "head cracked beneath my boot, cracked and emptied itself. The white neck lay stretched out in the dung, the wings twitched. . . . My heart, stained with bloodshed, grated and brimmed over."[10] Salter concludes the title story "Dusk" with a woman imagining a goose shot and thrashing about in the long grass: "bloody sounds coming from the holes in its beak. . . . The rain was coming down, the sea was crashing, a comrade lay dead in the whirling darkness."

The title of the first story in *Dusk*, "Am Strande von Tanger" (On the Beach at Tangier), alludes to a landscape by the Bohemian artist Wenzel Hollar (1607–1677). Salter confessed, "The title is pretentious, I know. I was in the phase where I thought, 'I'll floor the *New Yorker* with this title!'"[11] But his plan didn't work and they rejected the story. The characters long for the exotic ambience of Arab Morocco, with its permissive homosexuality and drugs, the decadence and corruption that had been described by Paul Bowles and Allen Ginsberg. This tale, written in Salter's distinctively precise and lyrical style, begins with a bold yet simple sentence fragment, "Barcelona at dawn," that contrasts to the title of the book. It takes place on one long, eighteen-hour day, from dawn to midnight. Three young expatriates— Malcolm, an American, and two Germans, his girlfriend Nico and her friend Inge—have been drifting about rather aimlessly and find themselves in a pivotal moment of change. Salter uses a subtle and allusive technique to indicate the delicate shifts in their lives.

In the beginning Malcolm and Nico, living together, are linked in parallel sentences to each other and to their exotic parrot Kalil. (His name means "Friend" in Arabic and is taken from the trendy pseudo-mystic Khalil Gibran): "Nico is asleep. . . . Kalil is asleep. . . . Malcolm is asleep." Malcolm had been drawn to Barcelona by an unnamed story ("Catalan Night" in *Open All Night*, 1922) by the French novelist and career diplomat Paul Morand, who made his name with impressionistic tales of night life in Europe in the 1920s.

As day breaks, the four stone spires of Antoni Gaudí's unfinished Sagrada Familia (Holy Family) church gradually appear. The most extraordinary sight in the city, the church is "a giant grotto whose skin is molded into a continuously curving, twisting construction, studded with stone sculpture and fragments of glass, china, tile, and mosaic."[12] The quiet, even saint-like architect had worked on this building from 1884 until he was killed by a streetcar as he walked to church on June 7, 1926—the day Malcolm was born.

Salter satirizes the idle and pretentious Malcolm, a would-be but non-creative artist who can't even begin to work. A narcissist and poseur, he admires his own body and wears the nonprescription round steel-rimmed glasses popularized by John Lennon. He's implicitly contrasted to Gaudí, a real artist whose mind conceived more than his hand could execute and who dedicated his life to an impossibly ambitious project. As Giorgio Vasari wrote of Leonardo da Vinci, "the cause of his leaving so many things imperfect was his search for excellence after excellence, and perfection after perfection."[13] Malcolm, however, expects celebrity and fame. He wants "to be an artist in the truly modern sense which is to say without accomplishments but with the conviction of genius. . . . His work is the creation of the legend of himself. So long as he is provided with even a single follower he can believe in the sanctity of this design." His "sanctity" also opposes the holy "*Sanctus, sanctus*" announced by Gaudí's lofty spires.

Their tranquil Sunday morning is interrupted by a phone call from Inge. Also from Hamburg, she'd shared a flat with Nico when they first came to Barcelona. She comes from a "low background," but falsely claims that her father is a surgeon. Inge is perpetually dissatisfied, frustrated and enraged. She's furious with her rich Spanish boyfriend who, after sleeping with her, has not kept his promise to call her. To get even, she calls and wakes him at 5 a.m. She impatiently yet pointlessly blows her horn at the slow cars on the way to the beach at Sitges, a resort on the Costa Brava, twenty miles down the coast from Barcelona. Once there, she won't go swimming. When Malcolm asks Nico what's wrong with Inge, she says "Everything" and then adds, "She's having her period." Fed up with Spanish men, Inge wants to go to America, to Rome and to Tangier. Malcolm and Nico have already been to Morocco, where he bought shorts made of blue Tuareg cloth and they picked up the parrot.

Despite all her faults, Malcolm is attracted to Inge, to her green eyes, white teeth, appealing mouth and deep tan, acquired (she claims) in only one day while bathing naked on the rocks. Nico, by contrast, has a wide mouth and can never get tanned, no matter how long she stays in the sun. Nico likes their monogamous life; Inge thinks a man needs a number of women. On the beach Malcolm listens with intense interest and heightened imagination as Inge takes an outdoor shower: "He can hear the soft slap and passage of her hands, the sudden shattering of the water on concrete when she moves aside." As the friends walk arm in arm through the town, Inge says, "People will think the three of us do it together." Sensing Malcolm's attraction, she plans to steal him from Nico. When they drive home with the sunroof open, the night is "so dense with stars that they seem to be pouring into the car."

The story portrays change in both setting and characters. The weather changes, as Malcolm predicted, and they are able to go to the beach. The streets of Sitges change from deserted in the hot midday lunchtime to crowded in the cool of the evening. Nico realizes that Malcolm, less intelligent than she, even stupid, is gradually changing. Dusk is "an hour of melancholy . . . when everything is ended." Inge, aroused by Malcolm's interest, suddenly changes from angry and sulky to laughing and happy. Nico becomes sullen and silent. Malcolm now swims with Inge, period or not, as he previously swam with Nico, who sits alone on the beach. Nico has also changed and somehow become a lesser person: "she is pierced by a certainty that Malcolm feels contempt for her. Her confidence, without which she is nothing, has gone." As Nico loses confidence in her ability to hold Malcolm, Inge confidently believes in herself, in her right to command and possess.

In Chez Swann, where they drink coffee, Nico falls asleep and then awakens to the sound of Spanish guitar music and singing. Malcolm, absorbed with and "poisoned" by Inge, can't hear it. In Proust's *Swann's Way* (1913), Charles Swann, obsessed and degraded by Odette de Crécy, finally realizes that she is not his type, that he's not attracted to her, that he actually finds her physically repulsive. At the end of Salter's story, Malcolm also emphasizes Nico's physical defects: her wide mouth and pale skin, small breasts, large nipples and big behind.

At the beginning of the story, Nico tells Inge that one of their parrots died last week and fears that Kalil (like herself) cannot live alone. Malcolm tells her to leave the parrot, whose bright colors recall Gaudí's rather gaudy church, in the sun. In a masterfully elliptical sentence about Kalil, Salter writes that "He blinks"—and then blinks no more. When Nico and Malcolm return to their flat, transformed by their expedition, they find the parrot dead. In the beginning of the story, Salter writes, the sleeping Nico "lies still, she does not even breathe"; in the end, Kalil's "breath has left his feathers." She sobs inconsolably for the dead bird and their dead love. Malcolm is committed to life, but not to life with Nico. Their bond is severed after Inge appears and the parrot dies. Inge's not as nice as Nico, but he wants her, for a change, anyway.

Nico's powerful father, whose three secretaries seem to confirm Inge's belief that a man needs a number of women, can no longer help her. Barcelona, which shares Tangier's western Mediterranean coastline, lies between Tangier and Hamburg on the Elbe. The rootless characters are torn between these places. The day that began with the great city at dawn ends with tears, darkness and the intimations of death.

"Twenty Minutes" dramatizes the brief time left between a riding fatality and a destined death. The accident takes place near Glenwood Springs, in a remote region of western Colorado. The rider is Jane Vare whose name suggests "dare." Jane resembles Salter's horse-country former wife, whose death he imagines in this story: "Tack on the kitchen table, mud on the wide-board floor. In she strode like a young groom in a worn jacket and boots. She had what they called a good seat and ribbons layered like feathers on the wall." The accident, which she watches while it happens, occurs suddenly as she approaches a familiar gate and the sun is going down: "At the last moment something happened. It took just an instant. [The horse] may have crossed his legs or hit a hole but he suddenly gave way. She went over his head and as if in slow motion he came after. He was upside down—she lay there watching him float toward her. He landed on her open lap. It was as if she'd been hit by a car."

This story was inspired by Hemingway's "The Snows of Kilimanjaro" (1936), in which a man dying in Africa remembers his past life in a series of flashbacks. He has vivid memories of his experiences in Greece, Austria, Turkey, Germany, the Rockies and trench warfare in Italy, and regrets "Now he would never write the things that he had saved to write." The story ends as his wife "did not hear him for the beating of her heart." [14] In Salter's story Jane remembers Manhattan, Sausalito, Haiti and jumping horses (like the one that killed her), and "all the things she had meant to do, to go East again, to visit certain friends, to live a year by the sea. She could not believe it was over." As she dies, "she could hear the pounding of her heart."

As the story shifts back and forth between the vivid past and morbid present, the light fades into dusk and darkness, the minutes pass and her brief time runs out. Her three main memories concern sexual frustration. She once boldly offered herself to a man by seductively asking, "You're not going to make me spend the night alone?" and was humiliated when he confessed that he was homosexual. A tall Englishman at the racetrack in Saratoga Springs took the initiative with the Quakerish gambit, "'I'd like to fuck thee.' 'Some other time,' she told him. 'I don't have another time. My wife's coming tomorrow. I only have tonight.' 'That's too bad. I have every night'"—except tonight with you. In her third memory her husband shocked her by suddenly announcing that "he was breaking off with Mara," who worked in his office. Jane was amazed that no friend had ever told her about his affair; her husband said, "I was sure you knew. Anyway it's over. I wanted to tell you. I wanted to put it all behind us." Instead, shocked and furious, she got out of the car and threw rocks at it. Each one of these concise dramatic episodes could be expanded into an entirely new story. At the last moment Jane recognizes the full significance of the accident: "In one unbelievable instant she realized the power of it, where it would take her, what it meant."

At the end of the story the driver of a passing car, after sex with a high school girl, sees her loose saddled horse, finds her and speeds her to the nearest town. But it's too late and she's dead on arrival. The driver belatedly realizes that it would have been better to have taken her to the nearby vet, who might have saved her and allowed her to live for more than twenty minutes. Theodore Roethke's "Elegy for Jane: *My Student Thrown by a Horse*," which also emphasizes the dying light, could have been written about the tragic life of Jane Vare:

> The sides of wet stones cannot console me,
> Nor the moss, wound with the last light.
> If only I could nudge you from this sleep,
> My maimed darling, my skittery pigeon.
> Over this damp grave I speak the words of my love.[15]

The title of "American Express" wittily uses the name of the travel company to announce its theme: speeding through life in search of pleasure. Like Phillip Dean in *A Sport and a Pastime*, Americans drive through a European country with a foreign girl. Salter's favorite plot also resembles his movie *Three* (1969), in which two male friends are sexually involved with the same woman. (There is also a threesome in "Am Strand.") The story takes place in October 1984. Frank and Alan, inseparable 37-year-old lawyers, eager for money and sex, start a firm called Frik and Frak, a slang euphemism for "fuck," and unexpectedly earn $13 million in a patent-case settlement. During their slavish work in Manhattan, "the city was divided into those coming up and those coming down," which recalls Micah 1:3: The Lord "will come *down*, and tread *upon* the high places of the earth."

The shy Alan gets divorced; he and the bold Frank, on a hedonistic quest, go to Europe with an American girl. After she leaves, the men pick up a complaisant Italian girl and travel around with her. Frank has to bribe the hall porter to allow Eda to sleep in his room. When they leave the hotel, staff whisper to each other in Italian that she's going to ruin, to wreckage, to dust. The wanderers drift aimlessly—mostly eating, drinking and screwing Eda—through Como, Rome, Venice: "the green water slapped as darkness fell"; Padua: "The stands were being set up in the market. It was before daylight and cool"; Verona: "the points of the steeples and then its domes rose from the mist"; Arezzo, Siena, Florence and finally: "So this is Spoleto. . . . Let's have some more wine." In one town the graceful curve of a woman "makes the square so perfect."

Alan, who feels some vital element is missing in him, is unhappy as a *terzo incomodo* (a third wheel) and decides to go home. Frank offers to strengthen their bond by sharing Eda with him. She had worried about how to explain her absence to her parents. When Frank explains the new arrangement she immediately understands and refuses his crude suggestion, but finally agrees. In New York a divorced woman, who needs money and can't find a suitable husband, had bitterly declared, "Women fall in love when they get to know you. Men are just the opposite. When they finally know you they're ready to leave." Alan is delighted with his new lover, who's restored his vitality. He sees the hotel porter drive off on his motorbike to buy rolls for breakfast and contrasts his own fortunate wealth and contentment to ordinary people who are coming down, "who live by wages, whose world is unlit and who do not realize what is above." The privileged Alan is not yet ready to leave Eda, though their precarious liaison could never be permanent.

"Foreign Shores" takes place in the Hamptons where Salter lived, and contrasts two women. The American shore is foreign to the Dutch *au pair* Truus (short for Gertrude). The title also suggests the alien shore of happiness that Gloria, the mother in the family, cannot reach. Though beautiful in her makeup, Gloria is divorced, bitter and miserable. Truus is efficient and takes good care of the five-year-old Christopher. On the beach, she's courted by Robbie, an attractive man who works for a pharmaceutical firm in Saudi Arabia—another foreign shore. They meet again at night, he flatters her and they have clumsy sex. Gloria suspects that Christopher, who likes to climb into Truus' bed and ride her like a pony, has erotic feelings for her and Gloria has actually seen his erection.

Robbie writes Truus letters that reveal his true profession. He recruits young women for porn movies and prostitution: "He went through Europe, city after city, looking for young people who in hotel rooms and cheap apartments . . . stripped and were immersed in a river of sordid acts." Gloria is horrified when she reads the letters, and finds that Robbie is trying to trap Truus and plans to exploit her: *"If you came to Europe it would be great. We would travel and you could help me. We could work together. I know you would be very good at it. The girls we would be looking for are between 13 and 18 years old. . . . Of course, there would be a lot of fucking, too."* Though Truus is naive and innocent, Gloria feels the girl is corrupting Christopher and immediately fires her.

Later on, Gloria sees a photograph in *Town and Country* of Truus, completely transformed, in a fashionable garden party in Brussels. Gloria is jealous and outraged that Truus has used sex to reach a grand social position, while she has been rejected by her lover and remains trapped in her lonely life. An unjust fate has reversed their roles and lumpy Truus is now on top: "The idea that there is an unearned happiness, that certain people find their way to it, nearly made her sick. . . . But then nothing, almost nothing, really made sense anymore."

The title "Lost Sons" refers to sons lost in battle and to the anti-hero Reemstma (Dutch like Truus), who was a lost son both at West Point and as a civilian at the reunion when most of his classmates were still in the army. A painter and outsider, he's a satiric portrait of Salter himself, who never really belonged with the military philistines. As a friend once asked Salter, "What are you doing this for? This isn't really the person you are."

Salter writes: "Reemstma had always been odd. Everyone wondered how he had ever made it through." Bewildered and disaster-prone during close order drill, he'd been awarded two unflattering nicknames. Scarcely recognized and mostly ignored at the class reunion, he's handed a used paper cup and, strangely insensitive to color, wears (and quickly changes) an ugly red-flowered tie made by his wife. She wisely refused to attend the reunion, where "there would be two weird people instead of one."

Reemstma seems to impress Kit Walker, a classmate's wife, by talking about his artistic creation of color and light. But his success—there's a waiting list for his pictures—means nothing to the soldiers, nor even to her. As she drifts away he feels the mood often evoked by Scott Fitzgerald, "A wave of sadness went through him, memories of parades, the end of dances, the Christmas leaves," compounded with the feeling of loss and regret, "The life he might have led came back to him." Classmates now pretend to nominate him during an election, but they are not serious and he "felt foolish. They had tricked him again. He felt as if he had been betrayed. No one was paying any attention to him." He finds Kit Walker, who has a grass stain on the back of her white dress and has had sex with a soldier who takes care to return separately from her. Reemstma doesn't realize the significance of the stain and mistakenly thinks, "she was not like the others." The repetitious last line, "*Der Schiff ist kaputt!*" refers to the Royal Navy sinking the German battleship *Bismarck* in the North Atlantic on May 27, 1944. It also suggests Reemstma's fate as cadet and classmate. Though he's a talented a painter, he still regrets his failure as a soldier. Success is meaningless unless people recognize it.

"Akhnilo," a nonce word that suggests the Latin *ex nihilo* (out of nothing, a word mentioned three times), is Salter's strangest and most Poesque story. In "The Tell-Tale Heart" (1843) the narrator believes that the increasingly loud ringing in his ears is the heartbeat of the old man he has killed. The police investigating the murder don't hear the throbbing sound of the beating heart, which forces the narrator to break down and confess. The police then tear up the floorboards and find the remains of the corpse.

Eddie Fenn, a 34-year-old married carpenter who'd gone to Dartmouth, has come down in the world and become an alcoholic. Untroubled by his condition, "he thought of failure as romantic," and has spent a drunken night lying outdoors and next to his car. Salter contrasts silence and sound, bright stars and black sky, dark and light as the night gradually turns to dawn. Fenn desperately searches for the source of the mysterious sound that wakes him up and pursues him. He is like the helpless toad tortured by a robin: "the crunch of abdomens, the passivity of the trapped." The horrific sound is variously described as a tone, signal, voice, call and cry. It emits an unintelligible language with four distinct, potentially revealing words that he hears but cannot remember.

Fenn crawls around the house and barn and climbs onto the roof of the porch. His wife asks him seven times, "What is it? What's wrong?" but he doesn't answer. She cannot help him and cannot hear the tormenting sound, which is completely inside his head. At the end he's overwhelmed and breaks down: "He shook his head. He was nearly weeping as he tried to pull away." Suddenly he slumped to the floor and sat there." The sound represents nothingness that may come from the soughing of the wind through the trees, a strange bird or insect, his own family or a noisy intruder; it could come from his guilt or fear, alcoholism or delirium tremens; it could be a nightmare, hallucination or ghost as it propels him into madness. The sound continues to haunt him, the mystery remains unsolved.

The title of "Dusk" expresses the melancholy mood of all the stories in this book. Mrs. Chandler, the heroine of this compressed and intensely emotional tale, is similar to Gloria in "Foreign Shores." Both women are bitterly disappointed in love, lonely and past their prime. We first see her standing in front of a red neon sign that ironically says PRIME MEATS. Both women could say, like Leopold Bloom contrasting his past and present in James Joyce's *Ulysses*, "Me. And me now." Mrs. Chandler had all the wifely talents: "She knew how to give dinner parties, take care of dogs, enter restaurants. She had her way of answering invitations, of dressing, of being herself. Incomparable habits, you might call them"—but they have become obsolete. As in "Twenty Minutes," there's a fatal accident—Mrs. Chandler's little boy had drowned—and her husband also makes a shocking confession of infidelity that destroys their marriage. The theme in both stories is "a fine woman whom no one now wanted."

Mrs. Chandler lapses into a sad depression: "She sat at night in the empty living room, almost helpless, not bothering to eat, to do anything. A fatal weariness had set in." Her last hope of happiness lies in her lover. Like Fenn in "Akhnilo," Bill is a fallen idol. He comes from an old and once-prosperous family, wears once-expensive clothes, and spends his time working as a handyman and playing golf. Like Mrs. Chandler's husband, Bill crushes her with a confession: he's returned to his wife and must end their affair. He's afraid she'll tell his wife everything; she promises to remain silent. She also suppresses the futile urge to reveal the emotions that have choked her heart and plead with him to stay with her: "The summer with its hope and long days was gone. . . . All gone now, pony, goose, boy." In "Dusk" the helpless dead bird, rabbit, snake and goose symbolize her gloom and her fate.

"Via Negativa," a variant of Christ's Via Dolorosa and one of Salter's best stories, traces the downward path of a failed writer. In this ironic self-portrait about Salter's long-time lack of recognition, Nile (the real name of his grandson) has thin hair and shabby clothes, bad teeth and stained fingers from smoking. Almost unknown, he has only a few uninteresting admirers, but still hopes for posthumous fame: "He is aware, however, that there is a great, a final glory which falls on certain figures barely noticed in their time, touches them in obscurity and recreates their lives." He's diametrically opposed to the wealthy and successful P., who wears expensive suits and handmade shoes, has a powerful face and rich head of hair. The crowd seems to part as P. struts down the street. Nile is also contrasted to W., who resembles Philip Roth. Famous at twenty for a *New Yorker* novella (like *Goodbye, Columbus*), he's attracted fifty eager young women over the years.

At a dreary required lunch with his mother and aunt, Nile seems to be "sleeping in the museum of his life." He then pays a disappointing visit to his lover Jeanine. Not realizing the implications of his talk, he mentions meeting his hated rival in the street. He thought, with all the money and attention W. was getting, that he was "going to hold out his ring for me to kiss." Ironically alluding to Isaac Babel's famous statement, "No steel could pierce a human heart as deeply as a period in exactly the right place," Nile jealously confesses that all he has is "A needle. If I pushed, it would go straight to the heart." He paradoxically adds, "There's fame worse than failure. . . . He's afraid of me because I've accomplished nothing."

As Nile watches her dress and put on makeup to please another man, he sees that someone has given her a bottle of expensive red Bordeaux. In a few subtle words Jeanine says that she can't see a film with him, refuses his sexual overture in her bedroom and won't say where she's going. To impress her and win her back, Nile claims that Viking is interested in his latest stories *Lovenights* (a variant of Salter's future book *Last Night*). She realizes that he's lying when he can't remember the name of the interested editor, and says "Good-bye," a final farewell. In *Light Years*, Viri had torn Nedra's beautiful dress. Nile now tears Jeanine's clothes, breaks her necklace and fantasizes about whipping her from room to room. He returns to his own dark room, tries to play Bach on his out-of-tune piano, plans to get a car, escape from Manhattan and drive all the way up the coast to Newfoundland. Meanwhile, in a fashionable neighborhood, Jeanine has an elegant dinner, a great contrast to Nile's dutiful family meal, with the seductive P. When Nile was with her the artery in her wrist was not beating. But when she's sexually excited and eager to sleep with her new lover, "her heart was beating slowly but hard." Success and celebrity always have sex appeal.

"The Destruction of the Goetheanum" takes place in Basel on the swift-moving Rhine, near the air base in Bitburg, Germany, where Salter was re-called to active duty in 1961. The obscure and ineffective title, which Salter awkwardly explains on the last page, cannot possibly represent the apogee and extinction of European high culture. In 1913 the muddled and fraud-ulent spiritualist Rudolf Steiner designed and built a hideous structure, named for Goethe, in Dornach, Switzerland, eight miles south of Basel. This Wagnerian *Gesamtkunstwerk*, including paintings and engraved glass, became the center of his crankish cult. Steiner claimed that from this for-tification, terminal and observatory "one could look into the soul." Like the Renaissance scholar Francis Bacon, but without his intellectual powers, he aimed "to encompass all of what was then human knowledge." On De-cember 31, 1922 (eleven years before the more famous Reichstag fire) the building burned, perhaps by arson, to the ground.

The unnamed narrator is a lonely, aspiring American writer who meets the charming young Nadine. (Like Nedra in *Light Years*, Nadine grew up in a small town in Pennsylvania.) This story repeats, without improving, some elements of "Via Negativa," which comes just before it in *Dusk*. Nadine is the disillusioned lover of another childish and selfish, failed and unknown author, William Hedges, who has infected teeth and is writing a story "The Goetheanum." He doesn't like to be alone, but has to be alone when he works. He's published one fragment in Rome, probably in the *Botteghe Os-cure*, and lives on the money sent by his rich brother-in-law. As in the earlier story, "men his age had made their reputations, everything was passing him by." But he absurdly believes that "he was following the path of greatness which is the same as disaster" and still vainly hopes "for something, some proof in the end that his talents had been as great as the others." As Hedges' life collapses the narrator, his half-hearted competitor, is humiliated and unsuccessful with the elusive Nadine who suddenly disappears. Hedges foolishly identifies with Steiner's megalomaniacal structure, believes in an absurd philosophy and doomed enterprise, and equates Oswald Spengler's decline of Western civilization with his own lack of talent and personal failure.

Salter portrays aspiring and failed writers who merely pretend to have talent. Craving recognition himself, he wonders if he will be admired or neglected, if success means public praise or merely satisfaction with his own work. A veil of melancholy shrouds the stories in *Dusk*, which have changing lights, sudden transitions, sentence fragments and shifting points of view; an elegant style, obscure allusions, satire, irony and wit. The web of relationships, the emotional entanglements, the tragic and exalted moments inevitably lead to disappointment and defeat, humiliation and loss.[16]

JIM AND KAY AT THE TABLE, JULY 2006

JEFF, KAY AND JIM ON THE BEACH

JEFF, JIM, KAY AND VAL ON THE BEACH

JIM

SEVEN

MEMORIES
AND MISFORTUNES
Burning the Days and *Last Night*

I

When Salter finished *Downhill Racer* and *Solo Faces*, he confessed, "I'm very tired of writing about people without education, intelligence or ideas," so he began to write about himself.[1] *Burning the Days* (1997) is not a traditional autobiography, but a judicious selection of Salter's experiences and memories, his loves and friends. He describes his family and boyhood, years at West Point, flight training, platonic love affair, first marriage, combat in Korea, recall to Air Force duty, life in Paris, screenwriting in Hollywood and literary companions in New York. The title suggests both the jet fuel he burned as a pilot and the intensity of his own young life. It also alludes to risk and celebrates survival. In Isaiah 43:2 the Lord comforts Jacob by assuring him, "When thou walkest through the fire, thou shalt not be burned."

Salter had given up two successful careers, fighter-pilot and screenwriter, turned his back on marriage and financial security, and now evokes the past. Four of his rather *recherché* chapter titles convey the mood of this memoir and suggest a range of cultural references that amuse or mystify. Pronaos, or introduction, is the entrance hall to a Greek temple; Icarus is the doomed flyer of Greek mythology; Ukiyo are the Japanese prints of ordinary life, the "floating world" that strongly influenced Impressionist painters; Dîners en Ville evokes his family life in France. Salter aims to rescue the burned past by writing about it: he has come through the fire and found a better life.

The metaphorical style is one of the glories of the book, and his descriptions of places and people are richly suggestive: grisly, pictorial, nostalgic and witty. War-blasted Manila "was half-destroyed; the tops were blown off the palm trees, the roads were ruined, the air filled with dust."[2] He admires the desert of Morocco, "its desolation and the brilliance of the light." He remembers in his beloved France, "the yellow headlights flowing along the road at night, the towns by a river, the misty mornings." Faces are theatrically lit by the dashboard of a car. Enemy planes suddenly appear like moving stars with "fateful glints." A burned face is a "glossy reminder" of an air crash. Pilots put down a plane "as gently as a glass figurine on a cabinet shelf, the wheels seem to touch with a feline softness." Salter writes of "the vast patience of the insane"; of people slowly emerging from the sea like details in a developing photograph; of "the heavens littered with stars, the earth strewn with lights"; of pristine women, "uncirculated, as they say of certain coins"; of a delicate young woman who "weighed sixty-two kilos, the absence of any part of which would have been a grave loss."

Salter's terse, finely chiseled Hemingwayesque sentences hint at deeper meanings: "Torture did not break him. Nothing could"; "His spine had been broken but not his will." In "In Another Country" Hemingway wrote, "In the fall the war was always there, but we did not go to it any more." Salter echoes this with "When the weather was bad, as it was that spring, we did not fly." Hemingway wrote in "The Killers," "'You're a pretty bright boy, aren't you?' 'Sure,' said George. 'Well, you're not.'"[3] In *Burning the Days* a woman tells Salter, "You're not very smart. You don't even know what I'm saying." In *Across the River and Into the Trees* Hemingway satirized his older rival Sinclair Lewis, whose cancerous skin looked "like Goebbels' face, if Herr Goebbels had ever been in a plane that burned, and not been able to bail out before the fire reached him."[4] Describing his agent, who had signed photos of Sinclair Lewis and Hemingway in his office, Salter wrote, in a subliminal recollection, that the man "looked like a naval lieutenant who had been burned in a turret explosion."

Salter's earliest memory was riding in a horse-drawn carriage. The Hudson was the river of his life when he lived in Manhattan, in West Point and in the towns between them—the setting of *Light Years*. The tall superior doorman at his family's posh apartment had been a lawyer in Poland and was scornfully known as the Count. Salter's mother—the youngest, most beautiful and most willful of four sisters—had spent a lively girlhood going to diplomatic parties in Washington.

His promising father made a fortune in real estate, then lost $70,000 in a bad loan and another $75,000 in the stock market. Like Charles Gould in Joseph Conrad's *Nostromo*, he put his faith in material interests and when his wealth disappeared he lost interest in life. Ruined, and ashamed to be seen, he would lie in bed for hours. Salter's father, distant from his son, played an ineffectual role in his sexual enlightenment. It began when Salter saw a naked woman through the window of a nearby apartment; continued when his father took him to a doctor whose vague explanations left him baffled; learned about masturbation from a priapic school friend; and completed his sentimental education by finding a hidden telltale pamphlet.

Salter's father had been first in his class at West Point in 1919 and Salter, following in his footsteps, graduated from West Point in 1945. Both men finished too late to fight in their contemporary world wars. His father was recalled to duty during World War II, Salter during the Cold War in Berlin. Salter had been accepted as an undergraduate at Stanford, but to please his father went to West Point. He was a natural alien and rebel whose demonic motto was *non serviam*, but he tried to fit in and become unnoticed. The rules of the military academy—the mindless hazing, the robotic discipline and hateful punishment—were a perpetual horror show. Like a skillful butler, Salter spent pointless hours polishing his breast plate and belt buckle. Cadets who failed secretly wept, wet their beds, sneaked away and even hanged themselves: "It was a place of bleak emotions, a great orphanage, chill in appearance, rigid in its demands." The army instructed its future soldiers to follow orders, however stupid and self-destructive; taught slavish submission rather then initiative and leadership. When I questioned Salter about this unsatisfactory tuition, he defended the humiliations as useful and necessary: everyone had to go through it and you got used to the training, which toughened you up and bonded you with your classmates. He was, at least, first in his class in military history.

To compensate for his father's weakness and failure, Salter became a fighter-pilot in the Korean War, won a gunnery championship and led an air-acrobatics team. Flight training, aloft in the unstructured air, was dangerous and exhilarating. He observed, with an eagle's eye, "the ground floating by with tidal slowness, the roads desolate, the rivers unmoving."

After getting lost at night and running out of fuel, he crashed into a house in Massachusetts. Salter recovered from this disaster; other pilots were not so fortunate. Their planes could be treacherous, could disintegrate when hit by enemy fire: "Pieces of metal were flying off, the whole carefully constructed machinery was coming apart miles above the earth, shedding wings, hurtling out of control." One friend ejected safely, then fell to his death: "Arms flapping, he would tumble endlessly, his parachute, long and useless, trailing behind." Another went into a vertical dive: "The body was destroyed beyond recognition. More than that can hardly occur."

Korea in 1952 was the real place for the right stuff: "You were not anything unless you had fought." The pilots were not allowed to attack the enemy airfields across the border in China. (In the Vietnam War they were forbidden to bomb Hanoi.) Their mission was to keep the Russian MIGs from attacking American bombers which, heavily laden and flying low, were heading north to destroy railroads and dams. In aerial warfare "the secret was simple: get in close, as close as possible, within fifty feet if you could, so close you could not miss." By risking everything Salter achieved his goal, redeeming both his father and himself.

His wartime experience, fascinating to read, was precious to him. But he strangely alternated between the ecstasy of aerial combat—the delirium of the brave—and the long hours on remote and boring bases: waiting, drinking, playing cards, swapping stories and taking, like a pasha, all the women he wanted. In 1957, the year after *The Hunters* was published, the promising lieutenant-colonel, destined for high rank, boldly—rashly—gave up his commission and became a professional writer. "As I walked into the Pentagon," to resign, he remarked, "I felt I was walking to my death." Art also demands risk. He was surprised to be retained after his plane crash and surprised again to be casually released when he should have been asked to stay.

Burning the Days, like his novels, has intensely erotic moments. A dashing, heroic figure, Salter is always aroused and tempted by sensual women. In his youth, he's filled with urges which the beauties sometimes "put down skillfully, like insurrections." In Honolulu he makes *il gran rifiuto* by not sleeping with the great love of his early life, his best friend's wife: "When Paula and I fell in love he overlooked it, for her happiness and to keep her, I suppose, and probably because he was sure of me." Since anticipation of sexual pleasure, which fulfills any fantasy, is often greater than the physical reality, their love was intensified by restraint rather than by consummation. As John Keats wrote of permanent promise, "For ever wilt thou love, and she be fair!"

Instead, Paula arranges his marriage. He is "bridled" (like a horse and to a bride) to an attractive, unspoiled, upper-class woman from the horse country of Virginia. He thought the quasi-vicarious marriage would last five years. It lasted for twenty-four and produced four children. When they were living in isolation in Grasse, near the Mediterranean coast of France, and he had no one to talk to about his work, he gave his wife a story and asked for her response. The abyss opened between them when she could neither understand nor encourage him: "'Well, what did you think?' 'About what?' 'The story.' 'I couldn't make head or tail of it.'" Salter's marriage, like his mother's, "had been wrong, she had known it early."

Salter is bitter and angry about the time he wasted making movies. He hated the fakery and tedious repetition; the aura of artificiality that both attracts and repels; the realization that "the best scripts are not always made." He quotes Cesare Zavattini—who wrote the finest postwar Italian films: *Shoeshine, The Bicycle Thieves, Umberto D.*—sadly confessing, "The cinema has failed." The money, the luxuries, the exotic locales, the famous stars, the sexual adventures were tremendously attractive. But he believed that working in the movies had turned him into a *poule*, a whore, for fifteen years. When a producer asked if there was a film in his latest novel, he caustically replied, "There's no film in anything I write, not even in scripts."

Salter's military education gave him an inordinate respect for sophisticated literary editors. But these men did not respect or envy his combat experience. In *Burning the Days* he does not discuss his writer-friends— Saul Bellow, Peter Matthiessen, George Plimpton and Richard Ford—but he exalts the obscure editors who helped him and would otherwise be forgotten. Robert Ginna was an ex-naval officer, writer and editor. He lived near Salter in Sag Harbor, "in painter's country, far out on Long Island: the flatness of the land, the incredible light." He tried and failed to make a movie with Salter; commissioned, as editor of *People* magazine, Salter's interviews with Vladimir Nabokov and Graham Greene; and published *Solo Faces* when he was head of Little, Brown. Unwilling to dispute his knowledge, Salter loved him and called him "the most successful man I have known, sure in his apprehension of life and in his values." He was even impressed by Ginna's phony woman-friend who falsely asserted, "Thomas Mann, God. His children, it was all incest." Mann wrote "Blood of the Walsungs" about incestuous twins, but his troubled homosexual and suicidal children were not incestuous.

Joe Fox, who published *Light Years* at Random House, also had some unimpressive qualities: "Harvard (swimming team captain), divorced (man about town), backgammon player, also squash, and acquainted with almost everyone." Like Ginna he was deaf to argument; he enjoyed (like many people) travel, ballet and parties. The foppish Ben Sonnenberg wore a flowing bow tie and carried a cane. The son of a wealthy advertising pioneer and art collector, he used his inheritance to found a literary quarterly, *Grand Street*, and published several of Salter's stories. When Salter's overambitious play failed, Sonnenberg cruelly declared, "I didn't like it."

Salter devotes thirteen pages to the most egregious example of undeserved admiration. He kissed Robert Phelps and wanted to kiss his "beautiful feet" as he lay on his deathbed. Phelps was an important but unfortunate influence on his life and brought out Salter's worst traits: uncritical adoration of Paris; worship of Colette, the mediocre Paul Léautaud and the anti-Semitic Marcel Johandeau; snobbery about expensive restaurants and costly wines; lapses into a precious mannered style; pretentious and irritating names of book titles and characters. Phelps condemned his own hopeless failure; Salter admired him. Like Ginna, Phelps also went in for salacious anecdotes. He claimed that the timid and inexperienced Duke of Windsor had married the duchess "because she was the finest fellatrix in Europe." Salter, a survivor, was drawn to lives like his father's that were achieved in agony: *il faut payer*. Ginna lost all his money, Sonnenberg was shattered by multiple sclerosis, Phelps was tormented and ravaged by Parkinson's disease. In a strange twist of taste, Salter adored Phelps but criticized Bellow.

The death of his daughter Allan reverberates through Salter's works. In *Burning the Days* he alludes to an unnamed story by Anton Chekhov about the effect of a child's death to explain his own feelings. In "Enemies" (1887) a doctor's son, aged six, dies of diphtheria. Right after that a frantic husband arrives and begs the doctor to save his dying wife. The doctor resists at first but finally gives in. When they reach the house, the husband discovers that his wife has faked her illness and sent him away so she could run off with her lover. The doctor is furious that the husband has dragged him away from his grieving wife and into his emotional chaos. The faithful wife has lost her child; the faithless wife has gained a lover. Chekhov observes, "It's an agonizing state! You most love those near you when you're in danger of losing them," and describes the all-pervasive "feeling of hopelessness and pain." The intense sorrow of death and betrayal do not bring the grieving characters together. As with Salter and his ex-wife, it drives them apart.

Robert Frost lost three children. When his son Carol shot himself, Frost—like Salter—was devastated, felt terribly guilty and tried to find an explanation for his death. But he also felt that Carol's stoical son had been strengthened by the tragedy and told him: "Disaster brought out the heroic in you. You now know you have the courage and nerve for anything you may want or need to be."[5] Salter recalled, "At the end of the summer in 1980 we drove East. I had been living in Colorado and after the death of my daughter decided, more or less, to go home. I was drawing the line beneath ten years." He tried to forget what had happened, but remembered that Lane Slate's son had been killed in a bicycle accident. Children also suffer and die in *Light Years*.

Salter's memoir illuminates the reality that inspired the novels. It describes the sleek but stranded Delage automobile; the theatrical producer who has scleroderma: "I put my hand on it. It was like a mummy's leg"; the sculptor whose bed is mounted on four tall columns: "you had to help her up, there was full complicity"; a woman who exclaims, like Nedra, "a man can always at fifty or sixty, start a new life, but a woman is used up," stripped of illusions but unable to say farewell; the model for Nedra herself: "her frankness and charm, the extravagance and devotion to her children. She smoked, drank, laughed raucously. There was no caution in her"; and a conclusion that echoes the ending of *Light Years*: "Feeling of courage. Great desire to live on."

Salter notes that in *A Sport and a Pastime* he hoped to transcend the pure concentration on eroticism and write something "licentious yet pure, an immaculate book filled with images of an unchaste world more desirable than our own"; that in *Light Years* he wished "to summarize certain attitudes towards life, among them that marriage lasted too long. I was perhaps thinking of my own." He wanted to (and luckily didn't) call this novel *Nyala*, an African antelope, or *Mohenjodaro*, an ancient city in the Indus Valley, and used the last four letters as the surname of Viri's closest friend.

Salter treasures writing but is uncertain about its lasting value. He believes "the only things that are important in life are those you remember" and "the thoughts of everything that happened, the notes that confirmed it make it imperishable." But he's also ambivalent about the power of words and believes, "To write of someone thoroughly is to destroy them. . . . Things are captured and at the same time drained of life, never to shimmer or give back light again." The words endure, but the real events and feelings are lost.

Truth in his memoir is also ambiguous. He recalls William Faulkner boasting that he'd been a flyer in France and came to believe it: it suited him to remember it that way. John Huston claimed that he'd fought at Monte Cassino and told his lover stories about it. When Salter tells her that Huston was a film director, not a fighter, she replies: "Well, he thinks he did. That's the same thing." Salter corrects Faulkner and Huston, insists that he is truthful and writes the version of reality that he remembers, but he is not an artist on oath and likes to improve his own stories. In his *Paris Review* interview he says, "You are perfectly entitled to invent your life and claim that it's true. . . . In great works of art there is a truth that transcends mere facts."[6]

Salter did not, as he claimed, publish his schoolboy verse in *Poetry* magazine. A few commonplace clips of his twelve-minute football film *Team Team Team* show players crashing against each other. But he vaguely maintains that "it had won a first prize at Venice," though there was no prize there for short documentaries and no evidence that he ever won anything. When an aspiring actress tells him that she's won a prize at the Taormina film festival, he asks, "which prize?" and she replies, "I don't know. Darling, I can't believe it."

Salter stretches the truth in a great sexual and spaceship fantasy, not meant to be taken seriously. On July 21, 1969, Buzz Aldrin and Neil Armstrong were launched into space from Cape Canaveral and became the first men to walk on the moon. Salter watches this tremendous event on television in a New York hotel while having sex with John Huston's former mistress, the unnamed Roman countess and painter Valeria Alberti. As the spaceship is explosively shot into the air Salter, with all-too-perfect timing, has a simultaneous orgasm: "she is writhing, like a dying snake, like a woman in bedlam. Everything and nothing, and meanwhile the invincible rocket, devouring miles, flies lead-heavy through actual minutes and men's dreams."

In *Burning the Days* Salter attempts to discover his true identity, to find his real self hidden among his many protean roles, and asks the crucial question: "Who are you?" Was he a fighter or writer, a screenwriter or

serious novelist? He realizes *"That person in the army, that wasn't me."* His
divided self is ready to abandon false roles and experience a conversion:
"I began to change, not what I was truly but what I seemed to be . . . to let
my true desires and real self live. . . . The road was leading elsewhere, to
what seemed a counterlife." Like Cortez in Keats' poem "On First Looking
into Chapman's Homer," Salter realizes that "at a certain point one stands
on the isthmus and sees clearly the Atlantic and Pacific of life. There is the
destiny of going one way or the other and you must choose." He "had come
very close to achieving the self that is based on the risking of everything,
going where others would not go, giving what they would not give." Finally,
he finds his real self and becomes a writer.

Sophisticated, wise and slightly cynical, Salter is still idealistic, at least
about his own work. *Burning the Days*, with its cunning indirection and
vivid narration of art and action, love and war, recalls André Malraux's *An-
timemoirs*. As in the novels, Salter finally realizes that "somewhere the true
life is being lived, though not where you are." He gave up a lot—glory, wealth,
prestige—to become a novelist, to create something lasting. He had "the rapturous dreams of an opium addict, intense but inexpressible," and wanted
"to achieve the *assoluta*"—as a great dancer becomes the *prima ballerina
assoluta*. "It is only in books," he believes, "that one finds perfection; only
in books that it cannot be spoiled. Art, in a sense, is life brought to a stand-
still, rescued from time." That is what he achieved. In his novels, the ideal
life is elusive and unobtainable. In the memoir, the ideal is found in art.[7]

II

In *Last Night* (2005) Salter compresses his stories like grapes to extract
their essence. The vivid characters rush through light and darkness as if
they were riding the Elevated train in New York. Dusk symbolizes the end
of the day and of life. Beautiful women, well endowed like a rich convent, ignite these sophisticated, satiric and sexy stories. They portray the deception,
guilt and betrayal of the beautiful and the disappointed, the rich and the
divorced. The characters frequently challenge the constraints of monogamy,
and their safe domestic present cannot match their past memories of youth-
ful sex in exotic locales. Salter's themes include broken marriages, mystical attraction, repressed agony, forbidden homosexuality, mutual betrayal,
emotional repression, perverse temptation and the limitations of charisma.

* * *

In "Comet" a man's second marriage disintegrates as his resentful and bitter wife exposes the faults of his first marriage and tries to destroy his indelible erotic memories of the past. Salter writes, "his persona was capable and calm. He'd gone to Princeton and been in the navy," past his prime but still a real man. He'd fallen in love with his retarded son's tutor and, after fifteen years of marriage, left his wife and three children. He realizes "he had done everything wrong in the wrong order." The tutor turned out to be an unfaithful call girl. But as he remembers his first ecstatic year with her in Mexico, he'd do it all over again: "driving down the coast for the weekend, through Cuernavaca, her bare legs with the sun lying on them, her arms, the dizziness and submission he felt with her as before a forbidden photograph, as if before an overwhelming work of art." It was thrilling love, "when you lose the power to speak, when you cannot even breathe." He had never felt such emotional intensity with either wife.

The gulf widens between husband and wife, and their marriage is doomed, when he takes her outside to witness a spectacular sight and she fails to see the bright tail of a whirling comet that is clearly visible. She says they can look for it again tomorrow; he says, "It won't be there tomorrow. One time only." He stares at the starry sky while she disappears across the lawn and trips on the kitchen steps. The past, Salter notes, "can't be changed. It can't be just turned into unhappiness." As he explained in an interview, "Comet" "is about a wife who, at a dinner, begins trashing her husband's life, his past, but in a way she can't because it was marvelous and it belongs to him, he lived it, it can't be touched."

The punning title of "Eyes of the Stars" refers to the stars in the sky and the eyes of film stars examined by the ophthalmologist. This satire on Hollywood begins with Teddy, a successful film producer and widow of an eye doctor. She's entered the world of fraudulence and dreams, and sees projects "on the way to realization or oblivion, sometimes both." The strangely named Boothman Keck is a rather passive, naive and married swimming coach. At the Los Angeles airport he escorts a famous movie star, Deborah Legley, who's been spoiled and corrupted by the movie business. On Teddy's film set "she turned out to be a monster. She made everyone wait, snubbed the director, and barely acknowledged the presence of the crew."

Teddy prepares caviar and invites them both to dinner. Deborah keeps Keck waiting outside her door and calls Teddy a boring idiot. She suggests they go out to eat without Teddy, and makes Keck cancel the dinner by claiming that Deborah's dog is sick. They drive to a restaurant, she picks a quarrel with the new owner of the place and they suddenly leave. On the way back Keck rescues a moth on the windshield. Deborah mocks him by asking, "Are you a Buddhist or something?" He wittily replies, while identifying with the insect, "No, I didn't know if he wanted to go where we're going, that's all."

Deborah recalls resisting an early attempt at seduction while in her teens. The older man had retrieved her lost earring, and she puts him off with "just the earring. . . . Let's not raise the curtain so fast." Continuing to be nasty and offensive to Keck, she declares, "One never has the human company one longs for. Something else is always offered." When she leaves the room, Keck phones Teddy and tells her "it's even worse if she likes you." Instead of being dismissed as a nonentity, you have to spend time with her and tolerate her insulting behavior. Teddy has had a far better life than the famous aging actress. At the end Teddy fondly recalls memories of her late husband. Like the husband in "Comet," she remembers her sexually exciting past: "the beer bottles rolling around in the back of the car when she was fifteen and he was making love to her every morning and she did not know if she was beginning life or throwing it away, but she loved him and would never forget."

"My Lord You" is a phrase from a sweet and sad eighth-century Chinese poem by Li Po, "The River Merchant's Wife," translated by Ezra Pound in *Cathay* (1915). In the poem the devoted and faithful wife, a contrast to the dissatisfied heroine of the story, addresses her distant husband: "At fourteen I married My Lord you. / I never laughed, being bashful. / Lowering my head, I looked at the wall. / Called to, a thousand times, I never looked back." Salter's story follows the ardent Ardis. He rapidly switches scenes from the remains of an elegant dinner party to the local library, the beach, the empty house of a poet and her own home.

The party is ruined by the late appearance of the dirty, drunken, intimidating and damaged poet Michael Brennan, a character based on Dylan Thomas. He's a parasitic self-proclaimed failure and genius, whose Venezuelan (third or fourth) wife has run off. He vividly recalls his *coup de foudre*: "She was walking by on the beach. I was unprepared. I saw the ventral, then the dorsal. I imagined the rest. Bang! We came together like planets." He dramatically quotes three passages from Ezra Pound's *Cantos*, refuses to eat and demands more drink. He seems to cast a spell on the shocked guest Ardis by boldly touching and then cupping her breast. After his close friend Deems (named after the music critic Deems Taylor) finally gets him out of the house, Brennan misses a curve in the road and cracks up his car.

In the library Ardis reads Pound's poems but can't find Brennan's. The librarian explains that in an act of self-censorship "he takes them away because unworthy people read them." At the dinner party she'd cryptically declared, "I think there's such a thing as sleeping with one man too many." In the library she remembers, "There had been one My Lord though she did not marry him." The one man too many is her husband, whom she refuses to sleep with after the party. Her sexual and marital frustration helps to explain her irrational, even mystical attraction to the disastrous poet.

On the way back from a sensual day at the beach, Ardis stops at Brennan's empty house and is terrified by the poet's huge dog, who embodies the spirit of his master: "She could hear the clatter of his nails like falling stones . . . his large, wet toenails gleaming like ivory." Suddenly, the dog disappears. On her second visit, Ardis searches for the poet throughout the house as the now-gentle dog follows her, and feels she's meant to be found there: "All she had never done seemed at hand." Surrendering to a wild impulse, she strips to the waist to reveal the breast Brennan once touched, ritually offers herself to the poet and awaits his arrival.

Her husband finds her and takes her home as the faithful canine stand-in follows them. Though Brennan was absent, he has a powerful effect on Ardis. She thinks, "My life has meant nothing," and is intensely unhappy with Warren, her lawyer and fixer husband. Brennan's dog, faithful to her, is now more important than Warren. As the dog moves wearily off, Ardis, liberated and rejuvenated, runs after him: "She seemed free. She seemed like another woman, a younger woman." This story, like several others, portrays a disappointed married woman who longs for the sexual thrills of the past. Led on by the dog, Ardis strives for an impossible, even self-destructive liaison with the poet.

In the ironic story "Such Fun" three close women friends discuss their money, sex and disappointments with alcoholic, unfaithful ex-husbands and lovers. They even express interest in the doorman and super of the apartment: "He's another story." Their gossipy but sad talk reveals their unhappy lives before the final shocking revelation.

The uninhibited Kathrin is, like Zelda Fitzgerald, "glamorous, uncaring. She had passion, daring." Salter writes that her defects were unimportant, "There was not much more to her than met the eye, but that had always been enough." She makes sexual revelations, prefers "on and off" to "off and on," compares eating oysters to swallowing semen and admits that she likes to be sodomized. Like many of Salter's women, she recalls happier days during the pastoral New England mornings when she first married: "She remembered driving to little summer theaters, the old iron bridges, cows lying in the wide doorway of a barn, cut cornfields, the smooth slow look of nameless rivers, the beautiful, calm countryside." Leslie, fixed in the bitter present, says men "remember you longer if you don't do it," and asks, "Have you ever decided this is as far as you can go?" in life and have no meaningful future.

Throughout the evening Jane has been silent and withdrawn, unable to break through the frivolous chatter. She can't tell her closest, egoistic friends—who don't want to hear her tragic news, would not understand her condition and are not able to feel her pain—that she'd spent the afternoon talking to a doctor before emerging onto the unreal street. She is doomed with Stage Four cancer, and there is no Stage Five. The friends long for their lost past; Jane has no future.

Salter's conclusion was influenced by Chekhov's early story, "Misery," in which a grieving cabman tries to tell his friends about his son's death, but no one will listen. At last, he confides in his horse. In Salter's story, Leslie says the evening has been such fun and Jane takes her awkward leave. In the taxi home she bursts into cathartic tears that streak her face and tells the driver of the confessional cab what she could not tell her friends: "[I'm] not sick. I'm dying of cancer." The driver, used to hearing so many strange people, doesn't know if she's really telling the truth. Death casts a glaring light on the other two women who are still playing sexual games.

In "Give," Anna, her little boy, her unnamed husband and his best friend Des who lives with them, seem blissfully happy on her 31st birthday, complete with flowers, rum cake and the present of a Cartier watch. Des, a successful but mentally unstable poet, has an ideal life: "That was his talent, to live as he liked, almost without concern, to live as if he would reach the desired end one way or another and not be bothered by whatever came between. . . . Everyone lies about their lives, but he had not lied about his." His poetry—

"*There lay the delta, there the burning arms*" and "*the light fluttering on the fronds*" (apparently written by Salter)—was "not about rivers uncoiling but about desire." The husband says the witty Des makes him feel joyous. They have common interests and tastes, a perfect meeting of the minds, though Des always knows more than he does. It was as if they "had sat in the same classes and gone to the same cities."

The husband and Anna have a custom called a "give," an undeniable request to stop doing something unpleasant or intolerable: "once a year, without causing resentment, you would be able to ask your husband or wife to stop this one thing." Seizing this privilege, Anna asks her husband to stop having sex with Des. He denies her accusation, but she's not persuaded and insists, "he has to leave. For good. If you want me to believe you, that's what it takes." With great reluctance and embarrassment he tells Des that Anna has discovered their homosexual secret. Bowing to her demands, he shatters their precious friendship and tells Des that he must leave. Des continues his glittering insouciant life in the Greek islands. The husband, devastated by the "injustice," follows Des' career "from afar, the way a woman does a man she was never able to marry." His rapturous admiration for and intellectual deference to Des resembles Salter's emotional friendship with the married Robert Phelps. Anna's discovery and accusation sound very like what the wife of the bisexual Phelps might have felt.

In Guy de Maupassant's famous story "The Necklace" (1888) that piece of jewelry destroys a life. A woman borrows a precious necklace to wear at a ball, loses it, and has to borrow an enormous sum to replace it. She ruins her marriage and life by slavishly working to pay the debt. Years later, the owner of the necklace tells her that the item she borrowed was a fake and made of paste. In "Platinum" Salter uses a similar motif of borrowed jewelry. A pair of precious borrowed earrings reveal to Brule that he and his son-in law Brian are having adulterous affairs with the same young woman, Pamela. When Brule, a successful lawyer, is cooking his birthday dinner, Pamela, who works at the U.N. and helps out at dinner parties, calls him "darling."

Brian seems to have a solid marriage and is especially close to his young precocious daughter Lily. But he is also ecstatically in love with Pamela: "the splendor and newness of her! He had known nothing like it." He's even more joyous than ever with his family: "The prohibited feeds the appetite for all the rest." When Brian confesses and claims the affair is not important, his furious wife throws him out of the house and says her father will kill him. Meanwhile, at a U.N. party in the Four Seasons, Pamela meets a handsome and wealthy Tunisian diplomat, who gives her a thousand dollars for her favors.

One morning Pamela sees and covets a pair of platinum earrings that belong to Brian's wife and that he picked up after they'd been repaired. She insists on borrowing them despite the risk and, unwilling to displease her, he reluctantly agrees. At another party Brian sees Pamela talking to Brule and wearing the telltale earrings. Brule summons Brian to lunch and, taking the high moral ground, hypocritically condemns Brian and orders him to give up Pamela so he can have her for himself. Brule thinks it's all right for him, but not for Brian, to sleep with Pamela. Brule warns that if Brian tries to expose him, he would deny the liaison and Pamela would back him up.

Sensing "something impending and unbearable," Brian desperately tries all day to get in touch with Pamela. Finally, she tells him the truth—a recurrent theme in this lying story—and promises to stop seeing Brule. She doesn't tell Brian that she's already rejected both lovers and replaced them with the attractive Tunisian Tahar (whose name means "pure" or "virtuous"). Salter concludes the story with Tahar's promise of exotic hedonism that can't be matched by her current lovers: "he offered a powerful intoxicant: darkened skin, white teeth, and a kind of strange perfume that clung even to his clothes. He offered rooms above the souk with a view of the city one could not even imagine, nights of an intense blueness, mornings when you had drifted far from the familiar world." Pamela has lied to both men and is being lured to a supposedly attractive life that cannot possibly match her expectations.

"Palm Court" refers to the lavish restaurant in the Plaza Hotel in New York where Noreen, a recently divorced woman, returns to Arthur, a wealthy Jewish stockbroker, for a last chance to recover their lost happiness. They had been deeply in love and together for three years, but a few brief incidents during that time foreshadowed Arthur's mistaken *gran rifiuto*. Noreen was once tied up and sodomized; their train to Westhampton hit a bicyclist; Arthur ate a forbidden lobster. When Noreen told him that she'd had a marriage proposal, he knew that he loved her, "that she was really giving him one last chance. He knew he should take it." But he failed to respond, and she made an unfortunate second-choice marriage, which "was as simple as a death, but lasted longer."

When they meet in the Palm Court twenty years later, Arthur is inevitably disillusioned: "she had gained weight, even her face showed it. She had been the most beautiful girl . . . even her clothes were hiding what she had been." Though she gives him a second chance, Arthur still can't emotionally commit himself and rejects her again by lying that he's engaged. Noreen can't compete with his idealized image of her youth, the best years of "her looks and wonderful laugh." In middle age her personal qualities don't seem to matter to him. She then offers herself to a homely and much older man. Arthur prefers to live with his past memories rather than accept the harsh reality of her present defects. In Salter's subtle variant of the Jamesian theme of the unlived life, Arthur knows he's made a terrible mistake and after she leaves he bursts into tears.

In "Bangkok" Carol, another ex-lover, turns up unexpectedly and offers herself to Hollis, a happily married man with a young daughter and a rare-book business. She tries to excite and tempt him with talk of fellatio, pedophilia and bondage, by recalling their ecstatic past and mocking his present sexually unexciting life. She wants to make him remember the past the way she remembers it. She seductively tells him she rarely has sex, which "never measures up, that's the trouble. It's never what it should be or used to be." She asks if he loved her and he vividly remembers: "You were incomparable. With you I felt I had everything in life, everything anyone ever dreamed of. I adored you." But on a foolish impulse she destroyed all they had. He returned from a trip and discovered that she was sleeping with someone else. Unlike Hollis, Carol "didn't know that real happiness lies in having the same thing all the time." He mistrusts her and believes she'd betray him again.

After recalling their great trip to Venice and saying she's inherited a lot of money from her father, she plays her trump card. Like Tahar, who'd lured Pamela to Tunisia, Carol invites him to have a sexually thrilling life with her and a beautiful friend in Bangkok. She urges him to leave everything, the pretend life of family and business, for "Travel. The Orient. The air of a different world. Bathe, drink, read. You and me. And Molly. As a gift" (another Threesome). As she draws him to her, he again remembers their blissful sunlit mornings on Hudson Street in Greenwich Village and repeats, "I knew I had everything life would ever offer." He still resists and she offers something even better than ecstasy—the anticipation of bliss to come when everything in his wildest imagination could be perfectly realized. Finally, after he rejects her and she forgets what she's learned about real happiness, Carol mocks him by saying, "I'll think of you lying in bed at night, bored to death with it all. . . . You missed your chance." But for once the man makes the right decision by rejecting her again and choosing to continue his tranquil and secure life. Salter said, " 'Bangkok' is about a woman's attempt at revenge."

"Arlington" ends with a funeral in the military cemetery in northern Virginia. Newell, an army officer, had been loudly drinking and fighting with Jana, his sexy, beautiful but unfaithful Czech wife. He would never forget her as "Naked she sat astride him and, caressing her own buttocks as he lay nearly fainting, began to ride." Westerveldt, a war hero and older colleague, had warned Newell that she was jeopardizing his career. When Newell was away, Jana slept with another officer and falsely claimed that he raped her. Helplessly in love with Jana, Newell stole radios from supply to get money for her, was court-martialed and sent to prison for a year. She didn't wait for him and married Rodriguez, who owned some beauty parlors.

Newell loyally and sacrificially attends Westerveldt's funeral at Arlington. Before the service begins someone asks, "who said, 'Let us cross the river and rest in the shade of the trees'?" These were the last words of the dying Confederate general Stonewall Jackson, which Hemingway used as the title of *Across the River and Into the Trees.* Like Reemstma in "Lost Sons," Newell is a complete (as well as a disgraced) outsider. He concludes, "He was loyal to her. It was one-sided, but that was enough." Salter dismissed this slight story as "really just a portrait with a kind of moral" about foolish self-destruction for a sensual but worthless woman.[8]

The ambiguous and ironically titled "Last Night" is Salter's masterpiece. It has a momentous theme, morbid ritual, tense buildup and shocking climax. Marit, suffering from terminal cancer that has traveled from her uterus to her lungs, has arranged a farewell dinner with her husband Walter and Susanna, a young family friend. Walter has agreed that after the meal he will administer a lethal injection prepared by her doctor: "What she had been was gone; it had been taken from her. The change was fearful, especially in her face." Morphine hadn't helped when terrible things happened to her. She tries to imagine what the world will be like without her, and consoles herself with thoughts of a calm transition to the afterlife: "the crossing was by boat, something the ancients knew with certainty." In the festive restaurant Walter orders two bottles of Cheval Blanc, a red Bordeaux, for $575 each.

Marit had no children; Susanna, Walter's lover, can still have them. Susanna is now everything to Walter; Marit means nothing. He begs Susanna to stay with him, but she can't bear to participate in the fatal procedure and goes out. Like a doctor, Walter conceals the razor-sharp syringe against his leg. He and Marit declare their *Liebestod*, and he effortlessly pushes the needle into her vein and injects the poison. Marit sighs, closes her eyes and lies back. Susanna, waiting outside in her car, comes back in and wonders if Marit knew about their affair. She seems to have punished Susanna by inviting her to dinner. Marit's death both releases and excites the survivors. Susanna is slightly drunk, Walter undresses her and kisses her gorgeous breasts: "He devoured her, shuddering as if in fright at the end and holding her to him tightly."

The next morning the supposedly dead Marit comes unsteadily down the stairs, like an Edgar Poe heroine emerging from the tomb, and discovers the guilty lovers. The fatal injection has merely put her to sleep. She begins to cry and says, "you must have done it wrong. . . . I thought you were going to help me. . . . I have to do it all over" and must prepare herself once again for death. Her traumatic appearance marks Walter's last night with the ashamed and horrified Susanna but not, as expected, with his bitterly revived wife.

The brilliant "Charisma" begins indirectly with two young women fantasizing about the still handsome and irresistible 79-year-old painter Lucian Freud, grandson of Sigmund and notorious piranha-like seducer of young girls. One of them has just seen Freud staring at Rembrandts in the Metropolitan Museum, and both agree that if they got the chance they would "fuck him."

The story then suddenly shifts in scene and characters to the love affair of the equally impressionable Leila Aaron and the notably charismatic Polo Millard. He has a dazzling smile, charm and power. There was "no one like him, his energy, his emanation . . . the intense pleasure he drew from life without coming to terms with it." In a restaurant Polo whispers something secret to Leila, leaves his phone number in her coat and something makes her call him the next day. He believes, with Islamic fatalism, that "it's all written . . . it was chance," tells her "we were predestined . . . we were meant to." The unnamed narrator abruptly remarks that after three months of marriage Leila jumped to her death from the eighteenth floor. But in a sleight of hand he also reveals that this was an alternate twist in the story; it never actually happened.

Like Lucian Freud, Polo loves high-stakes gambling and doesn't care about losing money. Like Eda in "American Express," Leila "didn't go places with men—her family would know," but also agrees to go with him. In the Bahamas he gambles, drinks, takes cocaine and introduces Leila to the drug—"but not that much." The reticent narrator, who later reads Polo's letters, reports that Polo "did things with her that I would have never dreamed." Leila allowed herself to be whipped and probably sodomized—Polo's way of expressing his hatred of his mother. Leila steeled herself not to cry out but could not prevent her moans and tears. She was afraid her roommate would see the slash marks, and destroyed all the photos Polo took to memorialize the occasion.

Leila marries someone else. Polo, like Lucian, is attracted to young girls, falls in love with a 16-year-old Brazilian and is rejected by her family. He inherits money from his late mother and continues to write Leila seductive letters from Italy and Egypt. He tries to lure her back by mentioning the portrayal of passionate love in the novels of Scott Fitzgerald and Lawrence Durrell, Leo Tolstoy's *Anna Karenina* and Gabriel García Márquez's *Love in the Time of Cholera*. Urging Leila to return, like Yeats' last mistress, he slightly misquotes Robert Herrick's "To Daffodils": "Stay, stay / Until the hasting day / Has run / But to the even-song." But charisma is not sufficient to save him and his bright lights are dimmed. Like Jane in "Such Fun" and Marit in "Last Night," Polo dies of cancer. The narrator, having told his tale, reappears to visit Polo's grave in East Hampton, but can't find it. He regretfully concludes: "it was just like him to have eluded me, in death as in life. To go where he could not be found. To escape the final questions" about the meaning and value of his dazzling faithless life.[9]

Salter emphasizes the decisive points of the narrative and ignores what lies between them. He suggests time and place by silence and fragmentary speeches. He enlivens the stories with evocative settings and mysterious events, and propels them toward a surprising climax.

EIGHT

INTELLECTUAL NOURISHMENT

There & Then, Life Is Meals and *Don't Save Anything*

I

Salter's extensive travels in Asia, Europe and Africa while serving in the Air Force gave him a lifelong taste for foreign parts. Like Samuel Johnson, he believed, "The use of travelling is to regulate imagination by reality, and instead of thinking how things may be, to see them as they are."[1] The witty and ironic photo by Jacques Lartigue on the cover of *There & Then* (2005) is a surrealistic image of an aquatic non-traveler. A neatly dressed mustached man wearing a solar topee, thick dark blind-man's glasses, shirt, tie and jacket, floats in a sausage-like rubber tube. His arms rest casually on the sides, one white hand hanging limply, and his legs and shoes stick out under the swirling sun-streaked water.

Pleasure Gardens, The Life We Admire or *Immortal Days* would have been more engaging book titles than the prosaic *There & Then*. The chapter titles are based on literary sources. The alluring but dangerous "Siren Song" comes from Greek mythology and Homer's *Odyssey*; "Paumanok," the Indian name for "fish-shaped" Long Island, from Walt Whitman's *Leaves of Grass*; "Nothing to Declare" from Oscar Wilde's pronouncement on arriving in America: "I have nothing to declare but my genius"; and "Roads Seldom Travelled" from Hamlin Garland's *Main-Travelled Roads*.

The eighteen disparate chapters consider mountain climbing and skiing; Colorado and Long Island; France and Japan; Basel and Trier; and cemeteries. Salter used details from guidebooks to flesh out these peripatetic and idiosyncratic essays, which were mainly written for travel magazines. He does not, like Paul Theroux, describe the hardships of travel but the attractive places that readers long to see. He captured the essence of the best locales, unspoiled and timeless in his memory and imagination, before they were irrevocably changed and lost by mass tourism. He sometimes refers to "we," but the only traveling companion he names is his son James on their bicycle trip in Japan. He'd agree with Rudyard Kipling's "The Winners": "Down to Gehenna or up to the Throne, / He travels the fastest who travels alone."

The book has no index and some flaws and errors. Salter's friends James and Gloria Jones are mentioned four times but not discussed. Salter loves France, but despite many trips has a weak grasp of the language. Les Halles is not "the only 'H' in French that is not elided." The chaste Hester Johnson was not the mistress of Jonathan Swift. The Imperial Hotel in Tokyo was not destroyed during the war but survived the bombing of 1944. You can't smell "the clean air of the open [North] sea" in Basel, which is 575 miles away. You certainly can't see Africa from Samoa, which is 9,200 miles distant. Salter does not identify the many allusions that enhance the pleasure and meaning of his essays.[2]

Salter's visual style draws the readers into his locales. Azay-le Rideau, a château on the Loire, "is built partly over a river. From the water side it seems to float on its own calm reflection." The Colorado "mountains are blue and there is a gentleness and grandeur that fills one with awe." Salter's "brown snake, perfect and slim, that withdraws in cool haste, coiling between rock and underbrush," recalls D. H. Lawrence's Sicilian "Snake": "[He] writhed like lightning, and was gone / Into the black hole, the earth-lipped / fissure in the wall-front."[3]

The chapters on mountain climbing and skiing provide the background for *Solo Faces* and *Downhill Racer*. Solo faces are dangerous routes climbed alone without good holds or a rope, "far beyond where mortals can go," far up "in some exposed place with nothing beneath but empty air." The Austrian Tyrol, where Hemingway had skied, "still has three great virtues: It is beautiful, friendly and cheap." St. Anton is a shrine for the sport, like Wimbledon for tennis and St. Andrews for golf. The downhill races reach 90 miles per hour, last for only two minutes and are decided by fractions of a second. The Austrian professionals know the terrain, "the short cuts and speed-building pitches."

In Kitzbühel, Salter takes lessons from the world-famous champion Toni Sailer, who has "the handsome, cold face of a man who has seen the heights." He tells Salter that courage, endurance and skill are needed for the toughest course, which has "extreme steepness at the start, abrupt changes of terrain and difficult turns." At the 1968 Winter Olympics in Grenoble, France, Salter and Robert Redford chose the real-life model for the hero in the movie. Klosters, Switzerland, where Irwin Shaw had lived and died, has the longest, twelve-minute ski run in Europe. Salter, who skied till late in life, had broken a foot, leg, arm and shoulder, remembered those fractures and used them in his writing. When his son broke his leg in Aspen, Salter stoically said, "shake it off, you'll be fine," until with tears in his eyes his son had to be carried down the mountain.[4]

In 1969 Salter bought a house in Aspen and spent the winters in the Rocky Mountains. The town was born with the discovery of silver in 1878, flourished for a short time and died in 1893 when silver prices disastrously fell. In the 1960s it was gradually transformed from a ruined mining town into a legendary ski resort. Salter spent summers in Bridgehampton, on Whitman's Paumanok, "which holds the promise of love affairs, novels written, barefoot life."

Half in love with easeful France, Salter devotes five rapturous chapters to his favorite country and admires the spiritual element in its hedonism: "France was unalterably different, ancient, stylish, beautiful, strange. . . . There was more than a hint of another life, free of familiar inhibitions, a sacred life, this great museum and pleasure garden evolved for you alone." He assumes the French have a "knowledge of the senses that includes carnal happiness."

His ideal provincial town, in southwest France, is Lectoure, whose name reminds him of the unnamed *lecteur* (reader). It has the most attractive qualities of the four summer houses he explores. The old man's game of *boule* (a kind of bowling), played close to the cathedral and under the trees, has "about the same pace as in convalescence." But these men do not embody Salter's stereotypes, "robust, open and courageous," a character that is not confined to Gascony. The town recalls the unrushed hours of Salter's favorite painter. Like Pierre Bonnard, Salter excludes historical and political events from his fiction: "Bonnard painted while the century roared past, the tremendous wars, crises, strikes, collapses, none of these are present in his work. There is no social content, only emotional."

"Roads Seldom Travelled" describes Salter's 1980 bicycle trip on the southern Japanese island of Kyushu with a guide, ten Australians and his

18-year-old son James. At night they bathed in deep steaming hot tubs, ate sitting on tatami mats and slept on hard pillows in country inns. James, a hardened rock-climber, found the guide oppressive and the Australians uninteresting, and read Lafcadio Hearn on Japan at night. In our interview, James recalled that he'd missed his flight to Tokyo, was a day late and hung over, but Salter didn't get upset about such things and wasn't angry. The room they shared was quiet and peaceful. Annoyed by the slow pace of the group, he shot ahead of the pack at his own speed. In James' childhood Salter was divorced, lived apart from his family and was absorbed in his writing. This great experience allowed them to spend more time together, gave his son a different view of his father and brought them closer than ever.[5] Salter notes that the dramatic suicide of the Japanese novelist Yukio Mishima by *seppuku* (ritual disembowelment) before a huge audience of soldiers "remains incomprehensible."[6]

"Evening in Basel," in which a woman describes her unhappy life—she's divorced and her small child is dead—supplies the background of Salter's story "The Destruction of the Goetheanum." Trier on the Moselle, with its vineyards and Roman ruins, is the setting of a secret liaison in *Cassada*. Revisiting the town, Salter recalls, "It wasn't this way before. I don't know what's happened. It's changed." He then searches for the real "Trier, the thing that has endured . . . the broken measure of what it once was."

In "Cemeteries" Salter writes that the Protestant Cemetery in Rome, where Keats and Shelley are buried, "remains perfect and still, rich with curious inscriptions and sleeping cats." One could add to his evocative survey of graveyards that Thomas Mann is buried near James Joyce in Fluntern cemetery in Zurich. Staglieno in Genoa has elegant statues and elaborate chapels. Highgate in London includes George Eliot, Cristina Rossetti, a statue of the weeping Alma Mahler and the massive bearded head of Karl Marx on a huge stone plinth. In Katha, Burma, fear of venomous snakes in the high grass made me look from a distance at the tombstones of the many young English men, women and children whose lives were cut short by incurable tropical diseases. Salter concludes that visiting cemeteries puts one in close touch with the illustrious dead: "There is a reality to being present at the grave. . . . The dead bring us to life, vivify us, give us scale. We are the unjoined part of them and at their graves we stand at our own."

In a crucial passage Salter explains that he esteems men who understand nature, machines and the weather that indicates when they can ski: men "who can do things, who know the names of trees and engine parts, the meaning of certain clouds and shifts in the wind. I admire the knowledge that takes time and solitude to acquire. Above all, I like men who do not put possessions first."[7]

II

The phrase "Life Is Meals" appears in *Light Years*, and in an interview Salter described how he and his wife wrote the book: "she went off somewhere and wrote some pages. I went off in an entirely different place and wrote some pages. Then we traded them and edited them."[8] When I got a proof copy, I offered to send Salter a list of forty typographical and factual errors (he even gave Shakespeare a line he never wrote). Though he was a meticulous writer, he was surprisingly unconcerned about the numerous mistakes, and wrote to me on May 29, 2006 that it was too late to make any corrections, the book had been sent to the printer. He'd be interested in my list unless there were truly shameful things. Occasional errors were catnip to reviewers, but they were not intentional. Though Knopf had produced an exceptionally beautiful volume, the careless editors caught only eight of the forty errors I had found and the rest were printed in the book in 2006. When the paperback edition was scheduled, Kay Salter urgently asked for my list of corrections, which they had misplaced. For many years Salter had been collecting scribbled and disorganized scraps of information on bits of paper for this book. When he gathered them together, he often relied on memory, did not check the original sources and allowed the errors to appear.

Life Is Meals began as the unpublished *Tasting Paris*, which has been mistakenly listed in Salter's bibliography. On January 12, 2007 he explained that *Tasting Paris* was a ghost book. It was contracted by Ecco Press, but Salter didn't like the production plans and cancelled the project. He had other offers for the book, but had not accepted them and was still revising.

The subtitle, *A Food Lover's Book of Days*, describes a year of eating sumptuously. A readable and quotable collection of thoughts and anecdotes inspired by an interest in food, it evokes the mood of Brillat-Savarin's *Physiologie du gout*, Ford Madox Ford's *Provence*, A. J. Liebling's *Between Meals*, Hemingway's *A Moveable Feast* and Robert Baldick's *Dinner at Magny's*. It also recalls the splendid feasts in the novels of Huysmans, Proust and Lampedusa, and in Ingmar Bergman's *Fanny and Alexander*.

This culinary calendar, which can be opened at random or read straight through, has entries for every day of the year, often pegged to birthdays of famous foodies. It evolved from the Salters' notebooks, recipes and reading, and includes "things of interest, bits of history, opinions, occurrences, odd facts," descriptions, philosophy, fantasy and poetry. Knowledgeable, lively and amusing, it is filled with *joie de livre* as well as *joie de vivre* and suggests a hedonistic yet civilized life. One recipe serves eight people or one gluttonous friend. The authors insist, with gusto, that it's impossible to eat less than five baklavas and that the aroma in the Turkish *Imam Bayeldi* "made the legendary priest faint from sheer joy." They mention dishes named for famous people: Chateaubriand Steak, Tournedos Rossini, Peach Melba and Bellini Cocktail; to which could be added Carpaccio Raw Ham, Beef Wellington, Beef Stroganoff, Bismarck Roll and Oysters Rockefeller.

The Salters write about food history and wine lore, favorite cookbooks and classic recipes, great chefs from Carême to Alice Waters and magnetic restaurants worth (as the Michelin guide says), "a detour." They emphasize French cuisine, with a nod at Italian, which became fashionable when spaghetti became pasta. There are social nuances and shopping hints, shrewd gossip and literary anecdotes, personal history and European travel, and dinners with writer-friends from Peter Matthiessen and John Irving to Jorie Graham.

They record memorable and disastrous dinner parties. On one forgettable occasion the food was bad, presentation chaotic, guests crowded. One angry man threw inedible roast beef onto the floor. (He could have said, "I've had a pleasant evening but this wasn't one of them.") Even worse was the fare served during the 1870 Franco-Prussian War when starving Parisians ate starving animals from the zoo: kangaroo, camel, elephant and bear.

The odd facts include cameo appearances of Marie Antoinette, who sipped some fortifying bouillon before being guillotined, and of John Ruskin, who became impotent after discovering that his bride had pubic hair. We discover that the scent of oranges was once used to mask the stench of theater audiences; that the name for apricots, which turn orange before they fully ripen, comes from the Latin word for "precocious"; and that the three native American fruits are cranberries, blackberries and Concord grapes. Extra-virgin olive oil "means lower acidity and hence, better flavor." The full-grown lobster, after complex molting, "is nocturnal, solitary, and territorial." The Salters are good on salt and mention Lot's wife, who turned into a pillar of it. We're also told that in the Middle Ages people consumed exotic fowl: "swans, storks, herons, cormorants, and turtledoves." But there's nothing about the delights of suckling pig and wild game—boar, deer, antelope, elk, bison, emu and ostrich—which I devoured during summers in Montana.

Czechoslovakia, home of Pilsner Urquell, has the highest per-capita beer consumption in the world; and fresh fruit is the best remedy for a hangover. There's a potent recipe for martinis, of which the alcoholic James Thurber remarked, "One is all right, two is too many, and three's not enough." The Salters could also have included the ingredients of Hemingway's delicious Papa Doble: white rum, and the juice of pink grapefruit and lime, as well as the famous paean of Samuel Johnson, "a hardened and shameless tea-drinker . . . who with tea amuses the evening, with tea solaces the midnights, and, with tea, welcomes the morning." [9]

The Salters describe aphrodisiacs—oysters, truffles and chocolate. Like Casanova, they emphasize "the sensual importance of dining, the opening act of so many seductions." Many luxurious restaurant scenes appear in Salter's fiction. The blissful connection between food and sex prompted Nabokov to observe, when a colleague complained that his students were spooning in the back row, "You're lucky they weren't forking." The Salters also essay two puns. In Turkey denying a wife coffee was *grounds* for divorce; fruit eaters live to a *ripe* old age.

The Salters mention significant moments in their private life. In the summer of 1973, when he was separated from his wife, they had their first breakfast together in Santa Fe, Kay cooked her first meal for him in Denver (Salter, across the table from her, "was everything") and they first lived together near the beach in Los Angeles. Three years later they took their first trip to France and moved into their house in Aspen. In 1985 their son Theo was born outside Paris.

The authors subtly remark "there are days, perhaps many, when you long to be somewhere else, and days when you are." In a passage reminiscent of Hemingway, a meal on the Greek island of Naxos evokes the joys of an Aegean summer: "We had lunch in a small mountain village named Kata Potamia [Down River] in a café overlooking parched brown hillsides. The tables were beneath trees with white-washed trunks. . . . The sound of cicadas, sometimes a great noise that rose with a rush and then fell, like a passing train." After lavish meals Salter swam, hiked, climbed up and skied down mountains to stay in shape.

Salter's most charming and irritating book is handsome and well il-lustrated, practical and anecdotal, snobbish and name-dropping. It offers self-help in the kitchen with advice about how to serve food and influence people. He rather smugly suggests that if you faithfully follow its guidance you will also have a friend-filled and gratifying life. It's meant to be an ideal gift for birthdays, weddings, anniversaries and holidays. As Graham Greene wrote of Ford's *Provence*, it is "an elaborate pattern of memories, historical and personal. The subject is the good life—as it should be lived by all the world."

In the *New York Times* of March 18, 2007, Stacie Stukin in "The Art of Feeding" quoted (to puff Salter's book) the most far-fetched of all his un-convincing claims: that in the last thirty years he "has thrown about 1,500 dinner parties with his wife Kay." This would amount to 50 dinners a year, or one every week, from 1975 to 2005. Since he was usually absorbed in his writing, took many trips abroad, drove annually from New York to Colorado and back in a two-week round trip, had several illnesses and accidents, and must have felt the inevitable social fatigue this boast was clearly impossible.

III

The title of *Don't Save Anything* (edited by Kay Salter and posthumously published in 2017) is contradictory. He saved everything, including notes and drafts. She put many of his uncollected essays and profiles, from the *Paris Review, Esquire* and *New Yorker* to *Food & Wine, European Travel and Life* and *Joe*, into this book.[10] But her choice of material is strange. She includes passages from *Dusk, Burning the Days, Gods of Tin, There & Then* and *Life Is Meals*, but inexplicably excludes important late work.

These essays, spinoffs from Salter's fiction, were published between 1974 and 2005. They reveal his wide-ranging interests and sometimes mention his marriages. Salter was delighted by the second chance with a new wife, who was younger, more interesting and more sexually exciting than his ex-wife. He called Kay a potent object and praised "the dreams she excites in others, the envy, the unexpected things she can say, none of them familiar, none of the wearisome stories about house and children." (Ann Salter never remarried.) Salter's second son, born when he was 60 and 30 years after his first child, was named Theo: "It was the second choice, but the first [unidentified] was even more exotic and sounded to his grandfather like the name of a foreign radio."

Always reverent about West Point—"once a fortress that guarded a river, it became a school to guard a nation"—Salter portrays two of its illustrious graduates. His perceptive essay on Eisenhower, an unexpected candidate for greatness, notes that unlike Napoleon and Grant he never commanded troops in battle. As his great rival Douglas MacArthur disdainfully commented, Ike "let his generals in the field fight the war for him." Like his powerful patron George Marshall, Ike "had hardly a single watt of military glory." Neither a great general nor a heroic one, this apparently ordinary man managed to reach the highest rank in the army. Salter's second military subject, Lieutenant General Sid Berry, his close contemporary (1926–2013), was a brilliant field commander with "the proper mixture of education, exposure at high levels, the sound of guns." Wounded and decorated in Korea and Vietnam, he became superintendent of West Point. He retrospectively admitted that America could not have won the war in Vietnam: "The political understanding and the staying power of the Communists were greater than those of our forces."

A war hero himself, Salter compares the attributes of downhill skiers and rock climbers to the qualities, perils and deaths of fighter pilots: "Courage, technique, finesse, strength and stamina" are needed by racers, who on steep chutes "go most of the way in the air." The great and inescapable danger in climbing "purifies it and gives it its rank. . . . The falls are brutal. Instantaneously, what amounts to a racer's existence explodes."

Salter skied with Toni Sailer and rock-climbed with another champion, Royal Robbins. He portrays Robbins as "a young, hatchet-faced Californian, aggressive, supremely talented, who had been famous since his teens." The climbing hazards are fear of heights, sudden rockfalls and blinding blizzards. The difficulties, especially when the rock face is past vertical and tilting toward the climbers, force them to grasp inches-wide cracks or hang by their hands from a foot-wide ledge. As if describing their skills, Alexander Pope wrote in "An Essay on Man," "The spider's touch, how exquisitely fine, / Feels at each thread, and lives along the line."

Like the greatest bullfighters, who take the most daring risks and suffer the most pain, "among serious climbers there is no such thing as not falling." Salter explains that "Robbins falls when he attempts something that is at the very limit of his powers, and it is his nature always to extend these limits. He expects a fall and is prepared for it." The ecstatic thrill, once he is off the ground, "is the feeling of being in another element, as distinct as diving into the sea." Yet rock climbing, a pointless exercise to most people, seems like Samuel Johnson's description of a dog walking on its hind legs: "It is not done well; but you are surprized to find it done at all."[11] Salter, with enthusiasm and first-hand experience, overcomes our resistance and makes the sport seem exciting.

Salter complained to Phelps that Aspen was boring and there was no one to talk to about intellectual subjects. But he makes the town seem interesting by emphasizing its mining history and modern transformation, its spectacular beauty in the Rocky Mountains and its world-class skiing. Despite the radical social changes from the era of the adventurous few to the present invasive rich, Aspen still has "the steep blue mountains, the wood fires, the trees bearing fresh snow." The scenic town belongs to what he calls "the true life": "At one point it is travel, at another a certain woman, at another a house somewhere with a view you will worship till you die." In a far-fetched comparison, he claims Aspen is like Paris—though these two places could hardly be more different.[12]

Like Scott Fitzgerald, Salter has the ability to invest everything with charm and enchantment. He emphasizes the romance of France, loves stories of attractive women who are always available and responsive, and tells salacious anecdotes: Bologna is famous for fellatio (techniques not specified). Sometimes, however, his rhapsodies on expensive dinners and pricey wines seem snobbish and spurious. His favorite Parisian restaurant, La Coupole, always has "the expectation of finding there le tout Paris . . . actors, intellectuals, journalists, musicians." But if Salter doesn't know any of them, he must gape at them like a tourist. When he cooked "authentic American cuisine" for French acquaintances, he gave them a corrosively hot Mexican chili.

The most interesting part of the book concerns Salter's true métier, writing and writers. He makes some incisive comments about writing in *Memorable Days*, and his best advice applies to himself as well as to Phelps: "You should really stop reading scripts and other perishables and concentrate on your own book." But it was always difficult to overcome inertia and begin to write, and he spoke of "that crisis of irresolution that precedes getting to work." Paralyzed by his own high standards, he was often dissatisfied with his writing: "I've struggled all day with a few paragraphs and only come up with two words that make me say ah, that's interesting." Like Franz Kafka who famously declared, "A book must be the axe for the frozen sea inside us,"[13] Salter struggled to reach and release his true self: "I'm hacking away at the surface, as at some kind of gray ice, trying to break through to what is underneath or I am dead."[14] He said Gertrude Stein wrote for praise, García Lorca to be loved, William Faulkner for glory. More modestly, Salter wrote to be admired, hoping for acceptance and approval. He liked to quote Jean Renoir's belief, "the only things that are important in life are the things you remember," but he thought art was greater than memory and "some things are better imagined than seen."

Salter, whose essay on Gabriele D'Annunzio (1863–1938) has the paradoxical subtitle "The Immortal Who Died," thought his "biographers are so poor. He needs someone with a scalpel, no sense of envy and an executioner's sense of pity"—not indulgent, but ruthless.[15] Salter doesn't attempt severe surgery, but offers a brief survey of D'Annunzio's war exploits, bizarre character and sinking reputation. He suddenly breaks the narrative in the middle and adds short ineffectual entries in alphabetical order, from A to O to V and W, on various aspects of the Italian's life and loves.

Fascinated by D'Annunzio, Salter states, "the writing was opulent, dazzling, sensuous. . . . He fought duels. He was detested by fellow writers, by decent people, the church, many critics, and not a few husbands. He was amoral, grasping, shrewd and the greatest writer in Italy." He was also a cad and, like most novelists, fictionalized the most sensational material. Salter calls *Il Fuoco* (The Flame of Life), about his ill-fated liaison with the great actress Eleanora Duse, "the most swinish book ever written."

D'Annunzio was a Great War aviator and hero who won the highest decorations and lost an eye in an aircraft accident. Salter doesn't mention D'Annunzio's greatest work, *Notturno*, his celebration of war when he was nearly blinded by that war wound. Salter sympathetically writes, "He experienced rapture, comparable only to the purest sensations of art and love. Some of his best descriptions are those of pilots who were his comrades and whom he could still recall vividly even when an old man." In 1919 he led a force of volunteers, the *Arditi*, into Fiume on the Adriatic coast east of Trieste, seized the city for Italy and held it for a year. But Salter notes, "No one, not even Byron, led so scandalous and unforgivable a life, and no one has seen his legend vanish more quickly."

Salter might have concluded that though the poet failed to harmonize his artistic talents with his political ambitions, he was able during a unique moment in history to gratify his personal fantasies with a poetic and political creation. His impressive careers—from Duse to *Duce*—as an aesthete, lover, warrior, adventurer, *commandante* and relic represent a paradigm and critique of the modern Italian character, which emphasizes appearance and emotion. After the seizure of Fiume, as much a *coup de théâtre* as a *coup d'état*, D'Annunzio could not transform the *bella figura* of a dramatic moment into a permanent and meaningful reality. But as E. M. Forster wrote, "By the time he died he had a number of books to his credit, a still larger number of mistresses, and the city of Fiume. It is no small haul."[16]

Isaac Babel, another man of action, was attached to the Red Cavalry during their postwar invasion of Poland. The stylistic antithesis of D'Annunzio, the Russian was concise and intense rather than extravagant and flamboyant. Salter admired and identified with Babel's themes of love and death, and noted the "rich element of sensuality in Babel's writing, sometimes implicit, glimpsed, sometimes clear." His tribute to Babel emphasized his courage in war and literary techniques. Like Hemingway, Babel believed "the strength came not when you could no longer add a sentence but when you could no longer take one away." Babel's morbid images were like Goya's *Desastres de la Guerra* but leavened by compassion. The mutilation and murder in his stories had "a kind of hopeless understanding and even forgiveness." Babel had a reckless affair with the wife of the Soviet Secret Police chief, and when Maxim Gorky died in 1936 he lost his protector. Before his execution Babel begged, "Let me finish my work," and his papers disappeared forever after his death. In 1940 Stalin murdered two of the greatest Russians, Babel and Trotsky.

Robert Ginna, editor of *People* magazine, sent Salter to Europe in 1975 to interview Vladimir Nabokov and Graham Greene. In Paris he wrote Phelps, "Nothing but difficulties here, trembling on the disastrous. Nabokov claims to be sick—I sent him a telegram saying 'Suddenly I am not feeling very well myself'—and Graham Greene has seen a copy of *People* and decided it is not suitable, this cheap little rag, for someone of his stature."[17] Finally, he persuaded these exhaustively interviewed writers to receive him. Extremely deferential and flattering in profiles rather than interviews, Salter described their backgrounds but gave surprisingly few direct quotations.

Babel had dismissed Nabokov's high style, multilingual puns, sly jokes and lofty knowledge with "he can write, but has got nothing to say"; Nabokov rejected Babel as a Soviet propagandist. Salter describes Nabokov's luxurious suite in the Montreux Palace Hotel on the shore of Lake Geneva in Switzerland. He says Nabokov had been the wealthiest modern writer and had lost everything—language, audience, social status, vast estates and inherited millions—and barely escaped after the Russian Revolution in 1917. (In Berlin in 1922 his father was assassinated by a Right-wing Russian monarchist.) His great theme is the lost past. Like *Swann's Way*, *Animal Farm* and *The Leopard*, *Lolita* was rejected by publishers everywhere and finally published by Olympia Press in Paris. Nabokov remarked, "I am not a famous writer. Lolita was a famous little girl." He wittily concluded that he likes bright people who understand jokes, and though his wife "is married to one of the great clowns of all time, she never laughs."

On January 15, 1975 Salter appealed to Greene as an impoverished fellow-writer. He said he was already in Paris, holding Greene's telegram expressing his strong disapproval of *People* magazine and refusing to see him. The problem was that Salter had come all the way to Paris. He was not on the staff of the magazine, had not been paid for all the time he'd spent, and was sure Greene would understand the problem. He begged, after coming so far, that Greene would at least meet him not as an interviewer, but as a fellow writer and admirer.[18]

Greene magnanimously relented, and Salter begins the essay (since George Orwell and Evelyn Waugh were dead) by calling Greene "the greatest living English writer." He's especially interested in Greene's long and close connection with the movies (his *Third Man* is superb). He mentions that when Greene was reviewing films he described Shirley Temple's "dimpled depravity" and suggested that 20th Century Fox was exploiting the child's sexuality. The studio then sued *Night and Day* and forced it to shut down. When I spoke to Shirley Temple about this in 1986, she was still angry about Greene's demeaning review and felt the magazine deserved to be suppressed.

Salter admires Greene's plots, cinematic dialogue and eye for sharp detail. He quotes Greene echoing the first page of *A Farewell to Arms* when complimenting his friend Evelyn Waugh: "In the Mediterranean you can see a pebble fifteen feet down. His style was like that." Salter repeats this image in his essay on Royal Robbins by commenting, "the Merced River is clear enough to see every pebble in its bed." He notes that Greene "lives in anonymity and quiet. . . . He is like one of his own solitary heroes, concealing untold depths of unhappiness and strength." Salter says that Greene's life is "as varied and glamorous as that of André Malraux," but since he was neither a soldier nor a politician, this claim is not convincing. After a serendipitous spinoff in September 1975, nine months later, Salter thanked Greene for generously recommending *Light Years* and persuading Bodley Head to change their mind and publish the English edition. On the dust wrapper Greene called the novel "A moving and subtle story of the loss of love, refreshingly free from the boring clichés of violence and pornography. If I read a better novel this year I shall have cause for gratitude." Two years later he told Greene that he was beginning a new book but was unable to sleep, apprehensive about setting out on a long journey that might not succeed.

Salter's last, previously unpublished essay, a lecture at the Woodrow Wilson Center in Princeton, is a furious, provocative and salutary attack on the faults of contemporary literary culture. He condemns the inability to read closely, the academic study of theory instead of serious fiction, "the displacement of literature, the devaluation of the word," the great leveling process and Noah's ark of inclusiveness, which forsakes "the traditional notions of what a liberal education should be." He boldly and accurately states "the edge has gone off discrimination" (in both senses) and asks, "In a country where Maya Angelou passes for a poet, Tom Clancy for a novelist, Tony Kushner for a playwright, what hope do words have?" This needs to be said, now more than ever, even if current readers are programmed to reject it. Salter would have been appalled to see, in the *New York Review of Books* (November 3, 2022), an ad for David Levine's drawings that prominently featured Zora Neale Hurston followed by William Shakespeare and James Joyce.

On September 24, 2008 Salter told me that his potentially intriguing article on the greatest things he'd seen in his life, written for *Men's Vogue*, was twice revised but never published. In *Don't Save Anything* Kay does not include several major essays: two on Hemingway and one on a famous emergency landing. "The Art of the Ditch" (*NYRB*, January 14, 2010) is Salter's expert and exciting account of a passenger plane that collided with a flock of geese. The birds had not crashed right into the windshield, so Captain Chesley Sullenberger could still see. But he could not restart the engines, which were destroyed and on fire, could not reach an airport and was forced to land on the Hudson River. "The need for power is obvious," Salter writes, "the pilot wants to be in complete control of the descent, holding it off just above a stall and allowing the tail to touch and then smoothly setting the rest of the fuselage down like a boat launched at more than a hundred miles an hour." After the pilot warned the passengers to brace for impact, the plane "touched the water at an optimum angle, nose slightly high, 120 knots. The left engine tore away, the plane's belly ripped open toward the rear, and the aircraft skimmed to a stop." All the passengers and crew survived, and the captain became a national hero.

Man of action and man of the world, pilot and athlete, traveler and sensualist, gourmet and bon vivant, Salter brings a lifetime of sophisticated experience to these elegantly written essays.

NINE

THE SUMMA

All That Is

Salter's last novel was eagerly awaited. He wittily told me that, like Antoni Gaudi's still unfinished cathedral in Barcelona, *All That Is* (2013) had been under construction forever. The slightly odd and deliberately vague title of *All That Is* recurs in variants throughout the book: "all she knew," "all he now was," "all that one loved" and (three times) "all of it," the latter meaning the full sexual act. He first mentioned the title when discussing the contrasts of *Light Years* in his *Paris Review* interview: "The book is the worn stones of conjugal life. . . . All that is beautiful, all that is plain, everything that nourishes or causes to wither."[1] He explained that the title "is deliberately ambiguous. It might represent everything related to human life—birth, love, loss, aging and maturing as a person—but it might also represent all that exists in the world."[2]

The hero's name, Philip Bowman, resonates with meaning. He has the same first name as Phillip Deane in *A Sport and a Pastime* (in which the phrase "all that is" first appears). Bowman's name signifies skill and courage. Bowmen won the great English triumph at Agincourt in 1415, celebrated in Shakespeare's *Henry V*. Sagittarius, a sign of the zodiac, is another archer who aims high to achieve victory and is thought to be adaptable and flexible. Isabel Archer, the attractive heroine of Henry James' *The Portrait of a Lady*, explores personal freedom and responsibility and—like Bowman—is betrayed by her great love.

Through portrayals of the ideal sensual life, Salter's novel of manners follows the glamorous tradition of Scott Fitzgerald. Bowman has rapturous dreams and wants to achieve perfection. He devotes himself to the fleeting hedonistic pleasures of landscapes, water, houses, views, parties, talk, taste, food and drink. Suggesting the allure of travel and evoking the spirit of place, the book moves restlessly from Manhattan, Long Island and the Hudson River Valley to lively scenes in England, France and Spain. En route to Granada, Bowman sees "the sunbaked country float past the window of the train, through his own reflection. There were hills, valleys, thousands upon thousands of olive trees."

Salter's major themes are war and love. The brilliant first chapter of *All That Is* returns to the military action of *The Hunters* and *Cassada*. Salter's exciting account of naval warfare near Okinawa shows how Bowman tests his courage and reveals his character. Though he does not play a heroic role in the battle, as navigation officer he's engaged in the major naval victory that leads to the conquest of Japan. The first sentence—"All night in darkness the water sped past"—suggests the speed of the ship, and thrusts the reader into the action. The enemy fire, a storm of steel, is as dense as swarming bees. During the suicidal kamikaze attacks, American sailors "watched with almost hypnotic fascination and fear as they came straight down through dense antiaircraft fire or swept in low, skimming across the water."

Salter writes that the American carrier-based dive and torpedo bombers came from out of the clouds, more than a hundred at a time. He describes the *Yamato*, which bore the poetic name of the Japanese nation, wounded and sinking as if it were a man.

> [It] had been built to be invulnerable to air attack. All of its guns were firing as the first bombs hit. One of the escort destroyers suddenly heeled over, mortally stricken and, showing the dark red of its belly, sank. Through the water twenty torpedoes streamed toward the *Yamato*, their wakes white as string. The impregnable deck had been torn open, steel more than a foot thick, men smashed or cut in two. . . . It was not a battle, it was a ritual, the death as of a huge beast brought down by repeated blows. . . . Waves swept over it and men clinging to the deck were carried off by the sea in all directions. As it went under, a huge whirlpool formed around it, a fierce torrent in which men could not survive.

A historian described the battle that took place on April 7, 1945—five days before Franklin Roosevelt died. After fifteen American aerial attacks on the Japanese ship, the *Yamato*'s hull listed at 90 degrees and was almost vertical in the water. When its ammunition broke loose and exploded, the ship rolled over and plunged to its grave 450 fathoms below: "the American planes had disposed of the world's biggest and best battleship in well under two hours, just over a hundred miles off the Kyushu coast [of southern Japan]. There was only a little hyperbole in Samuel Morison's conclusion that this quick dispatch of the world's mightiest warship ended 'five centuries of naval warfare' based on competition between surface ships." [3]

All That Is was strengthened by the influence of Joseph Conrad as well as Fitzgerald. A crucial incident (also recalled later in the novel) was inspired by the famous scene in Conrad's *Lord Jim* (1900). Jim, a merchant marine officer, dishonors himself by jumping off a sinking ship that's carrying Moslem pilgrims to Mecca. Puzzled by his own cowardly behavior, he recalls: "I had jumped. . . . It seems. . . . It was as if I had jumped into a well—into an everlasting deep hole." [4] When Bowman's ship is hit in battle, his friend "Kimmel had jumped. . . . He became a kind of legend. He'd jumped off his ship in error. . . . He jumped overboard in the middle of the ocean during a big attack. That was the last time I saw him." Jim is punished for his impulsive act; Kimmel achieves a kind of fame.

Salter based his central character on his own life. Bowman was born in 1925, an only child, with an aged mother and absent father. He drives an old car, lives in Piermont on the Hudson and in Bridgehampton, and dislikes Mexico. When the wife and children of Bowman's friend Eddins are asphyxiated in a train fire, he feels responsible and guilty, as Salter did after Allan's death, and compares it to an air crash: "If he had been on the train, somehow this wouldn't have happened. He had failed them. . . . [It was] like something fallen from the sky, a great engine detached from an airliner high above and unseen and unheard hurtling down, death had struck, destruction, plunging into life like a sharpened stake." Most important, Salter and Bowman long for a different, superior life, unconstrained by bourgeois morality or behavior.

The novel describes forty years of Bowman's life from 1945 to 1984. His wartime naval service had made his existence seem more intense and real, and all his postwar sexual encounters attempt to recapture the thrill of combat. After graduating from Harvard after the war, he becomes—like Robert Ginna and Joe Fox—a successful book editor: "He liked reading the manuscripts and talking to the writers, being responsible for bringing a book into existence, the discussions, editing, galleys, page proofs, jacket." With more experience, he saw the darker side of the fight for literary prominence. The struggle among poets for important prizes or a secure academic job "was often the result of intense self-promotion, flattery and mutual agreements."

This bookish novel is filled with subtle allusions and literary anecdotes, from Byron's death in Greece and Lorca's execution in Spain to Pound's incarceration in a madhouse and Hemingway's description of gangsters in "The Killers."[5] Bowman has a wide acquaintance and there's a Tolstoyan profusion of characters, many divorced and alcoholic. Delineated in a few striking phrases, they make vivid cameo appearances, often very late in the novel, and then vanish.

Two of Salter's literary patrons and two prominent publishers (three of these men are Jewish) appear in the novel. Bowman has a frosty job interview with the wealthy Mr. Kindrigen, based on the father of Ben Sonnenberg, the editor of *Grand Street*. The father had virtually invented the business of public relations: "He could arrange anything in newspapers and magazines—for ten thousand dollars, it was said, he could put someone on the cover of *Time*." Though Bowman was a naval officer and Harvard graduate, Kindrigen refuses to exert his power and influence, and curtly orders him to "Go home."

The tall and elegant Malcolm Pearson, based on George Plimpton of the *Paris Review*, comes from a wealthy family. He wears expensive clothing and thinks of becoming a history professor, if only to annoy his father. Later on, he walks with a cane and disapproves of things. Salter doesn't mention Plimpton's handsome looks, extraordinary athletic ability, innovative journalism, and central role in the social scene in New York and expatriate Paris. Though the prestigious Farrar Straus and Giroux never originally published Salter, he treats the rich, luxury-loving Roger Straus, Robert Baum in the novel, reverently. Bowman works contentedly for the charming and confident Baum, who runs an informal office, pays little for books and brings out serious literature. Unlike Straus, Baum had been an army sergeant and seen action in the war, "from which he had emerged whole and unharmed, and had given him his credentials." There's a striking contrast between the real-life characters based on the classy and elegant George Plimpton and on the crude and aggressive Roger Straus. (I knew both of them.) Salter took what he wanted from his friends to make a literary point.

Salter was also impressed by the Austrian-born, English publisher George Weidenfeld, the model for the portly Bernard Wiberg (a variant of Wiborg, the maiden name of Fitzgerald's friend Sara Murphy). Wiberg "was resplendent in his dark, bespoke suits, and his self-regard, while great, was no greater than his success." Like Pablo Picasso and John Maynard Keynes, he married a ballerina; like Baum, he published many Nobel Prize winners. He became Sir Bernard and owned a valuable painting by Francis Bacon. Salter offers a brief account of Bacon's character, the antithesis of the respectable Wiberg. A slave to dark sadistic homosexual lovers, Bacon was fascinated and disgusted by the flesh: "He belonged to the nether world with its bitchy language, gossip and betrayals. . . . His lovers had drunk or drugged themselves to death. . . . He never painted over on a canvas. It was always once and for all."

Salter's style is pure and elegant, his dialogue sophisticated and witty. One indolent character has "the handsome face of someone who had never done much." "Photos from the summer curling" suggests couples curling up in the summer. A friend not seen for years hasn't changed a bit, "except for his appearance." Another companion asks Bowman, "'Whatever happened to that sultry girl who was having an affair with your rich father-in-law?' 'He died, you know.' 'He did? It was that intense?'" There's a fine account of a dangerous, near fatal swim in the ocean: "It was deeper. The bottom was gone, his foot could no longer touch it. He fought against the panic. He was rising and falling in the swells, the waves thundering."

Bowman inhabits the literary world, but his main career is sexual. Several women in the novel, when avidly seeking liaisons, are angry and have grievances. One bitterly believes, "Never give men your best. They come to expect it" and are disappointed when they don't get it. Others, still attractive in middle age, want to gain a lover before they lose their looks. Bowman's women, usually separated or divorced and often starved for sex after months, even years, of celibacy, are immediately attracted to him and frequently take the exciting active role. He's never rejected, but not ashamed to record his occasionally inadequate performance. The 26 brief, seductive sex scenes are not, as in *Sport*, the obsessive focus. More lyrical than lubricious, they are placed in the social context of the novel. Bowman seeks the perfect place, penetration, potency, prolongation and pleasure. In his symphony of sex both lovers are in complete harmony.

Salter describes the sex scenes with subtlety and wit: "They made love simply, straightforwardly—she saw the ceiling, he the sheets," as the self-absorbed lovers do not look at each other in this strangely detached encounter. With an English lover Bowman "went in slowly, sinking like a ship, a little cry escaping from her, the cry of a hare." The best sex scene combines sexual and religious ecstasy: "He loved everything, her small navel, her loose dark hair, her feet with their long, naked toes in the morning. Her buttocks were glorious, it was like being in a bakery, and when she cried out it was like a dying woman, one that had crawled to a shrine."

Bowman travels to London for business and social contacts, to Spain for glamour and pleasure, to Paris for a bitter seduction. Memories of the war sometimes surface and link Bowman the sexual adventurer to Bowman the naval officer. England, seen from the approaching plane, is green and unknown beneath broken clouds. The country recalls memories of the recent war: the catastrophic retreat of the British army from Dunkirk, "encircled and trapped on the Channel beaches," and the destruction of the British ships *Prince of Wales* and *Repulse* near Singapore on one fatal day, December 10, 1941. "The far-off sinking of the warships that were thought to be indestructible" recalls the destruction of the *Yamato* in Pacific waters at the beginning of the novel.

At Wiberg's lavish costume party, Bowman meets Enid Armour whose name suggests "I need *amour*." Following the usual pattern, he soon undresses her and takes her to bed: "They made love as if it were a violent crime, he was holding her by the waist, half woman, half vase, adding weight to the act. She was crying in agony, like a dog near death. They collapsed as if stricken. . . . She was trembling like a tree about to fall, her cries were leaking beneath the door." Brutality, art, pain, morbidity, stroke, chaos and flood all combine to intensify and exalt the sexual experience.

They travel to Spain, and visit Madrid, Toledo, Seville and Granada.[6] They taste the exotic food, watch the flamenco dancers and recall García Lorca's great poem on the death of the matador Ignacio Sánchez Mejías. Salter notes that Lorca was executed by the fascists for his homosexuality and his Left-wing politics. Enid is the great love of Bowman's life. Though separated from her husband, she's still under some strange obligation to him and unwilling to leave London. Years later she writes to Bowman, as if to intensify the pain of his loss, "*The days I spent with you were the greatest days of my life.*"

Returning from London to Manhattan, Bowman shares an airport taxi with Christine. Like Enid, she is estranged from her husband (who is Greek), and has a teenaged daughter, Anet. He and Christine have an instant rapport, eat in a Greek restaurant and swim in the ocean. He feels free to do anything with her: "He rubbed his cock slowly above her raised cunt as if bathing its length. Finally, he seated it. There was a long lovemaking in which his mind went blank." Self-enclosed and oblivious to the outside world, "they neither saw nor heard the rain."

Bowman links his emotional and financial life to Christine, which ignites a disastrous series of events. She becomes a real estate broker and finds him an ideal house in Bridgehampton for $120,000. He takes out a mortgage for $65,000, borrows $8,000 and pays $47,000 in cash. She moves into the house and helps pay the mortgage, and he's blissfully happy with her on weekends and holidays. The snake enters his Eden when she meets Ken Rochet and ricochets to that secret lover. Bowman is then shocked to learn that she's suing him for the ownership of the house, falsely claiming that it was bought in both their names because she couldn't qualify for a mortgage. Since there was no written agreement, "it became her word against his, and the jury decided in her favor. She was awarded title. The house was gone. Only afterwards did he learn that there was another man." She has betrayed him, first with a lover, then with a theft. He feels humiliated by the loss of Christine and his house, by his own foolish love and reckless trust in her. He bides his time and plans to get even for her treachery.

In the past, when Anet returned from school, Bowman had tried to be step-fatherly but felt emotionally intense with her. He comforts her when she's stung by a bee and frightened by a thunderstorm. After his break with Christine, he sees Anet, now age 20, in a Long Island train station. They arrange to meet, and he suggestively tells her about how Picasso seduced the beautiful young Marie-Thérèse Walter, fell in love with her and taught her about sex. Bowman and Anet smoke Moroccan hashish in a tiny pipe bowl and get high together. She has reluctant and passive sex with him, and he invites her to Paris. He shows her the sights, takes her to delightful restaurants and sleeps with her: "He wanted it to last a long time. When he felt himself going too far he slowed and began again. He could hear her saying something into the bedding. He was holding her by the waist. Ah, ah, ah. The walls were falling away. The city was collapsing like stars." The world responds to their convulsions.

Then, while she's sleeping, he writes a cruel note: *"I'm leaving. I can't bother now to explain."* He pays the hotel bill, drives away (like the Sam Waterston character in *Three*) and feels only the slightest guilt. Christine is furious to hear about Bowman's sexual revenge. Instead of explaining his real motive, she blames Anet, not herself, and screams at her: "He wanted to show you were a little slut. He didn't have to try very hard. . . . You are stupid. You're a stupid little girl."

At the end of the novel Bowman recalls his erotically satisfying and emotionally devastating life. Sex and sensual memories had given him the greatest pleasure as well as the deepest pain. Alluding to his ex-wife Vivian, to Enid and Christine, he thinks: "He'd been married once, wholeheartedly, and been mistaken. He had fallen wildly in love with a woman in London, and it had somehow faded away. As if by fate one night in the most romantic encounter of his life he had met a woman and been betrayed." Bowman discovers that he could love women deeply, then suddenly dislike, even despise them.

Critics of the novel accepted Salter's negative portrayal of his hero, who takes cruel and unconscionable revenge on his lover Christine. The London *Observer* called *All That Is* "superb." The *Guardian* noted, "though it's less than 300 pages long, the sharpness and abundance of observed detail give it an epic quality."[7] In the *Independent* Geoff Dyer wrote, "Salter has produced a strange masterpiece, a novel that seems a summing-up of much that he groped towards in his long middle period."[8] In striking contrast to the early denigration by Anatole Broyard and Robert Towers, Michael Dirda, who'd written the Foreword to Salter's correspondence with Phelps, proclaimed that "Salter and his friends are not just transformed, they are transfigured, made radiant." He praised "Salter's gravely serious, precise and musical prose, the close attention to the diction and rhythms of every phrase and paragraph."[9]

All That Is concludes with Bowman, aged 60, meditating on time and death, and on Charon rowing him across the Styx. His memories recall the idea of reality in the epigraph: "everything is a dream, and only those things preserved in writing have any possibility of being real." This belief recalls Calderón de la Barca's play *La vida es sueño* (Life is a Dream) and Virginia Woolf's statement, "Nothing has really happened until it has been recorded."[10] Salter aims to capture in poetic prose the evanescent moments of life. As in Proust, art is life perfected and rescued from time before it disappears.

Battered after three losses, the self-absorbed, embittered and vengeful Bowman (an archer who's missed his mark) remains idealistic and still believes in love. He finds pleasure elusive but, romantic and longing for the unattainable, takes his latest lover to experience the exotic ambience of Venice. Like Thomas Hardy, in his late eighties Salter continued to write well and produced an impressive work of art, a worthy successor to *A Sport and a Pastime* and *Light Years*.[11]

TEN

STRANGE CAREER

Fame is the spur that the clear spirit doth raise.

—MILTON, "Lycidas"

Salter's masterpieces—*A Sport and a Pastime*, *Light Years* and *Burning the Days* place him, after Saul Bellow and Vladimir Nabokov, as the best postwar American novelist. His lyrical evocation of people and places, of luxurious decadence and the danger of death, are unsurpassed. But his two best novels had poor reviews and sold few copies, and he did not achieve fame until much later. On September 7, 1997, when Salter had been writing for forty years, the former Marine pilot Samuel Hynes observed in the *New York Times Book Review* that "his reputation is of a curious kind; no single book of his has a secure place in the canon of modern fiction. As a writer he is both known and not known." Why were Salter's early novels ignored for so long, and why did his literary reputation revive when he was in his seventies and eighties?

By the mid-1970s, Salter had abandoned two successful careers: one delayed his progress as a novelist, the other derailed it. He was a fighter pilot in the Korean War and the screenwriter of four films. His well-paid work in Hollywood enabled him to return to writing fiction, and he enjoyed an astonishing resurgence of creative power and late success. Salter published eight books in the forty-four years between 1956 and 2000. In his eighties he published ten books in thirteen years.[1]

A fighter pilot combines the skill of a brain surgeon with the risk of a matador. Salter surrendered his life whenever he got on a war plane, and the chance of death made his existence seem even more precious. He recalled in an interview that many pilots "got killed early on. There were a lot of accidents. Those I had as real friends, maybe half a dozen, for some reason, they're all dead."[2] The macho emphasis in the fighter squadrons was on drink and daring; anything else was suspect. Amid all the alcohol, gambling and whoring, Salter dreamed of being a novelist, even a great one.

In this intellectual vacuum, he secretly wrote his first novel, *The Hunters*. He published it under the pseudonym of James Salter to disguise his authorship, protect his military career and hide the identity of the pilots he portrayed in his fiction. *The Hunters* sold a respectable 12,000 copies. His second war novel *Arm of Flesh* was a disastrous attempt to imitate William Faulkner's use of multiple narrators in *As I Lay Dying* (1930). It got very little notice, failed to sell and vanished without a trace.

Salter decided to follow Rilke's advice in "Archaic Torso of Apollo": "You must change your life." He explained that "reading about the lives of others is one of the things that gives us courage to change our own, the courage to struggle against our own."[3] He came to believe that his true life belonged in the literary world, not the Air Force, that "there is the knowledge of the senses that includes carnal happiness, and a greater knowledge that comes from intellect and reason."[4]

In 1957, when Salter sold the screen rights of *The Hunters*, he left his promising career after twelve years in the Air Force. In the terrible descent from fighter pilot to nonentity, he feared he'd made a disastrous mistake. After the money from the film rights ran out, he lived a hand-to-mouth existence for several years. In his version of a rags-to-riches story, he even tried selling swimming pools to wealthy neighbors. We don't know who employed him and what he earned; he might have worked for one summer and sold three pools. But he did have his Air Force pension, his pay from joining the Air National Guard and his wife's money from her wealthy family.

Salter had an engineering degree. Conscious of having lived in a cultural void, he deferred to editors with more sophisticated backgrounds and was powerfully influenced by the dilettante and literary snob Robert Phelps (1922–1989). Born in Elyria, Ohio, and educated at Oberlin College, he had a wife and son but was secretly bisexual. In his elegy on Phelps, Richard Howard wrote: "[You] were satisfied—or so you asserted—with patching up Colette" in five anthologies, and making flower arrangements of other prose by the homosexual writers Jean Cocteau and Glenway Wescott.[5] Salter took the surname of the hero of *A Sport and a Pastime* from Peter Deane, the coauthor with Phelps of the anthology *The Literary Life* (1968). He repeatedly praised this scrappy scrapbook and used anecdotes from it in his lectures, *The Art of Fiction*.

Salter corresponded with Phelps during the 1970s, but when his friend developed Parkinson's disease and found it difficult to write they drifted apart. In April 2013 Salter wrote me that he was in love with Phelps, not homosexual love, but in love with his tastes and what he represented. Salter eagerly adopted Phelps' Francophilia: his fondness for French phrases and admiration for precious and pretentious writers, especially Paul Léautaud (1872–1956), the eccentric, pet-obsessed, theater critic and diarist, and the married bisexual Colette, whom Phelps absurdly equated with Marcel Proust. Questioning, for once, his worship of Phelps, Salter quoted Judith Thurman, Colette's biographer, who said Colette wrote only half a dozen great letters. The others were all unrevealing and constrained. He was, naturally, astonished by this.[6] Reading Colette and Léautaud had a negative effect on Salter and encouraged him to occasionally indulge in mannered precious prose. He would have learned much more from his natural allies: Albert Camus' virile and heroic *The Plague* and André Malraux's description of aerial combat in the Spanish Civil War in *Man's Hope*.

The English novelist Geoff Dyer, noting Salter's innovations, remarked that "creative writing courses emphasise the importance of point-of-view and p.o.v. characters. Salter blows much of that stuff out of the water."[7] After the austere prose of his early war books he was no longer interested in traditional narrative and chronological structure, and used a radically different style and form in his third and fourth novels, *A Sport and a Pastime* and *Light Years*. Salter told Phelps (punning in French on his own name) that his sentence fragments—which suggest broken thoughts and incomplete speech—are "going to have many beautiful jumps, *sauts*, perhaps it will be a ballet."[8] One puzzled critic noted that "Salter jumps the gap from one kind of time to another, from broad narrative time to tight episodic time, without a safety net, trusting the reader to follow him."[9] Salter also alienated readers by killing his main characters at the end of the novels: Connell in *The Hunters*, Cassada in *Arm of Flesh*, Dean in *Sport*, Nedra in *Light Years*.

Salter's titles—*Light Years*, *Dusk* and *Last Night*—were increasingly dark. But other titles were prosaic and flat rather than poetic and suggestive: *Cassada*, *There & Then*, *Memorable Days*, *Don't Save Anything*. His original title for his last, vaguely named novel, *All That Is*, was the potentially disastrous *Toda*. He wrote, "Some names are like magic. Unforgetta-ble."[10] But Geoff Dyer wittily called the principals in *Light Years*, Nedra and Viri, "possibly the most irritatingly named characters in literature."[11] Salter also used obscure, even pretentious, titles for the stories in his first collec-tion, *Dusk*: "Am Strande von Tanger," "The Destruction of the Goetheanum" and the invented word "Akhnilo."[12]

Sport portrays the intense sexual relations of a Yale dropout and an electrically responsive French shop girl. In the 1960s the explosion of sexual liberation and corresponding freedom to describe it had not reached the still-staid editors, critics and professors. Salter recalled that Doubleday was embarrassed by *Sport*, didn't know what to do with the provocative book and failed to promote it: "They were holding it like it was a pair of dirty socks."[13] In 2005 he added, "Nobody wanted to review it. It was too sexual. . . . Now, in an era when even anal sex is discussed on prime-time TV, the book is completely inoffensive."[14]

The perceptive George Plimpton, whose Paris Review Editions copub-lished the novel with Doubleday, praised "its purity of style and its sensu-ality, which quickly attracted a cult following that has continued to grow over the years."[15] But influential critics took the opportunity to attack *Sport*, while savagely condemning *Light Years*, in both the *New York Times* and the *New York Times Book Review* in June and July 1975. Robert Towers' savage review of *Light Years* focused on Salter's unusual style, condemned the relentlessly poetic prose and unearned lyricism. *A Sport and a Pastime* sold fewer than 3,000 copies; *Light Years* sold only 7,000 and was remain-dered a year later. The contemptuous response to Salter's best novels in the two most influential newspapers damaged his reputation. These depress-ing and discouraging blows struck two months before the break-up of his twenty-four-year marriage and scarred him for several decades. Bloodied but unbowed, Salter continued to write and await recognition. As he ob-served in his story "Via Negativa": "there is a great, a final glory which falls on certain figures barely noticed in their time, touches them in obscurity and recreates their lives."[16]

Salter was still in a weak position when *Light Years* appeared. Unlike his close friends, George Plimpton and Peter Matthiessen (as well as Norman Mailer and John Updike), he had no powerful Harvard connections. He got a late start and didn't publish his first novel until he was thirty-one. Though he taught at several universities, he did not have a secure salary nor an influential post at a university. He did not solidify his reputation by belonging to a prestigious group: the New York intellectuals, the Beat poets or the postwar Paris buddies around William Styron and James Jones. The last two, as well as Salter's more famous contemporaries—J. D. Salinger, Norman Mailer and Joseph Heller—were all extremely productive after they returned from World War II. Scholars wrote their biographies and published their letters; they got a great deal of critical attention and were commercially successful. Despite his formidable achievements, Salter struggled for recognition during the first half of his literary career.

Salter was often called "a writer's writer," a term he disliked. This distinction excluded him not only from readers, but also from writers' groups in the Hamptons where he lived. When Heller and Mario Puzo suggested inviting him to join their group, other members objected and claimed "he was too good a writer" and would not fit in.[17] More aggressive in the air than on the ground, and unfamiliar at first with the maneuvers of the literary world, Salter did not have the theatrical and provocative persona of a Truman Capote or Gore Vidal, and was not good at promoting himself. But a new generation of patrons—Plimpton, Ben Sonnenberg and Jack Shoemaker of North Point Press—were more insightful and adventurous. Salter was determined to stay alive until his five novels were recognized.

Salter had written *The Hunters* on an Air Force base, surrounded by his rowdy comrades. When writing at home after leaving the service he moved from solidarity to solitude and had to be alone—preferably with the children away and the house empty. Insecure and uncertain, he confessed, "I just didn't have deep enough confidence to go on, and I suppose that let me stray away from writing for periods. I lived this life for at least five or seven years, not writing anything important."[18] Needing money to support his family, he interrupted his literary career by writing screenplays from the mid-1960s into the following decade. His Guggenheim application was rejected in 1972, he published only one volume between 1979 and 1997, and during most of the 1980s all his books were out of print. In this hiatus, between his mountain-climbing book *Solo Faces* (1979) and his stories in *Dusk* (1988), he wrote book reviews, travel essays and high-level journalism.

Salter repeatedly emphasized that novels were much more difficult to write than nonfiction, and it took courage to continue. He could not force himself to write on schedule every day and explained, "it's either because of the press of affairs or I just haven't brought myself to a position where

I'm ready to write anything down."[19] He always felt a crisis of irresolution before starting to work. He began without ego or expectation, and waited, like Hemingway, for something *true* to come. He didn't have writer's block, but was constrained by a more subtle impediment: "I have failure to write, or am too distracted to. I have occasional lack of belief. If I really feel futility, I read something like *The Iliad*."[20] When composing a story he had to "gather every resource, prepare for a struggle of weeks, even months, and every moment the danger of giving up, giving in."[21] Alluding to Samuel Beckett's "You must go on. I can't go on. I'll go on" in *The Unnamable*, he found writing as hard as rock climbing and exclaimed: "you come to these places and say to yourself, I can't do this, I know I can't do this, I'm certain I can't do it, but I have to do it. I know I have to."[22] He later explained his motives for writing: "I've written to be admired by others, to be loved by them, to be praised, to be known."[23]

Echoing T. S. Eliot's lines in "The Hollow Men" on the fatal crevasse between conception and completion—"Between the idea / And the reality / Between the motion / And the act / Falls the Shadow"—Salter told Phelps, who was permanently blocked on his second novel: "All week I've tried to write a story, I know everything about it, I can almost read it and yet I can't seem to write a single paragraph which interests me. It's like looking for something in the dark, there's such a huge amount of chance in writing."[24] As he struggled to complete *All That Is*, he wrote to me in July 2006 about the contrast between his ambition and achievement: "You have caught me at the tail end of life. I thought I would snatch the fire from the gods but each time came away with a piece of wood that only smoldered a little."[25]

Salter had an idiosyncratic way of collecting his fictional material. He scribbled random notes on odd pieces of paper, even on menus, stuffed them in his pockets and scattered them around his chaotic writing tables. Finally—like Isis gathering the remains of Osiris—he combined them with his journals and fit them all together. When we drove to the beach in Bridgehampton, I sat on bits of his future work and he carefully locked his old car to make sure no notes would escape. He wrote in longhand, feeling the words on the page, then labor-intensively typed, corrected and retyped on a heavy old machine. He felt writing involved "a lot of self-hatred, a lot of despair, a lot of hope and a lot of just absolute effort."[26] He remembered that Picasso painted and Thomas Mann wrote late in life, and remained like Ford Madox Ford, "an old man mad about writing." Like the old man described in Cicero's *De Senectute*, who planted trees that would never bear fruit in his lifetime, Salter published two posthumous works: on writing and a collection of essays. Salter's range was narrow but he looked in deep. He wrote literary essays only on Gabriele D'Annunzio and Isaac Babel and rarely considered politics, art or music. In a letter to Joe Fox, Salter said he was inspired by the work of his favorite artist. He often conceived and wrote his fiction while thinking of the life and paintings of the solitary and intimate Pierre Bonnard. The artist had spent his entire life outside the art schools and main movements of his era, and once described himself as floating between "intimacy and decoration."[27]

His satiric stories in *Last Night* portray the disappointed, even disastrous love affairs of rich and privileged, sybaritic and spoiled, high-strung and vulnerable, sad and guilty people. The alluring women who ignite his fiction are stripped of illusions, but unable to say farewell and escape from human bondage. The title and contents of *Life Is Meals* were strongly influenced by Liebling's *Between Meals*, which has that rare quality, charm, and celebrates a hedonistic yet civilized life.

Just before his literary rocket took off Salter, using a sexual metaphor, alluded to his own undervalued work: "There are books that can be skimmed and fully grasped and others that only yield themselves, so to speak, on the second or even third reading. . . . There are many writers and many of some magnitude, like the stars in the heavens, some visible and some not, but they shed glory."[28] In his *Paris Review* interview he contrasted the admiration that authors receive in France with their lack of recognition in America: "the dissatisfaction of poets, their feeling that the culture, the nation, did not give them the honor or respect they deserved."[29]

But recognition, though late, was on the way. James Wolcott wrote in *Vanity Fair* that Salter was "the most underrated underrated writer, whose best novels are all brilliant."[30] An editorial in *Esquire*, where Rust Hills had published many of his stories and essays, declared that *Sport* is "one of the great literary works of our day" and that Salter "has been more appreciated by more serious literary authors than has any other modern American writer."[31] Saul Bellow praised him as an "exceptionally talented" author whose fiction "turns me around, gives me new bearings, changes my views,"[32] and Salter also got printed endorsements from many other distinguished writers.[33]

Dusk won the PEN/Faulkner Award, but nine of the eleven stories had been rejected by the *New Yorker* and Salter had never produced the kind of bland, facile, made-to-order stories they wanted. He finally published a story and five articles in the *New Yorker*, and had a perceptive profile and obituary by Nick Paumgarten. After decades of neglect, *All That Is* was enthusiastically praised in the *New York Review of Books* by Joyce Carol Oates and Michael Dirda. Salter told me that "Bob Silvers has it in his head that I can write about aviation matters," and he contributed six pieces, including two on flying.[34]

In a resurgence of literary power Salter became more self-assured, assertive and effective in promoting his own work. His reprints were admired in a more sexually liberated time; his interviews in Plimpton's *Paris Review*—and 22 others collected in *Conversations with James Salter*—projected a wise and sympathetic image. Picador in London reprinted *Sport*, *Collected Stories* and *All That Is*, and paid exceptionally well for them. On November 20, 2012 Salter told me that these books in Britain, France, Germany, Holland and Italy had the biggest sales of his life. His *Collected Stories* "got a big English advance (Picador) within a stone's throw of six figures. This is for me *unexampled*." The English and French publishers, he ruefully informed me, "claim to have discovered me at the very lips of the grave."[35]

His daughter Nina, whose small publishing company in Paris, Editions des Deux Terres, translates English writers into French, launched her father on the front page of *Le Monde* and the cover of *Lire*. *All That Is* became a bestseller and sold 70,000 copies in France.[36] Salter's new agent, Amanda Urban at Curtis Brown, connected him to Knopf, which brought out the stories in *Last Night*, the handsomely produced *Life Is Meals* and *All That Is*. Salter told me that he'd done more to promote his last novel than for any other book and the publicity had left him with a prickled feeling. Knopf did nothing to promote it.

Over the years, as Plimpton had predicted, word gradually spread about Salter's extraordinary intellect and style. Writers who felt he'd been unfairly ignored or condemned were eager to praise his virtues. Readers were now more tolerant of the anal sex scenes in *Sport* and this novel, with *Light Years*, became exciting literary discoveries. An excellent retrospective essay on *Sport* by Sarah Hall in the *Guardian* argued that the novel transcended the sexual theme and revealed Salter's almost miraculous transformation fifty years after it first appeared: "Since its publication in 1967, during the decade of sexual revolution, *A Sport and a Pastime* has set the standard not only for eroticism in fiction, but for the principal organ of literature—the imagination. What appears at first to be a short, tragic novel about a love affair in France is in fact an ambitious, refractive inquiry into the nature and meaning of storytelling, and the reasons we are compelled to invent, in particular, romances."[37]

Salter's late torrent of books reignited his career in an extraordinary way. Between 1982 and 2013 all his novels and stories were reprinted in paperback and widely praised the second time around. He rewrote, revised and reissued them, sometimes with prefaces by himself, and was fortified by many extremely favorable reviews and interviews. But all the photos in Salter's late books and articles about him show him in old age, which may have discouraged younger readers.

Several reprints had introductions by important contemporary writers whose judgments were perceptive and persuasive. Reynolds Price declared in the Farrar, Straus edition that "*A Sport and a Pastime* is as nearly perfect a narrative as I've encountered in English-language letters, a brilliant and heartbreaking portrayal of young sexual intoxication."[38] In his Introduction to the Penguin *Light Years*, Richard Ford agreed: "It is an article of faith among readers of fiction that James Salter writes American sentences better than anyone writing today. . . . It is an immensely readable, luminous novel . . . that radiates gravity, great intelligence and verbal virtuosity."[39] The Irish novelist John Banville enthusiastically wrote in the Picador edition of *Collected Stories*: "Salter is a magician, and his marvels are exquisitely wrought yet exert a muscular grasp of the everyday realities of life."[40]

In 2014 Salter gave three well-paid but rather casual lectures at the University of Virginia. He then made triumphant processions to pick up a stream of honors and awards. He was elected to the American Academy of Arts and Letters in 2000; he won the PEN/Malamud Award for excellence in short fiction in 2012; and in 2013, when Zeus descended in a shower of gold, he got the first Windham-Campbell literary prize, a staggering $150,000. He told me that all the other winners were young authors who got the prize to encourage their writing: "For me, it's to enable me to stop."

During the late success in his last decades, as the honors and awards poured in, the victorious Salter regained confidence, overcame his creative inhibitions and began to write with full-throated ease. He was now able to publish his uncollected works in books: his war fiction, stories, travel articles, correspondence, interviews, lectures and essays. Despite the hiatus in mid-career, he always remained faithful to his dominant subjects: aerial combat, sophisticated society and sexual relations. Success, beginning with *Burning the Days*, enabled him to spend several years on *All That Is*. Michael Dirda concluded his review of the novel by stating, "after years of being 'becalmed,' James Salter has now rightly come to be regarded as one of the great writers of his generation." [41]

When Salter described his ancient contemporary, the actor Kevin McCarthy, who'd starred in his play *The Death Star*, he seemed to be portraying himself: he's in his nineties, a bit rumpled, with white uncombed hair, still glamorous for a man his age. On June 10, 2015, two dozen friends gathered in the Sag Harbor home of Maria Matthiessen (widow of Peter) for a dinner to celebrate Salter's clear-minded 90th birthday. His end came in a sudden rush. On June 19th, while exercising in a gym, he had a fatal heart attack.

Salter had a rare combination of talents and achievements. He was a fighter pilot and Francophile, downhill skier and mountain climber, novelist and screenwriter, expatriate and traveler, epicurean and sensualist. A war hero himself, he hero-worshipped combat generals and astronauts, champions on fast snow and high peaks, European film directors and literate editors. His tribute to William Styron revealed his own values: "He was a person of conviction regarding what was good and what was not in the world and also in literature, especially the novel. He became what he always dreamed of and worked for, a writer, a famous writer." [42] Salter and Styron were born one day apart in the same year. He called Styron a friend, though not a close friend, and thought Styron was superior to him in achievement and status. [43]

Salter's first two books portrayed flying. The cruel reception of his next two innovative novels discouraged him and accentuated his perfectionism. His detour into well-paid screenwriting interrupted his serious work. It took time for the social change of the 1960s to alter the hostile response to his novels. Eventually, as his style and subject matter became more acceptable, authors and reviewers began to see the high quality of his writing. In his late career, as the Zeitgeist finally caught up with him, he moved from outsider to insider, from cult figure to successful writer, from obscurity to fame. Unlike Marcel Proust, Franz Kafka and Tomasi di Lampedusa, who died before their work was recognized, Salter lived long enough to become celebrated while he was still alive. [44]

ELEVEN

FRIENDSHIP AND RECOLLECTIONS

I

On July 18, 2005 I wrote to Jim for the first time, cold, in Bridgehampton, Long Island. I discussed the influence of Hemingway and Fitzgerald on his work, mentioned some places we'd both lived in (Colorado and Japan) and my meetings with his friends: James Dickey, Irwin Shaw, James Jones, Joseph Mankiewicz, Joseph Losey and Patrick Leigh Fermor. Jim responded on August 6 to what he called my "astonishing letter" and exclaimed: "I was stunned to learn that Dickey was a navigator. He posed as a pilot and one night in Paris, the night we met, told me that if we'd been in the air at the same time he'd have shot my ass down. I see now what with, a sextant. He was a big blowhard, constantly interrupting with imitations of movie actors. But he could write, I agree with you."[1] Jim and I had an immediate temperamental affinity, and could write and talk about subjects of great interest to us. Writing is a lonely profession and we were delighted to have struck sparks. Many of his friends had died, and I was an admirer and late substitute.

During the last decade (2005–15) of his long life Jim sent me eighty letters, postcards and emails. He usually typed one-page, single-spaced letters on oversized A4 stationery with letterheads of exotic hotels, sent to him by friends, from Estonia to China, from the sailboat *Olinka* to (disappointingly) Days Inn in Hays, Kansas. His letters discussed writers, reading and readings, family and friends, travels and teaching at Virginia and at Duke (where he was pleased to earn $20,000 for one week), movies and Hollywood, his books and my books (especially *Hemingway* and *Edmund Wilson*), and his resurgence of literary power and astonishing late success.

He wrote frankly about his early sexual adventures, money and awards, writing schedule and writing problems. I sometimes addressed him as "Tuan Jim," after the hero of Joseph Conrad's Malayan novel. Since my mother's maiden name and his original name was Horowitz, I fancied that we might be distantly related. I also found that in John Huston's film *The Misfits* the 1939 Meyers biplane, which drove the wild mustangs out of the mountains and into captivity, was actually flown by a pilot named Ken Salter. While visiting a friend, I discovered that his father and Jim's father had been in the same class at West Point. I saw a photo of Jim's father in the yearbook and confirmed that he'd been first in his class.

As our friendship developed Jim wanted to read everything I wrote. I sent him eight of my books and he generously praised, never criticized, my work. Like my late friend J. F. Powers, it amused Jim to pretend that I was the great author and he the humble drudge. When I asked his advice about selling my screenplays, he replied, "You are dramatically overqualified to write movies. I don't particularly like them. If I go to [work on] one it's with uneasiness. I don't like being in the hands of a director."

Before my first visit he defensively warned me, though he was extremely sophisticated and well read, "am afraid you're going to find me a little more uncultured than you expected." When I sent him a list of more than sixty errors in the appalling edition of his letters to Robert Phelps, he seemed far less troubled than I was. "Cher Maître," he wrote, "Far from being angry, I am dazzled by your immense and rightfully proud knowledge of all these matters and persons. What you dashed off in an hour or two is far beyond my own knowing." We strongly disagreed about book editors. He admired and depended upon them, I found them (except for Aaron Asher and Peter Davison) obstructive and incompetent. I was convinced that all the students who got a C- in my English classes had taken revenge by becoming editors.

We mostly discussed literature, and Jim noted the difference between modern poets, such as Robert Lowell and John Berryman, and novelists: "The poets decided to be manic and destroy themselves. The novelists did otherwise, but then a novel requires a lot of organization and persistence, they had to keep their heads." He especially admired and taught Hemingway's "The Short Happy Life of Francis Macomber" and observed, "Hemingway is very affected and can be annoying, but the story, its structure and pace as well as its tone are so good." Edmund Wilson he adored and often referred to as an inspiring literary touchstone who represented lost values:

"Wilson seems to represent, both because of when he lived and what he was, a last brave flaring of literature's long eminence. At the same time, reading about him fills one with courage and desire." Wilson's motto from Deuteronomy 31:6, cut in Hebrew letters on his gravestone, was "Be strong and of a good courage."

In a grumpy mood, Jim compared Wilson's apogee to the robotic mindlessness of our own time and declared, "We are swimming in sewage, aren't we? The culture seems to be accelerating and heading, as if towards an irresistible black hole, towards the screen, television, computer, movie house." Jim was violently against the younger George Bush, hated reading about politics and didn't care who won the next election. But he also believed that culture moved in cycles and that there would be a return to a healthier society—though not yet.

Jim was always perceptive about writing. Reading through thousands of pages of his unpublished journals before selling them to the University of Texas, he noted the dominant themes: "I find them filled with the same preoccupations that are in my novels: the sexual life and its paramount presence in life, interesting or clever dialogue, profiles of individuals, occasional incisive observation, self-analysis, and descriptions of incidental women. . . . There are [also] descriptions of other writers and judgments of them and many intensely personal entries about my unhappy first marriage."

Using a flight metaphor, he also expressed his cardinal principles as a novelist, which should be carved in stone in all the writers' "workshops": "Don't try to include everything, hold the irony, do not abandon characters—stay with them, persevere, be yourself, the best character with the most wonderful phrases is the author, lift off early." When his exact but distant contemporary William Styron died, Jim took it as a personal blow: "Styron's death, long desired by him according to his son-in-law, and following some terrible final rounds, has hit me more than usual. I've known him since the early 1960s . . . but we were never close. I feel close now."

I published two articles and two reviews about Jim's work, for which he was excessively grateful: "The review of [*Life Is Meals*] is *wonderful*, all one hopes, more than one deserves. More than two deserve. . . . Many, *abundant* thanks." He gave me some useful background about his story "Am Strande von Tanger" and wrote that I made him see his work in a new way: "I feel elevated to another level, your perceptive analysis of 'Am Strande' is an adjunct to Literature. Well, I am very grateful. More than that, it made me want to read the story, and it's interesting that you point out connections I was unaware of." Pleased to accept my homage to him with *Samuel Johnson*, he replied (though most of his friends were writers), "I've never had a book dedicated to me before. . . . It's thrilling."

Though I'd caught him "at the tail end of life," he'd achieved his greatest recognition during his final years. He lived modestly but had, like Scott Fitzgerald, a weakness for the wealth and luxury he'd tasted in Hollywood, and was pleased to be with people who played polo and were rich together. "We were in Egypt in February," he wrote in 2010, "cruising up the Nile with [the English publisher] Christopher and Koukla MacLehose, and the Peter Matthiessens. I'm sure you've been there. The legendary tombs and temples were crowded, everything was crowded, Abu Simbel was a 3-hour bus ride each way from Aswan which was crowded, but the days spent sailing up and down the river are what I'll remember, feeling of timelessness."

On June 15, 2015, five days after his birthday and four days before his death, he wryly told me, "I've just had my ninetieth birthday, try to imagine that. . . . [I'm] writing a couple of reviews for the *New York Review of Books*, one on David McCullough's *The Wright Brothers*, a book I doubt you'd be inclined to read."

Jim inscribed 26 various editions of his books for me. The three best, signed in three different ways, were:

A Sport and a Pastime: "To Jeffrey. Represents, I think, the apogee. Very fondest, Jas."

All That Is: "To Jeffrey, one of its first and certainly most diligent readers. With great affection, James Salter."

Burning the Days: "Dear Jeffrey—you were born just a bit too late to be included—Affectionately, Jim."

I valued his approval more than any other writer's. A friend said the best thing about my *Thomas Mann's Artist-Heroes* (2014) was Jim's comment: "This brilliant and intensely rich book fills one, from the beginning, with the desire to know more—all there is—about Mann and the stories and novels that brought him to preeminence as Germany's greatest modern writer and important moral force. This is a wonderful book written with verve. Thomas Mann, his person, themes, obsessions and art have been of lifelong interest to Jeffrey Meyers, who brings to them the background and breadth that supreme literary art and the tremendous decades from 1900 through the 1940s deserve." This really was "an adjunct to Literature."

II

We lived on different coasts of America and managed to meet only twice: for three days each time, in June 2006 and July 2007, at his home in Bridge-hampton. But our letters paved the way for stimulating and sympathetic encounters. Jim had short-cropped white hair, high forehead, blue eyes, pointed nose, uneven teeth, a sturdy build and rugged good looks. His artist friend Donald Sultan described his speech in *The Hamptons* (July 17, 2015): "His voice was deep and resonant with a slight pause between sentences, as if he were thinking over the way he said it even as he began the next. I have met only a few people in my life who were so measured in their intimate conversations."

He was in great shape for a man of eighty-one and tackled a wind-blown balloon on the beach before his young grandson could catch it. He was an amusing raconteur and attentive host. Greeting me while leaning against the frame of his open front door, he expected to be bigger than me and allowed, "you're taller than I expected." Referring to *Julius Caesar* and punning on "short of money," he recalled that Robert McCrum in the *Guardian* (March 24, 2007) "interviewed me and described me as 'shortish,' unkindliest cut. I've been short but never shortish." Sizing me up, he said he disliked my stagy, professional author's photo, wearing a Córdoba hat, and thought I looked better in person.

All four desks in his house were piled high with papers and left no space to work. The books spilled chaotically out of the narrow shelves, and though he offered to give me a copy with his introduction to Irwin Shaw's *The Young Lions*, we couldn't find the book. My wife and I stayed in a bed-and-breakfast place on our first visit. The following year Jim gave us the upstairs master-bedroom. His Corgi, who was named Paavo after the Finnish runner and slept with Jim and Kay, was recovering from an operation and couldn't climb the narrow circular staircase. Jim let the garden grass grow high and liked "to see the wind blow through it." He also rented a small flat on West 45th Street in Manhattan, which Kay used to write and see plays and films. They met during the filming of a television show just after Kay graduated from college and, she affirmed, "he educated me."

Jim withdrew from the summer social life in order to write. But he found the winters in Bridgehampton, where he could work without interruption, were too cold, bleak, boring and depressing to bear. So each year after Christmas they took a week to drive to Aspen. Paavo didn't like flying, and Jim wouldn't trust anyone to drive his dog, papers and possessions to Colorado. He still skied downhill in Aspen, despite the high altitude and his arthritis, and played tennis singles with Matthiessen on "millionaires' courts" in the Hamptons. Speaking of local lavish parties, Jim had "wondered where the beautiful people had gone to, but there they were, all in their thirties and some of the women in little else."

Jim had four children from his first marriage, and had struggled to educate them all at the University of Colorado. His twins, son James and daughter Claude, were "completely unintellectual." Jim's first wife still lived in Aspen, but he was "only in touch with her by necessity." His daughter Nina (with a long "i") looks like him and was in Bridgehampton when we visited. She lives in Paris and runs her own small publishing company, Editions des Deux Terres, which translates English-language authors, including Kazuo Ishiguro and Ruth Rendell, and publishes them in French. Briefly married to a Frenchman when she was twenty, she has a well-behaved, bilingual son, Nile, then about ten years old. Pretty but not enticing, Nina was still jealous of Kay's happy marriage and resented me for diverting Jim's interest during our visit. She sulked and was mainly silent during dinner, and sat apart on the beach. Angry and aggressive, hostile and rude, she'd rather be feared than liked. She behaved childishly, was obviously unhappy and seemed to be battling demons.

Kay said she'd been that way since childhood, was usually much worse, and Kay was glad to have me there to ease the tension. Nina demanded more attention than Jim could supply. He seemed apprehensive that she might explode, but was patient and tolerant: a good father. When Jim opened a bottle of Macon, I said the name sounded like an obscene word in French. Nina contradicted me and, tired of tangling with her and thinking she knew more French than I did, I dropped it. I later confirmed that *con* means "cunt" in French and "Ma con" had suggested that to me. Nina was more innocent than she seemed; Jim thought she "just didn't get it."

Theo, Jim's son with Kay, had been to Lawrenceville and was then a junior at Bowdoin. He spent summers as an intern on Wall Street and with a theater company. Jim had grave doubts about a theatrical career, but wanted to let him have a shot at it. He liked traveling in Europe with Theo and appreciated the liveliness he generated when he was home.

Jim liked to reminisce about his glory days in the Air Force. But he was not sorry that he'd left to become a writer in 1957 after the successful publication of *The Hunters*. Some of his old comrades had made four stars. Most, retired for thirty years, played golf and ranted against the liberals. He remembered the huge air ace Robert Olds—six feet, two inches; 230 pounds—who "begged to be a fighter pilot in a small cockpit." But he added, "heroes are more often made up than true." He described experiencing the effects of oxygen deprivation during training: he started to play cards but quickly passed out. He also explained that if a stowaway tried to hide in the wheel case of a plane he would die of suffocation before he froze to death.

Jim went to a few meetings of the American Academy of Arts, but felt like a renegade who didn't belong with all the respectable oldies. "Can you see me with those guys?" he asked. The main advantage of being in the Academy is that "you can say you're in the Academy." He preferred to break a solemn mood and liven things up with some jokes. Gloria, wife of James Jones, asked while dancing next to two gays who were dancing together, "My man has a hard on. Does yours?" A hostess asked Nabokov, who arrived at a Cornell dinner party during a snowstorm, "Did you come in a troika?" "No, a Buicka." At a diplomatic reception the British foreign minister asked an attractively dressed person to dance and was told, "I don't dance. I'm not a woman. I'm the archbishop of Lima."

Jim then ranged through friends in the literary world. Sarah, widow of George Plimpton, could be difficult with biographers. She wanted to protect her young daughters from knowledge of her husband's amorous adventures. Saul Bellow, after hesitating, finally decided to marry a woman (Susan Glassman) with a mustache. His last young wife (Janis Freedman) was a devoted mouse. Jim's closest friends were Peter Matthiessen, living near Bridgehampton and married to a German woman from Tanzania, and the screenwriter Lorenzo Semple in Santa Monica. He thought Richard Ford had the good life. He'd been at an artist's residence in Berlin for six months, and just sent a postcard saying *Off to Paris today—two months*. "He and his wife have a glancing sort of marriage." Jim asked about my meetings in Spain with the writer Gerald Brenan and with the matadors Antonio Ordóñez and Luis-Miguel Dominguín. He liked Dominguín's charmingly formal way of greeting me, "A sus órdenes" (at your orders), and repeated it several times.

Jim was at his best when talking about writing. He used to appear in *Esquire*, but thought the magazine was now garbage and would no longer contribute. He had a new agent who's "big at ICM," went into Vintage paperbacks before signing with Knopf for *Last Night* and *Life Is Meals*, and was annoyed that the publisher wouldn't pay for his plane ticket from Aspen to Berkeley when I invited him to speak. *A Sport and a Pastime* he wittily called "a cross between Henry Miller and Henry James." *Light Years*, with the exotically named heroine Nedra, was not about his first wife but about the conceptual artist Barbara Rosenthal, who had a rather sad and disappointing life. *Life Is Meals* was inspired by a published literary calendar. Showing me his original notes and large colored chart, and noting my appreciative interest, he remarked, "you have a way of gaining one's confidence." Knopf didn't push the book, which sold 16,000 to 17,000 copies, and earned beyond his advance. (Shrewd writers know that if you make your advance you weren't paid enough at first.) He's now known as a high-toned foodie writer. He was just starting his new novel, *All That Is*, but didn't like to talk about it in case it didn't work out.

We were supposed to feel honored by an invitation to the first big social event of the Hamptons' summer season: a lavish party thrown by the literary agent Ed Victor. Jim dressed up for the occasion in a dapper white suit and royal blue tie. One friend cattily asked if he had rented it and when he had to return it to the store. By contrast to his elegant attire, we drove up the long driveway to the valet parking in Jim's deliberately chosen old wreck of a car, of which he was inordinately proud. He insisted on locking it himself because some of his notes were still floating around inside. The jalopy also provided a notable contrast to Victor's pretentiously parked Rolls Royce, which symbolized the party's vulgar display of wealth and power.

Blythe Danner, actress and mother of Gwyneth Paltrow, and Candice Bergen looked delightfully attractive. But there were few intellectual faces. The only other writers I saw amid the swarm of agents and editors were Kurt Vonnegut, who looked ill and died the following year; the journalist Ken Auletta, who seemed to be constantly preening before an invisible mirror; and the biographer Robert Caro. When Caro politely asked what I was working on and I replied, "Johnson," he tensed up and exclaimed, "wait a minute"—as if to say, "I'm the one who writes about Johnson around here." But he appeared relieved as I added, "Samuel, not Lyndon." I was enraged at the financial exploitation of writers, who earned so little, by middlemen who

made so much. Jim, who'd been around much longer than me, was resigned
to the fact that "authors are nothing." Nina said the party was a "shark feed,"
but couldn't specify who were the sharks and who the prey.

As we left the next morning both Jim and Kay said they appreciated our
considerable effort to get to the end of Long Island and thanked us for coming. Kay, in friendly fashion, kissed me good-bye on the lips. Nina, though
glad to see us go, refused to permit frenchified kisses on both cheeks and
saw me off with a stiff, extended handshake. I asked Jim, "Shall we continue
to correspond?" he replied, "Yes, but not so often" and I suggested once a
month. The ever-hostile Nina then interrupted with, "Wait a minute. I get
only two letters a year," and wanted us to cut down our correspondence to
her level. We ignored her injunction and continued to write in our usual
way. In Jim's next letter he graciously wrote, "It was such a pleasure to meet
you both. I can't say I had no idea—I suspected it would be. After a certain
point it's not easy to make friends."

After we'd bought the plane tickets for our second visit, Jim and Kay
had a last-minute change of plans and we arrived the day after their exhausting flight from St. Petersburg, Russia. Their nine companions on the
trip included Peter and Maria Matthiessen, Jean Kennedy Smith (sister of
President Kennedy), Rose Styron, the sculptor Jack Zajac, an English editor and a scout from the French publisher Gallimard. Jim had rented a flat
with two other couples, a bit far from the city center and from the others
in the group. Taxis were difficult to find and, pushed from both sides in a
crowded bus, his pocket was picked. They never met any Russians, but the
weather was fine and he especially liked seeing Nabokov's old mansion and
Anna Akhmatova's museum at Fotanka House. They sat through the entire
Sleeping Beauty from 7 to 11:30 p.m., and then ate scrambled eggs at their
flat. Though Petersburg was famed for its beauty, he thought it was ugly
and didn't much like it. He thought Moscow, which he didn't visit, must
be a horror. Russian food and service were, as always, poor but expensive,
especially when traveling with rich, free-spending friends. Though he hated
flying and the journey cost a lot, he had a good time and felt it was worth it.

On the first night in Bridgehampton, Kay served a simple summer dinner of cucumber, tomato and onion salad, spaghetti carbonara, watermelon
and Blackstone red California wine. The second night, when the Matthiessens came to dinner, we had stuffed avocado, broiled flounder, creamed
potatoes dauphinoise, Spanish flan and Blackstone red. Matthiessen, with-

drawn and unresponsive, looked terribly gaunt, seemed to be ill and close to death. He said authors now needed an agent who could also edit, but that Jim's agent Binky Urban couldn't edit anything. He praised Becky Saletan as a good editor—though she did absolutely nothing for my two books at Harcourt while dancing attendance on Peter. At dinner Jim gently teased Kay about her pronunciation of *macedoine* and Macedonia, and some aspects of her taste in cooking, When she seemed hurt, he stroked her hand, said he was sorry and promised not to tease her again.

Like Fitzgerald and Faulkner, Jim had swallowed the Hollywood bait and was fond of recalling those prosperous and fantastical years. Omar Sharif, who'd starred in *The Appointment*, told Jim that David Lean used to invite the *Lawrence of Arabia* actors into his tent for tea, while the huge crew waited to start work, and asked their ideas about the scene to be shot that day. Lean then deftly maneuvered them into doing precisely what he wanted. Robert Redford had called Jim about a month ago, said he wanted to keep in touch with old friends and invited him to tea at a New York hotel. But Redford had broken with several former friends, and Jim was still resentful about having to change the original script of *Downhill Racer* to make Redford look heroic.

Jim had met his great friend, the Yale-educated Lorenzo Semple (who died in 2014), in Aspen. Semple immediately propositioned Jim's attractive first wife and suggested they go to a motel. Semple's wife later found incriminating photos of his long-time mistress. Semple was reluctant to attend a dinner of French aristocrats at Lectoure in southwestern France. But at the end of the elaborate feast and while seated between two beautiful Swedish twins, he made a long speech in French and was applauded by the fifteen guests. Jim wrote *Avalanche Express* (1979) with Semple. The studio liked their script and flew them to London, but the director rejected it: a great waste of time, but good money. As an example of the deep corruption in Hollywood, he told the story of the writer who got a $500,000 contract for a script he never had to write. Jim went to a Hollywood party with a girl who said, "There's Brad Pitt. I blew him. Do you think he'd remember me?" Jim couldn't resist remarking that she'd "be easy to spot on her knees."

The next morning Jim apologized for his "drunken ranting" against the movies. In fact, he wasn't drunk and told amusing stories. To counter his condemnations of all the film producers and directors, I mentioned meeting and admiring Billy Wilder, Fred Zinnemann, Joseph Mankiewicz and

Walter Mirisch. Jim agreed that they were all fine men, but exceptions to the rule.

After a few bottles of wine at dinner, Jim had moved on to contemporary writers. He disliked both Salman Rushdie and his work. Though Rushdie had all the qualifications except the ability to write, he thought his recent knighthood would help him snag the Nobel Prize. Asked about the most impressive contemporary writers, he jokingly replied that Joseph Heller had great hair, almost like Einstein's, and that Philip Roth was supposed to be very funny. William Gaddis, who used to live in Bridgehampton, loved movies and was disappointed that none of his novels had ever appeared on the screen. When they went to the movies together, Gaddis would laugh with an appreciative "heh, heh." Jim had dinner with the recently widowed, eighty-five-year-old Arthur Miller, who turned up with Agnes Barley, a young woman in her twenties. Miller, he said, could be ponderous and boring, and we agreed that Tennessee Williams was a much better playwright. Jim's negative comments were based on his exceptionally high standards and reflected his belief that until recently he'd never had just recognition and rewards as a writer. Like Edmund Wilson, Anton Chekhov was his literary touchstone, and he quoted the poignant line from the end of *The Cherry Orchard*, "You're going away, leaving me behind?"

He'd read my life of Hemingway, but wanted to know more and asked me for some insider stories about him. He was greatly interested in Kay Morrison, married to a Harvard professor, who had simultaneous affairs with Robert Frost and his hostile biographer Lawrance Thompson. He questioned me about my revealing interview with Kay's daughter Ann. Eager to tell her story she said, "I've been waiting all my life for you to come." Ann's ex-husband, on the scene at the time, didn't understand the sexual complications until he'd read my life of Frost. Jim also questioned me about my friendship and correspondence with a sexually adventurous English novelist, Francis King, whom I later described in *Remembering Iris Murdoch* (2013).

Reading and writing were always favorite subjects. Jim liked to read slowly and aloud, and wondered how I could absorb everything when reading so fast. I quoted Samuel Johnson's belief that no man ever read a book through. I was writing an essay about Jim's work and promised to show it to him when it was accepted, but I wanted to express my own interpretation, not his. Quoting D. H. Lawrence, "Never trust the artist. Trust the tale," he agreed. By chance I heard, while staying with Jim, that my twenty-page piece had been accepted and would appear in the *Kenyon Review* (Spring 2008).

He mentioned Alex Vernon's book *Soldiers Once and Still*, about Hemingway, himself and Tim O'Brien. Vernon discussed Jim's early West Point story, "Empty is the Night," in *Pointer*. Jim said the title was not a deliberate allusion to Keats's "Ode to a Nightingale" and Fitzgerald's *Tender Is the Night*, but thought Vernon should have spotted the echo. "Vernon's interested in war," Jim said, "I'm interested in writing." He didn't show the work to Kay and another friend until it was finished, and revised again when they'd read it. The phone rang a lot while we were there, perhaps because they'd been away for a few weeks. But he planned to withdraw from social life, as he did the previous summer, and concentrate on his work.

Like Nina in 2006, his dog Paavo caused serious problems in 2007. Thirteen years old, half blind and very sick, he was having chemotherapy for incurable cancer "to give him one more good year." At breakfast on our third and last day Paavo, after a bad night, had a convulsive fit while his brown eyes gazed desperately at his master. Jim rushed him to the vet, but he died an hour later. He returned with the dead dog wrapped in a blanket, dug his grave in the garden and then worked off his angst at the gym. I felt it was a great release for the poor animal and was glad to escape to the beach. Jim and Kay were both grief-stricken—she cried all afternoon—and could not go out to dine with us that night.

The next morning Jim, regretful about missing our last dinner, was especially kind and attentive. He gave me one of his shirts, asked about how my wife and I had met at UCLA and married while I was teaching in Japan. He wanted a photo of our daughter, who seemed "to come out of *Vanity Fair*." We ended bookishly as Jim wrote down the titles of little-known works, including Edmund Gosse's *Father and Son*, L. P. Hartley's *The Go-Between* and J. F. Powers' *Morte D'Urban*, which I especially admired.

Tough but tender-hearted, Jim loved Phelps, flew to Shaw's deathbed and wrote an emotional farewell letter to Matthiessen. He led a charmed life: came from a wealthy background, attended prep school and West Point, was a handsome ladies' man, survived a dangerous air crash and 100 missions as a fighter pilot, had four screenplays made into movies, had five children, created three literary masterpieces, achieved late recognition and honors, was greatly admired by leading writers, lived to 90 and died suddenly.

I regret that I didn't know Jim when he spent winters in Aspen and I was teaching at the University of Colorado. He could have stayed with me when driving west to Aspen; I would have seen him frequently, invited him to read and teach in Boulder. It's sad to have lost 30 years of potential friendship, but I treasure my decade of comradeship with Jim—a heroic man, lively companion and brilliant writer.

TRIBUTES

Many distinguished novelists have paid tribute to Salter's achievement:

Tom McGuane: "I liked much of Salter's work very much, some not so much, and don't know all of it. I liked *The Hunters*, *Solo Faces* and *Cassada* more than the critics, was fascinated by *A Sport and a Pastime* despite its creepiness, loved *Burning the Days*, his great short stories like 'Last Night,' and consider *Light Years* to be among the most annoying books I've ever read. 'Viri'? Gimme a break. Writers like Cheever, Sebald and Salter produce great work striving for something they wish they were, a WASP in Salter's case. I knew Salter and, net-net, revere him and his work."

Edna O'Brien on *Light Years*: "Brilliant, moving and full of truth."

Saul Bellow on *Light Years*: "I hope that a great many people will read *Light Years*. It is a delicious book. . . . Mr. Salter's gentleness and his poetry are what we most need in these clattering, roaring, distracting times."

Jhumpa Lahiri on *Light Years*: "[I admired his] sentences so precise, so clean, so fervent and yet so calm. . . . I loved the mood of the book, which was sober and sophisticated, but also casual, playful. I loved its structure, restrained and orderly, while at the same time loose and unspooling. I loved its intimate texture and its images. . . . Reading Salter taught me to boil down my writing to its essence. To insist upon the right words, and to remember that less is more. He taught me that a plot can be at once a straight line and a collage, that tense and perspective are fluid things."

Anita Brookner on *Light Years*: "[There is] an immense nostalgia for the settled state, not merely for happiness but for trust, for the knowledge that one will not be betrayed. That this once existed, and was willfully brought to an end, imparts an aura of tragedy to an exasperatingly familiar scenario. The marriage in question is treated as something so ideal that the only possible progress is downwards, towards, if not ruin, then certainly expulsion. . . . The theme is grief."

Norman Mailer on *Solo Faces*: "A fine, exciting and sensitive novel."

Irwin Shaw on *Solo Faces*: "A beautifully written and thoroughly engrossing story of high adventure."

John Irving on *Solo Faces*: "A terrific novel—compelling, sad, wise and kindhearted. Mr. Salter's prose is rare and stunning. How energizing it is to read a novel with a real hero in it—and a real hero he is."

Peter Matthiessen on *Dusk*: "There is scarcely a writer alive who could not learn from his passion and precision of language."

Richard Ford on *Burning the Days*: "Brilliant. Sentence for sentence Salter is the master."

Susan Sontag on *Burning the Days*: "Salter is a writer who particularly rewards those for whom reading is an intense pleasure. He is among the very few North American writers all of whose work I want to read, whose as yet unpublished books I wait for impatiently."

Joyce Carol Oates on *Burning the Days*: "[It is] prose of uncommon subtlety, intelligence and beauty . . . so rich in its observations, so poetically precise in language. . . . [It is] one of the most engaging and beautifully composed recent memoirs."

Joseph Heller on *Burning the Days*: "What a wonderful book, by a sensitive author who is romantic, intelligent and superbly balanced. It is a serene account of a surprising diversity of experiences, but it also a history of my time."

Michael Herr on *Burning the Days*: "[It] is a classic memoir, alive with amazing people, fabulous events, extraordinary stories of war and love and the great wide world. Through the sheer and sensual force of his writing (and nobody writes more beautifully), James Salter hasn't only recollected the past, he's reclaimed it."

Michael Ondaatje on *Burning the Days*: "A wise and sensual memoir. [It] contains some of the best flying writing I have read as well as vivid and dark portraits of men in the floating world of filmmaking and publishing. Salter writes his self-portrait by focusing on what has shaped him, by showing what he has loved and admired and feared to become in others. You cannot put it down."

Julian Barnes on *All That Is*: "A consistently elegant and enjoyable novel, full of verve and wisdom."

Edmund White on *All That Is*: "This masterpiece is a smooth, absorbing narrative studded with bright particulars. If God is in the details, this book is divine."

John Irving on *All That Is*: "A beautiful novel, with sufficient love, heartbreak, vengeance, identity confusion, longing and euphoria of language to have satisfied Shakespeare."

Geoff Dyer on *All That Is*: "Mastery, eventually, is an indifference to how things are meant to be done. Or, as Salter himself says of Francis Bacon, he never 'tried to conform to any idea of the artist, which allowed him to become a greater one.' Exactly."

NOTES

ONE. A RESTLESS LIFE

1. "James Salter: Novelist, Traditionalist, Seeker of Clarity," *Weekend* (Yale University), September 13, 2013.
2. All of Salter's letters to me were written in his last decade, between August 6, 2005 and June 15, 2015—four days before his death.
3. James Salter, *Burning the Days* (NY: Random House, 1997), pp. 33–34.
4. Letter from Salter to Peter Matthiessen, March 1, 1991, Humanities Research Center, University of Texas, Austin (HRC).
5. *Memorable Days: The Selected Letters of James Salter and Robert Phelps,* ed. James McIntyre (Berkeley: Counterpoint, 2010), p. 121.
6. Quoted in Salter's Memorial Service, July 28, 2015.
7. James Salter, "Eliot Stanton," *Horace Mann Quarterly,* 24 (Summer 1942), 13.
8. *Burning the Days,* pp. 107–124.
9. James Salter, *All That Is* (NY: Knopf, 2013), pp. 37, 240, 216, 46.
10. Paul Grondahl, "State Author bangs the drum as noisily as he can," *Times Union* (Albany, NY), 1997.
11. Noreen Tomassi, Interview with James Salter, *Center for Fiction,* n.d.
12. *Conversations with James Salter,* ed. Jennifer Lavasseur and Kevin Rabalais (Jackson: University Press of Mississippi, 2015), p. 90.
13. Jann Wenner and Corey Seymour, *Gonzo: The Life of Hunter Thompson* (NY: Little, Brown, 2007), pp. 102, 118.
14. Zachary Leader, *The Life of Saul Bellow: Love and Strife, 1965–2005* (NY: Knopf, 2018), p. 148. Salter referred to Lionel Trilling's influential book *Sincerity and Authenticity* (1972).
15. James Salter, *Don't Save Anything,* Preface by Kay Salter (Berkeley: Counterpoint, 2017), p. 255.

16. *Memorable Days*, p. 57.

17. Leader, *Bellow*, pp. 149–154.

18. James Salter, *The Art of Fiction* (Charlottesville: University of Virginia Press, 2016), pp. 58–59.

19. *Memorable Days*, p. 122.

20. Leader, *Bellow*, pp. 149–154.

21. Postcard from Bellow to Salter, no date, HRC.

22. Saul Bellow, *Letters*, ed. Benjamin Taylor (NY: Viking, 2010), p. 520.

23. Sally Gall, "James Salter: Style is the Writer," *Bomb* Magazine, July 10, 2015, pp. 21, 30.

24. James Salter, *There & Then: Travel Writing* (Washington, DC: Shoemaker & Hoard, 2005), pp. 9, 15, 94, 43, 57, 66.

25. Robert Phelps, Foreword, Colette, *Earthly Paradise: An Autobiography* (NY: Farrar, Straus and Giroux, 1966), pp. vii–viii.

26. Joseph Blotner, *Robert Penn Warren: A Biography* (NY: Random House, 1997), p. 366.

27. *Memorable Days*, pp. 78, 59, 110, 164.

28. *Burning the Days*, pp. 267–268; Interviews with Salter's twin children, Claude Salter, Aspen, September 13, 2022, and James Owen Salter, Bozeman, Montana, September 15, 2022.

29. Jeffrey Meyers, *Hemingway: A Biography* (NY: Harper and Row, 1985), p. 177.

30. *Memorable Days*, p. 129.

31. James Salter, *Gods of Tin: The Flying Years*, ed. Jessica Benton and William Benton (Washington, DC: Shoemaker & Hoard, 2004), p. 42.

32. Letter from Salter to Robert Ginna, October 27, no year, HRC.

33. *Memorable Days*, p. 183.

34. *Conversations*, pp. 80, 75.

35. *Art of Fiction*, pp. 8–9.

36. *Memorable Days*, p. 153.

37. *All That Is*, pp. 181, 113–114.

38. Interview with James Owen Salter.

39. *Burning the Days*, p. 216.

40. *Burning the Days*, pp. 194–216.

41. Edward Hirsch, "James Salter," *Paris Review* Interview, 127 (Summer 1993), 69.

42. *Burning the Days*, p. 207.

43. Letter from Irwin Shaw to Salter, January 5, 1965, HRC.

44. Letter from Peter Matthiessen to MacArthur Foundation, July 28, 1991, HRC.

45. Letter from Salter to Matthiessen, early 1990s, HRC.

46. Letter from Salter to Matthiessen, March 27, 2014, HRC.

47. *Memorable Days*, p. 52.

48. *Burning the Days*, p. 276.

49. *Don't Save Anything*, p. 95.

50. James Salter, "Peter Matthiessen (1927–2014)," *New Yorker*, April 14, 2014.

51. "James Salter," *Weekend*, September 13, 2013.

52. Kay Salter, "Wednesdays," *Narrative*, November 2015.

53. *Don't Save Anything*, p. 107.

54. Letter from Salter to Matthiessen, December 14, [2013], HRC.

55. *Art of Fiction*, pp. 21, 75–76.

56. James Salter, Hadada Acceptance Speech, *Paris Review*, June 22, 2015.

57. Letter from Salter to Robert Ginna, November 11, 2000, HRC.

TWO. FIGHTER PILOT

1. *Don't Save Anything*, p. 215.

2. James Salter, "Text," *West Point* (Zurich and NY: Stemmle, 2001), p. 9.

3. *Don't Save Anything*, p. 220.

4. Daniel Sutherland, *Whistler: A Life for Art's Sake* (New Haven: Yale UP, 2014), pp. 31–32.

5. *Gods of Tin*, p. 24.

6. *All That Is*, p. 169.

7. James Salter, "Lost in Air," *New Yorker*, March 18, 2014.

8. *Art of Fiction*, p. 25.

9. Max Hastings, *The Korean War* (NY: Simon & Schuster, 1987), pp. 255, 258.

10. James Salter, Review of William Langewiesche, *Fly By Wire*, *New York Review of Books* (*NYRB*), January 14, 2010.

11. Hastings, *Korean War*, p. 259.

12. Mike Benitez, "The Korean War and the Phoenix of Flight Leadership, Part II," *War on the Rocks*, October 23, 2017.

13. Hastings, *Korean War*, pp. 256–268.

14. *Gods of Tin*, pp. 60, 63, 89, 101.

15. Alex Vernon, *Soldiers Once and Still: Ernest Hemingway, James Salter and Tim O'Brien* (Iowa City: University of Iowa Press, 2004), p. 131.

16. *Burning the Days*, p. 302.

17. *Art of Fiction*, p. 52.

18. *Paris Review* Interview, p. 74.

19. Antonio Díaz Oliva, "An Interview with James Salter," *Asymtote*, 2022.

20. *Conversations*, p. 183.

21. Michael Carlson, Obituary of Salter, *Guardian*, June 22, 2015.

22. Grondahl, "State Author," *Times Union*, 1997.

23. Wilfred Thesiger, *The Life of My Choice* (NY: Norton, 1987), p. 115.

24. James Joyce, *Dubliners* (London: Penguin, 1962), p. 220.

25. James Salter, *The Hunters* (NY: Vintage, 1999), p. 3.

26. Antoine de Saint-Exupéry, *Wind, Sand and Stars*, trans. Lewis Galantière (London: Penguin, 1969), p. 147.

27. Richard Hillary, *The Last Enemy* (London: Pan, 1956), pp. 43, 17.

28. W. B. Yeats, *Collected Poems* (NY: Macmillan, 1959), pp. 133–134.

29. Sybille Bedford, *Aldous Huxley: A Biography* (NY: Knopf, 1974), p. 659.

30. Lee Server, *Robert Mitchum* (NY: St. Martin's, 2001), p. 319.

31. *Conversations*, p. 174.

32. Hemingway, *Across the River and into the Trees* (NY: Scribner's, 1950), pp. 225–226.

33. *Burning the Days*, p. 168.

34. James Salter on dust jacket of *Cassada* (Washington, DC: Counterpoint, 2000).

35. Ernest Hemingway, *Short Stories* (NY: Scribner's, 1938), p. 8.

36. William Cowper, "The Stricken Deer," in Louis Bredvold et al., *Eighteenth Century Poetry & Prose* (NY: Ronald Press, 1939), p. 891.

THREE. THE FATE OF PLEASURE

1. James Salter, Introduction to *A Sport and a Pastime* (NY: Modern Library, 1995), p. viii.

2. James Salter, *A Sport and a Pastime* (San Francisco: North Point, 1985), pp. 9–13.

3. Ford Madox Ford, Introduction to *A Farewell to Arms* (NY: Modern Library, 1932), in Jeffrey Meyers, ed., *Hemingway: The Critical Heritage* (London: Routledge & Kegan Paul, 1982), p. 156.

4. *Don't Save Anything*, p. 60.

5. James Salter, Introduction to Donald Sultan, *New Poppy Paintings* (NY: Ameringer & Yohe Fine Art, 2004). See Rainer Maria Rilke, *Letters to a*

Young Poet, trans. M. D. Herter (NY: Norton, 1963), p. 30: "The artist's experience lies so unbelievably close to the sexual, to its pain and its pleasure, that the two phenomena are really just different forms of one and the same longing and bliss."

6. *Paris Review* Interview, pp. 78–79.

7. Introduction to *Sport*, p. viii.

8. James Joyce, *Ulysses* (NY: Vintage, 1986), p. 462.

9. Salter, Introduction to *Sport*, p. vii.

10. D. H. Lawrence, "A Propos of *Lady Chatterley's Lover*," *Phoenix II*, ed. Warren Roberts and Harry Moore (NY: Viking, 1968), p. 508.

11. D. H. Lawrence, *Lady Chatterley's Lover* (NY: Signet), p. 232.

12. *Paris Review* Interview, p. 77.

13. Lord Byron, *Byron's Poetry*, ed. Frank McConnell (NY: Norton, 1978), p. 22.

14. *Memorable Days*, pp. 95, 72.

15. Thessaly La Force, "Possible Titles for *Light Years*," *Paris Review*, April 8, 2011: Salter's final choices included *Estuarial Lives*, *Last Year*, *Next Year*, *Luminous Ashes* and *Last Traces*.

16. Alex Bilmes, "James Salter: The Greatest Writer You've Never Read," *Esquire*, June 21, 2015.

17. Yeats, *Collected Poems*, p. 187.

18. Salter, *Light Years* (NY: Vintage, 1995), pp. 53, 117, 183.

19. *Art of Fiction*, p. 60.

20. *Conversations*, p. 104.

21. James Meek, Review of *All That Is* and *Collected Stories*, *London Review of Books*, June 20, 2013.

22. Richard Ford, Introduction to *Light Years* (London: Penguin, 2007), pp. vi–vii, ix, xi. *Light Years* also has important literary allusions:

> 95—"nothing in abundance"—Plato, The Golden Mean: "nothing in excess."
>
> 170—"his character, his fate"—Heraclitus: "Character is fate."
>
> 173—"It's finished"—John 19:30: *consummatum est* (It is finished), Christ's last words on the Cross.
>
> 21—"is death so warm, so easeful?"—Keats, "Ode to a Nightingale": "I have been half in love with easeful death."
>
> 31—"that's not what I am at all"—Eliot, "The Love Song of J. Alfred Prufrock": "That is not what I meant, at all."

FOUR. SOPHISTICATED STYLE

1. Michel Dirda on the dust jacket of *Burning the Days*.

2. Ford, Introduction to *Light Years*, p. v.

3. Scott Fitzgerald, *The Great Gatsby* (NY: Scribner's, 1925), pp. 6, 180.

4. *Art of Fiction*, p. 19.

5. James Salter, Introduction to A. J. Liebling, *Between Meals* (1959; San Francisco: North Point, 1986), pp. ix, xxi.

6. "James Salter," *Weekend*, September 13, 2013.

7. *Memorable Days*, p. 181.

8. Gall, "James Salter," p. 29.

9. Edgar Allan Poe, "Ligeia," quoting Francis Bacon, *Complete Tales and Poems* (NY: Vintage, 1975), p. 655.

10. *Don't Save Anything*, p. 116.

11. *Memorable Days*, p. 127.

12. Henry James, "The Middle Years," *Selected Short Stories*, ed. Quentin Anderson (NY: Holt, Rinehart and Winston, 1957), p. 165.

13. Scott Fitzgerald, *The Crack-Up*, ed. Edmund Wilson (1945; NY: New Directions, 1959), p. 31.

14. Fitzgerald, *The Great Gatsby*, p. 69.

15. James Salter, *Still Such: An Elegy* (NY: William Drenttel, 1992).

16. *All That Is*, pp. 203, 253.

17. Fitzgerald, *Crack-Up*, pp. 28–29.

18. James Salter, "Bangkok," *Last Night* (NY: Knopf, 2005), p. 111.

19. *There & Then*, p. 14.

20. Fitzgerald, *Great Gatsby*, p. 182.

21. *Light Years*, p. 3.

22. Fitzgerald, *Great Gatsby*, p. 118.

23. *Sport*, p. 169.

24. Oliva, Interview, p. 11.

25. *Memorable Days*, pp. 190–191, 97.

26. *There & Then*, p. 26.

27. *Conversations*, p. 128.

28. James Salter, Review of Hemingway, *The Garden of Eden*, *Washington Post Book World*, June 1, 1986.

29. Hemingway, *Across the River*, pp. 51–52.

30. James Salter, Review of Paul Hendrickson, *Hemingway's Boat*, *NYRB*, October 13, 2011.

31. *Memorable Days*, p. 126.

32. *Paris Review* Interview, p. 86.

33. *Don't Save Anything*, pp. 15–16.

34. *Memorable Days*, p. 153.

35. Ernest Hemingway, *Dateline: Toronto*, ed. William White (NY: Scribner's, 1985), pp. 421–422.

36. *All That Is*, p. 67.

37. John Simon, "In Memoriam, James Salter," *Uncensored John Simon*, June 22, 2015.

38. *There & Then*, p. 113.

39. *There & Then*, p. 135.

40. Ernest Hemingway, *The Sun Also Rises* (NY: Scribner's, 1926), p. 247; *All That Is*, p. 290; *Light Years*, p. 123.

41. Ernest Hemingway, *Death in the Afternoon* (NY: Scribner's, 1932), p. 123; James Salter, "Cinema," *Dusk and Other Stories* (San Francisco: North Point, 1988), p. 76.

42. Hemingway, *Short Stories*, p. 207; "Cinema," *Dusk*, p. 91.

43. Hemingway, *Short Stories*, p. 170; *Light Years*, p.172.

44. Hemingway, *Short Stories*, p. 273; "Comet," *Last Night*, p. 11.

45. Ernest Hemingway, *A Farewell to Arms* (NY: Scribner's, 1929), p. 3; *Don't Save Anything*, p. 140.

46. Ernest Hemingway, *For Whom the Bell Tolls* (NY: Scribner's, 1940), p. 70; *All That Is*, p. 254.

47. *Memorable Days*, p. 34; Hemingway, *Across the River*, p. 71; *Memorable Days*, p. 18.

48. *All That Is*, pp. 44, 162.

49. T. S. Eliot, "Tradition and the Individual Talent," *Selected Essays, 1917–1932* (NY: Harcourt, Brace, 1932), p. 4.

FIVE. UNICORN IN THE STABLE

1. *Paris Review* Interview, p. 95; *Conversations*, pp. 7, 8.

2. *Burning the Days*, pp. 209, 237, 209.

3. "As They Were: American Masters Through the Lens of James Salter," Armory Show, New York, March 8–11, 2012.

4. Letters of Peter Glenville and Martin Poll, May–October 1965, HRC.

5. Sidney Lumet, *Making Movies* (NY: Vintage, 1996), pp. 8–9.

6. *Burning the Days*, p. 269.

7. *Conversations*, pp. 123, 9, 12.

8. Bilmes, "James Salter."

9. *Burning the Days*, p. 270.

10. James Boswell, *Life of Johnson* (London: Oxford UP, 1961), p. 1068.

11. Salter, "Cinema," *Dusk*, p. 76.

12. *Burning the Days*, pp. 116, 124.

13. Letters of Irwin Shaw and James Salter, HRC.

14. *Burning the Days*, p. 271.

15. *Memorable Days*, p. 9.

16. *Burning the Days*, p. 270.

17. *Paris Review* Interview, p. 96.

18. Robert Redford, *Downhill Racer* Interview, Criterion DVD, 2009.

19. Quoted in William Dowie, *James Salter* (NY: Twayne, 1998), p. 33.

20. *Burning the Days*, p. 235.

21. George Orwell, "The Sporting Spirit," *Works*, ed. Peter Davison (London: Secker & Warburg, 1998), 17:442.

22. Pauline Kael, *Deeper into Movies* (NY: Bantam, 1974), pp. 57–59.

23. *Memorable Days*, pp. 92, 127; *Conversations*, p. 144.

24. *Memorable Days*, pp. 141, 159, 160.

25. Joseph Conrad, *Victory* (1915; Garden City, NY: Doubleday, 1957), p. 164.

26. *Don't Save Anything*, p. 135.

27. Dinitia Smith, "A Fighter Pilot Who Aimed for Novels but Lives on Film," *New York Times*, August 13, 1997; *Burning the Days*, p. 299.

28. *Conversations*, p. 8.

29. *Memorable Days*, p. 49.

30. *Burning the Days*, pp. 336–338, 210.

31. Ian Hamilton, *Writers in Hollywood, 1915–1951* (NY: Harper & Row, 1990), pp. 145, 136, 153.

32. S. J. Perelman, *Don't Tread on Me: Selected Letters*, ed. Prudence Crowther (NY: Penguin, 1987), pp. 173, 172.

33. Anonymous, Letter to Jeffrey Meyers, July 5, 2022.

34. *Memorable Days*, p. 49.

35. Bilmes, "James Salter."

36. *Don't Save Anything*, p. 280; *Conversations*, p. 111.

37. Jeffrey Meyers, *Edmund Wilson: A Biography* (Boston: Houghton Mifflin, 1995), p. 248; Charles Baker, *American Writers. Supplement IX* (NY: Scribner's 2002).

38. *Paris Review* Interview, p. 97.

SIX. DANGER AND DISILLUSION

1. William Wordsworth, *The Prelude*, in *Oxford Authors*, ed. Stephen Gill (Oxford: Oxford UP, 1964), p. 452.

2. Percy Shelley, "Mont Blanc," *Poetry and Prose*, ed. Donald Reiman and Sharon Power (NY: Norton, 1977), p. 91.

3. John Ruskin, "The Mountain Glory," *Modern Painters* (London: Routledge, 1907), IV.352.

4. Mirella Tenderini, *Gary Hemming: The Beatnik of the Alps* (Holyhead, Wales: Ernest Press, 1995), pp. 76–77, 139.

5. W. H. Auden, *The Ascent of F6*, in *Two Great Plays* (NY: Modern Library, 1937), pp. 154, 173.

6. James Salter, *Solo Faces* (San Francisco: North Point, 1988), p. 15.

7. Thomas Mann, "Death in Venice," in *Death in Venice and Seven Other Stories*, trans. H. T. Lowe-Porter (NY: Vintage, 1963), pp. 9–10.

8. *Burning the Days*, p. 348.

9. *Dusk*, p. 76.

10. Isaac Babel, "My First Goose," *Collected Stories*, trans. Walter Morison (NY: Meridian, 1960), pp. 75, 77.

11. *Conversations*, p. 106.

12. Lawrence Gowing, ed., *A Biographical Dictionary of Artists* (NY: Facts on File, 1995), p. 235.

13. Giorgio Vasari, *Lives of the Artists*, trans. E. L. Seeley (NY: Noonday, 1957), p. 152.

14. Hemingway, *Short Stories*, pp. 54, 77.

15. Theodore Roethke, *Collected Poems*, (Garden City, NY: Doubleday, 1975), p. 98.

16. These stories appeared in the *Paris Review*, *Grand Street* and *Esquire* between 1968 and 1988.

SEVEN. MEMORIES AND MISFORTUNES

1. *Memorable Days*, p. 180.
2. *Burning the Days*, p. 129.
3. Hemingway, *Short Stories*, p. 26.
4. Hemingway, *Across the River*, p. 87.
5. Jeffrey Meyers, *Robert Frost: A Biography* (Boston: Houghton Mifflin, 1996), p. 277.
6. *Paris Review* Interview, p. 98; *Light Years*, p. 246.
7. Salter's allusions, as always, reveal his reading and values, and illuminate the text:

> 214—"God bless us, a thing of naught"—Shakespeare: *A Midsummer Night's Dream.*
>
> 91—"I am the master of my fate"—W. E. Henley: "Invictus."
>
> 49—"The time you won your town your race"—A. E. Housman: *A Shropshire Lad.*
>
> 68—"[bred to a] harder thing than triumph"—W. B. Yeats: "To a Friend Whose Work Has Come to Nothing."
>
> 64—"They shall not grow old as we who are left grow old"—Laurence Binyon: "For the Fallen."
>
> 307—"You must change your life"—Rainer Maria Rilke: "Archaic Torso of Apollo."
>
> 111—"you could discover death as quickly by fleeing from it"—Somerset Maugham and John O'Hara: "Appointment in Samarra."
>
> 132—"Come now and let us go and risk our lives unnecessarily"—Isak Dinesen: *Out of Africa.*
>
> 75—Peter Slavek—character in Arthur Koestler: *Arrival and Departure.*

8. *Conversations*, p. 93, for quotes on all three stories.
9. These stories appeared in *Tin House, Esquire, Paris Review* and *New Yorker* between 1993 and 2003. "Charisma" appeared in Salter's *Collected Stories.*

EIGHT. INTELLECTUAL NOURISHMENT

1. Samuel Johnson, *Letters, Volume II: 1773–1776*, ed. Bruce Redford (Princeton: Princeton University Press, 1992), p. 78.

2. Eleanor of Aquitaine's unforgettable epitaph: "Here lies Henry's daughter, wife and mother—great by birth, greater by marriage, but greatest by motherhood." Robert Browning's poem on Marshal Lannes is "Incident of the French Camp"; Kipling's *I am paid in full for service* from "The Galley-Slave"; *Good-Bye to All That* is the title of Robert Graves' autobiography; John Betjeman's *"Dear old, bloody old England"* from "A Lincolnshire Church"; Delmore Schwartz's *"narrow and tall on all sides"* from "The Commencement Day Address." Salter's "Then there is the next day and the day after that and on and on" echoes *The Great Gatsby*: "What'll we do with ourselves this afternoon? . . . and the day after that and the next thirty years?" Salter says, "Shoes were an important element in [Luis] Buñuel's art"; foot fetishism dominates *The Diary of a Chambermaid*.

3. D. H. Lawrence, "Snake," *Complete Poems*, ed. Vivian de Sola Pinto and Warren Roberts (NY: Viking, 1964), p. 351.

4. Interview with James Owen Salter.

5. Interview with James Owen Salter.

6. Using an eyewitness account, I explained his motives in "Mishima's Suicide," *Michigan Quarterly Review*, 49 (Fall 2010), 606–610.

7. The essays in this book were published in *Le Nouvel Observateur, Esquire, Antaeus, New York Times, New York Times Magazine, European Travel and Life, Traveler, Outside* and *Hamptons* between 1981 and 1992.

8. *Light Years*, p. 25; *Conversations*, p. 79.

9. Samuel Johnson, *Oxford Authors*, ed. Donald Greene (Oxford: Oxford UP, 1984), p. 509.

10. The headings and chapter titles echo literary works: "Why I Write" from Orwell's essay; "Odessa, Mon Amour" from the film *Hiroshima, Mon Amour*; "Confidential Agent" from Graham Greene's novel; "Many Splendored Thing" from Han Suyin's novel; "The Immortal Who Died" from D. H. Lawrence's *The Man Who Died*; "Man Is His Own Star" from Emerson's "Self-Reliance"; "Eat, Memory" from Nabokov's *Speak, Memory*; "Once and Future Queen" from T. H. White's *The Once and Future King*; "Snowy Nights in Aspen" from Henry Miller's *Quiet Days in Clichy*; "Words' Worth" a pun on the poet's name.

11. Boswell, *Life of Johnson*, p. 327.

12. When I asked for Puccini's opera "Gianni *Schic*chi" in Aspen, they sent me to a ski shop.

13. Franz Kafka, *Letters to Friends, Family and Editors*, trans. Richard and Clara Winston (NY: Schocken, 1977), p. 16.

14. *Memorable Days*, pp. 8, 6, 38, 25.

15. *Memorable Days*, p. 166.

16. Jeffrey Meyers, "Gabriele D'Annunzio," *A Fever at the Core* (London: London Magazine Editions, 1976), pp. 110–111.

17. *Memorable Days*, p. 136.

18. Letter from Salter to Graham Greene, January 15, 1975, Boston College Library.

NINE. THE SUMMA

1. *Paris Review* Interview, p. 80.

2. *Conversations*, p. 172.

3. George Feifer, *Tennozan: The Battle of Okinawa* (NY: Ticknor & Fields, 1992), p. 30.

4. Joseph Conrad, *Lord Jim* (NY: Modern Library, 1931), p. 111.

5. Salter laces his novel with his characteristic literary allusions to enhance the meaning and the reader's intellectual pleasure:

> 12—"A pillar of flame . . . a biblical pillar"—Exodus 13:22: "the pillar of fire by night."
>
> 57—"cast into darkness"—Matthew 22:13: "cast him into outer darkness."
>
> 92—"our war over abducted women"—Helen and the Trojan War.
>
> 282—"clean in body, clean in mind"—Juvenal: *"mens sana in corpore sano."*
>
> 188—"in the middle of life"—Dante, *Inferno: "Nel mezzo del cammin di nostra vita."*
>
> 95—"all hope had to be abandoned" and 289- "people absolutely without hope"—Dante, *Inferno: "lasciate ogni speranza voi ch'entrate."*
>
> 60—"When lovely woman stoops to folly"—Oliver Goldsmith: *The Vicar of Wakefield.*
>
> 266—"she had a good feeling . . . as if she could hug herself"—James Boswell, *Journals*: "I hugged myself."
>
> 153—"a house named Crossways"—George Meredith: *Diana of the Crossways.*
>
> 55—"There's a wonderful one in Thomas Hardy"—Hardy's poem: "A Thunderstorm in Town."

213—"quartered out there?"—Rudyard Kipling, "Gunga Din": "quartered safe out here."

89—"Virginia, the Catherines and Janes"—Virginia Woolf and the heroines of *Wuthering Heights* and *Jane Eyre*.

140—the dissolute son who "must always be taken in"—The Prodigal Son in Luke 15:31 and in Robert Frost, "The Death of the Hired Man."

191—"At the foot of the Ngong Hills"—Isak Dinesen, *Out of Africa*: "I had a farm in Africa at the foot of the Ngong hills."

160—"Age doesn't arrive slowly, it comes in a rush"—Ernest Hemingway, *The Sun Also Rises*: Mike went bankrupt in two ways, "Gradually and then suddenly."

134—"He rarely met a writer he didn't like"—Will Rogers: "I never met a man I didn't like."

211—"that's going to go down in infamy"—Franklin Roosevelt on the Japanese attack on Pearl Harbor: "a date which will live in infamy."

6. Several errors, not caught by Knopf, appear in the novel:

143—Newmarket is in Suffolk, not Norfolk; northeast, not north, of London.

122—Madrid *does* have a river: the Manzanares flows through the city.

125—Lorca's city was Granada, not Seville.

288—The Amazon and Rio Negro meet in Manaus, very far from where Elizabeth Bishop lived in the hills of Ouro Preto with Lota (not Lolta) Soares.

173—Modigliani, not Apollinaire, had a French mistress who jumped out of a window and killed herself. And Modi, not Apollinaire, had a Russian lover, the poet Anna Akhmatova.

88—Ezra Pound broadcast pro-fascist and anti-Semitic tirades *throughout* the war, and was ruined in 1945, not 1941.

7. James Lasdun, *Guardian*, May 11, 2013.

8. Geoff Dyer, *Independent*, May 13, 2013.

9. Michael Dirda, *NYRB*, June 6, 2013.

10. Nigel Nicolson, *Virginia Woolf* (London: Penguin, 2000), p. 2.

11. In May 2013 London Review Limited Editions published 75 signed copies of an exceptionally luxurious version of *All That Is* with the finest printing, paper and leather binding. The exotic multilingual names of these

ingredients sound like those on expensive French menus in *Life is Meals*: "50 of which have been quarter-bound in Harmatan fine natural grain leather and Nettuno Oltremare sides with a letterpress label on Zerkall Toned cotton paper, numbered 1 to 50. All copies have maroon and blue head and tail bands, coloured tops and Media Indigo endpapers, and are housed in Dubletta 3252 slipcases lined in Suedel."

TEN. STRANGE CAREER

1. These ten books were *Gods of Tin: The Flying Years* (2004), *Last Night* (stories, 2005), *There & Then* (travels, 2005), *Life Is Meals* (gastronomy, 2006), *Memorable Days* (correspondence with Robert Phelps, 2010), *All That Is* (novel, 2013), *Collected Stories* (2013), *Conversations* (interviews, 2015), *The Art of Fiction* (on writing, 2016) and *Don't Save Anything* (essays, 2017).
2. *Conversations*, p. 86.
3. *Memorable Days*, p. 89.
4. *There & Then*, p. 23.
5. *Memorable Days*, p. xxv.
6. Letter from Salter to Peter Matthiessen, December 8, no year, HRC.
7. Geoff Dyer, Review of *All That Is*, *Independent*, May 13, 2013.
8. *Memorable Days*, p. 73.
9. James Meek, Review of *All That Is*, *London Review of Books*, June 20, 2013.
10. *All That Is*, p. 172.
11. Geoff Dyer, *Otherwise Known as the Human Condition* (Minneapolis: Greywolf, 2011), p. 159.
12. Salter named his daughters Allan Conrad, Nina Tobe and Claude Cray.
13. Smith, "A Fighter Pilot Who Aimed for Novels."
14. *Conversations*, p. 102.
15. Quoted in David Haglund, "James Salter in the *New Yorker*," *New Yorker*, June 20, 2015.
16. *Dusk*, p. 120.
17. Tracy Daugherty, *Just One Catch: A Biography of Joseph Heller* (NY: St. Martin's, 2011), p. 426.
18. Bilmes, "James Salter."
19. *Paris Review* Interview, p. 59.
20. Gall, "James Salter."

21. *Memorable Days*, p. 142.

22. *Paris Review* Interview, p. 85.

23. *Art of Fiction*, p. 33.

24. *Memorable Days*, p. 11.

25. Jeffrey Meyers, *Resurrections: Authors, Heroes—and a Spy* (Charlottes-ville: University of Virginia Press, 2018), pp. 87–88.

26. Rachel Cooke, "James Salter: The Forgotten Hero of American Litera-ture," *Guardian*, May 11, 2013.

27. Letter from Salter to Joe Fox, July 23, 1974, HRC.

28. James Salter, "The Paradise of the Library," *New Yorker*, July 19, 2012.

29. *Paris Review* Interview, p. 90.

30. James Wolcott, "Remembering James Salter," *Vanity Fair*, June 22, 2015.

31. "Editorial Note," *Esquire*, August 1984, p.101.

32. Saul Bellow, Letter to Salter, August 5, 1975, quoted in Dowie, *James Salter*, pp. x–xi.

33. Salter was praised by his close friends George Plimpton, Irwin Shaw and Peter Matthiessen as well as by Norman Mailer, Joseph Heller, Edmund White, John Irving, Michael Ondaatje, Julian Barnes, Susan Sontag and others. There is only one brief reference to Salter in the biographies of Plimpton, Shaw and Heller; none at all in the lives of the other writers, nor of Salinger, James Jones, Vonnegut, Capote, Styron, Vidal, Updike, Roth and Raymond Carver.

34. Meyers, *Resurrections*, p. 89.

35. Meyers, *Resurrections*, p. 89.

36. The translations included *Un bonheur parfait* (*Light Years*) and *Et rien d'autre* (*All That Is*). He was also translated into Spanish: *Juego y distrac-ción* (*A Sport and a Pastime*); Italian: *La solitudine del cielo* (*The Hunt-ers*) and *L'arte di narrare* (*The Art of Fiction*); and German: *Verbrannte Tage* (*Burning the Days*) and *Lichtjahre* (*Light Years*).

37. Sarah Hall, "Beautiful and brutal: how James Salter set the standard for erotic writing," *Guardian*, February 17, 2017.

38. Reynolds Price, Introduction to *A Sport and a Pastime* (NY: Farrar, Straus and Giroux, 2006), p. xi.

39. Richard Ford, Introduction to *Light Years* (London: Penguin, 2007), pp. v, ix, xi.

40. John Banville, Introduction to *Collected Stories* (London: Picador, 2013), p. xiv.

41. Michael Dirda, *NYRB*, June 6, 2013.

42. James Salter, Review of William Styron, *Selected Letters*, *NYRB*, January 10, 2013.

43. Letter from Salter to Ginna, November 3, 2006.

44. Despite all the positive reviews and journalistic praise during Salter's last decade, there are still only two books about him—William Dowie's introductory Twayne volume (1998) and one third of Alex Vernon's work on writers and war (2004)—and nothing in the last twenty-six years. It's time for a revival.

ELEVEN. FRIENDSHIP AND RECOLLECTIONS

1. All quotes from Salter are in Meyers, *Resurrections*, pp. 84–100.

BIBLIOGRAPHY

WORKS BY SALTER

Books

The Hunters. NY: Harper, 1956. Revised edition: Counterpoint, 1997, Preface by Salter, pp. xiii–xv; Vintage, 1999; Penguin, 2007.

The Arm of Flesh. NY: Harper, 1961.

A Sport and a Pastime. NY: Paris Review Editions and Doubleday, 1967. Bantam, 1968; North Point, 1985; Modern Library, 1995, Intro. by Salter, pp. vii–ix; Farrar, Straus and Giroux, and Picador, 2006, Intro. by Reynolds Price, pp. vii–xi.

Light Years. NY: Random House, 1975. North Point, 1982; Vintage, 1995; Penguin, 2007, Intro. by Richard Ford, pp. v–xiv.

Solo Faces. Boston: Little, Brown, 1979. Penguin, 1980; North Point, 1988.

Dusk and Other Stories. San Francisco: North Point, 1988. Penguin, 2008. Modern Library, 2010, Intro. by Philip Gourevitch, pp. ix–xiii.

Still Such: An Elegy. NY: William Drenttel, 1992. Prose poem.

Burning the Days: Recollections. Random House, 1997. Vintage, 1998.

Cassada. Washington, DC: Counterpoint, 2000. Foreword by Salter. Revised version of *The Arm of Flesh*.

Gods of Tin: The Flying Years. Ed. and Intro. by Jessica Benton and William Benton. Washington, DC: Shoemaker & Hoard, 2004.

Last Night: Stories. NY: Knopf, 2005. Vintage, 2006.

There & Then: Travel Writing. Emeryville, California: Shoemaker & Hoard, 2005.

Life Is Meals: A Food Lover's Book of Days. With Kay Salter. NY: Knopf, 2006.

Memorable Days: The Selected Letters of James Salter and Robert Phelps. Ed. James McIntyre. Foreword by Michael Dirda, pp. ix–xx. Berkeley: Counterpoint, 2010.

All That Is. NY: Knopf, 2013. London Review Bookshop Limited Edition, 2013; Vintage, 2014.

Collected Stories. London: Picador, 2013. Intro. by John Banville, pp. vii–xiv.

Conversations with James Salter. Ed. Jennifer Lavasseur and Kevin Rabalais. Jackson: University Press of Mississippi, 2015.

The Art of Fiction. Charlottesville: University of Virginia Press, 2016. Intro. by John Casey, pp. vii–xxxvii.

Don't Save Anything. Berkeley: Counterpoint, 2017. Preface by Kay Salter, pp. xi–xiv.

Poems, Stories and Articles

Nine Poems in *Horace Mann Quarterly*, 22 (Spring 1940–Summer 1942).

"Empty is the Night," *Pointer*, 22 (October 6, 1944), 6, 27–28.

"The Last Christmas," *Pointer*, 22 (December 15, 1944), 6–7.

Interview with [Lt. General] Sid Berry, *People*, 2:10 (September 2, 1974).

Interview with Antonia Fraser, *People*, 3:7 (February 24, 1975).

Interview with Vladimir Nabokov, *People*, 3:8 (March 17, 1975). Extract in Nabokov, *Think, Write, Speak*. NY: Knopf, 2019. P. 449.

Interview with Graham Greene, *People*, 5:2 (January 19, 1976), 65–67.

Interview with Han Suyin, *People*, 6:19 (November 8, 1976).

"D'Annunzio: The Immortal Who Died," *Paris Review*, 75 (1979), 180–198.

Introduction to A. J. Liebling's *Between Meals: An Appetite for Paris*. San Francisco: North Point, 1986. Pp. ix–xxi.

Review of Ernest Hemingway, *The Garden of Eden*, *Washington Post Book World*, June 1, 1986, pp. 1–2.

"The Captain's Wife," *Esquire*, 105 (June 1986), 130–139.

Review of Scott Donaldson, *John Cheever*, *Los Angeles Times Book Review*, July 17, 1988, pp. 1, 3.

"America and Japan: 50 Years Later," *New York Times*, December 7, 1991, p. 22.

Edward Hirsch, "James Salter: The Art of Fiction," *Paris Review*, 127 (Summer 1993), 54–100.

"Sacred Things." *The Water's Edge*. Photos by Sally Gall. San Francisco: Chronicle Books, 1995.

"Passionate Falsehoods," *New Yorker*, July 28, 1997.

"Comment" on Clinton and Lewinsky, *New Yorker*, September 27, 1998.

"Some for Glory, Some for Praise." *Why I Write: Thoughts on the Craft of Fiction*. Ed. Will Blythe. Boston: Little, Brown, 1998. Pp. 34–40.

"Text." *West Point*. Photos by Marcia Lippman. Zurich and NY: Stemmle, 2001. Pp. 5, 9, 33, 71, 103, 127.

Introduction to Donald Sultan, *New Poppy Paintings*. NY: Ameringer & Yohe Fine Art, 2004.

Gioia, Dana, ed. "Salter Reading from *Burning the Days* and *Why I Write*." *Operation Homecoming: Writing the Wartime Experience*. National Endowment of the Arts Audio, 2004.

Foreword to Irwin Shaw, *The Young Lions*. Chicago: University of Chicago Press, 2009. Pp. vii–ix.

"On Richard Seaver," *New York Review of Books*, March 12, 2009.

Review of William Langewiesche, *Fly By Wire*, *NYRB*, January 14, 2010.

Review of Andre Dubos, *Townie: A Memoir*," *NYRB*, April 7, 2011.

Review of Paul Hendrickson, *Hemingway's Boat*, *NYRB*, October 13, 2011.

"The Paradise of the Library," *New Yorker*, July 19, 2012.

Review of William Styron, *Selected Letters*, *NYRB*, January 10, 2013.

"Lost in Air," *New Yorker*, March 18, 2014.

"Peter Matthiessen (1927–2014)," *New Yorker*, April 14, 2014.

Hadada Acceptance Speech, *Paris Review*, June 22, 2015.

Review of David McCullough, *The Wright Brothers*, *NYRB*, August 13, 2015, pp. 4, 6.

"Life into Art," *Paris Review*, 214 (Fall 2015), 229–243.

Filmography

Downhill Racer, 1969. Writer.

The Appointment, 1969. Writer.

Three, 1969. Writer and director.

Threshold, 1983. Writer.

WORKS ON SALTER
Films, Books and Articles

Jim Case. *The Artist in America*. Documentary film, 1971.

Margaret Miller, "Glimpses of a Secular Holy Land," *Hollins Critic*, 19 (February 1982), 1–13.

"Editorial Note," *Esquire*, August 1984, p. 101.

Reynolds Price, "Famous First Words," *New York Times Book Review*, June 2, 1985, p. 3.

Robert Burke, "Interview with James Salter," *Bloomsbury Review*, 8 (May–June 1988), 3, 6, 18.

Arne Axelsson. *Restrained Response: American Novels of the Cold War and Korea, 1945-1960*. Westport, Conn., 1990. Pp. 81–8, 145, 148.

Adam Begley, "A Few Well-Chosen Words," *New York Times Magazine*, October 28, 1990, pp. 40–43, 80–85.

Richard Cohen, "No Fool Like an Old Fool," *Washington Post*, March 15, 1992.

William Dowie. *Dictionary of Literary Biography: American Short Story Writers Since World War II*. Detroit: Gale, 1993. Pp. 282–287.

Paul Grondahl, "State Author bangs the drum as noisily as he can," *Times Union* (Albany), 1997.

Dinitia Smith, "A Fighter Pilot Who Aimed for Novels but Lives on Film," *New York Times*, August 13, 1997, p. 13.

William Dowie. *James Salter*. NY: Twayne, 1998.

Eric Weinberger, "Salter's Flight Path," *Nation*, 272 (March 12, 2001), 34–36.

Charles Baker. *American Writers. Supplement IX*. Ed. Jay Parini. NY: Scribner's, 2002.

Alex Vernon. *Soldiers Once and Still: Ernest Hemingway, James Salter and Tim O'Brien*. Iowa City: University of Iowa Press, 2004.

Michael Cocchiarale, "'The Most Dangerous Way': James Salter's *Solo Faces* and the Escape from Modern Sport," *Aethlon*, 22 (2004), 117.

"James Salter." *Contemporary Authors Online*. Detroit: Gale, 2006. [1–7].

Stacie Stukin, "The Art of Feeding," *New York Times*, March 18, 2007.

Robert McCrum, "How to be the hippiest act in town even in your eighties," *Guardian*, March 24, 2007.

Jeffrey Meyers, "Salter's Gift," *Kenyon Review*, 30 (Spring 2008), 92–111.

Jeffrey Meyers, "James Salter's 'Am Strande von Tanger,'" *Notes on Contemporary Literature*, 38 (September 2008), 2–5.

Robert Redford. *Downhill Racer* interview. Criterion DVD, 2009.

Todd McCarthy. *Downhill Racer* pamphlet. Criterion DVD, 2009.

"James Salter." *Contemporary Literary Criticism*. Volume 275. Detroit: Gale, 2009. Pp. 244–277.

Benjamin Percy, "The Nameless Pioneer: James Salter's 'Akhnilo,'" *Ecotone*, 6 (2010), 150–155.

John Thompson, "James Salter on Sex and Writing," *Gentlemen's Quarterly*, January 13, 2010.

James Salter: A Sport and a Pastime. Documentary film, 2011.

Porochista Khakpour, "*Light Years*," *Paris Review*, April 6, 2011.

Jhumpa Lahiri, "On *Sport*," *Paris Review*, April 7, 2011.

Ian Crouch, On *Sport*, *Paris Review*, April 7, 2011.

Thessaly La Force, "Possible Titles for *Light Years*," *Paris Review*, April 8, 2011.

Kate Petersen, "An Interview with James Salter," *Paris Review*, April 11, 2011.

Nick Paumgarten, "James Salter's Last Book," *New Yorker*, April 15, 2013, pp. 42–51.

Rachel Cooke, "James Salter: The Forgotten Hero of American Literature," *Guardian*, May 11, 2013.

"James Salter: Novelist, Traditionalist, Seeker of Clarity," *Weekend* (Yale University), September 13, 2013.

David Kirk Vaughan, "James Salter's Pilots and Wingmen, Then and Now," *Journal of Literature and Art Studies*, 4 (2014), 895–901.

Mary Norris. *Between You and Me: Confessions of a Prom Queen.* NY: Norton, 2015. Pp. 108–109.

Helen Verongos, Obituary, *New York Times*, June 20, 2015, p. A-20.

David Haglund, "James Salter in the *New Yorker*," *New Yorker*, June 20, 2015.

Nick Paumgarten, "Postscript: James Salter, 1925–2015," *New Yorker*, June 21, 2015.

Alex Bilmes, "James Salter: The Greatest Writer You've Never Read," *Esquire*, June 21, 2015.

Michael Carlson, Obituary, *Guardian*, June 22, 2015.

John Simon, "In Memoriam: James Salter," *Uncensored John Simon*, June 22, 2015.

James Wolcott, "Remembering James Salter," *Vanity Fair*, June 22, 2015.

Dorothy Hom, "James Salter—An Appreciation," *Southampton Review*, June 22, 2015.

Alexander Chee, "Sex and Salter," *Paris Review*, June 24, 2015.

Jhumpa Lahiri, On *Light Years*, *Paris Review*, June 26, 2015.

Rupert Thomson, "My Hero: James Salter," *Guardian*, June 27, 2015.

Sally Gall, "James Salter: 'Style is the Writer,'" *Bomb*, July 10, 2015.

Donald Sultan, "Tribute to James Salter," *The Hamptons*, July 17–30, 2015, p. 2.

Nate Brown. "Things American: Writers Remember James Salter." *American Short Fiction*, July 22, 2015.

Derek Mong, "The Poet's Salter: An Appreciation," *Kenyon Review* online, July 29, 2015.

Kathleen Alcott, "Food in Salter," *Paris Review*, October 23, 2015.

"Elizabeth Ann Altemus." Obituary, *Aspen Times*, December 3, 2015.

Will Mackin, "Writing Like Flying," *New York Times Magazine*, December 27, 2015.

Jeffrey Meyers, "Remembering James Salter," *Sewanee Review*, 124 (Spring 2016), 333–343.

Sarah Hall, "Beautiful and brutal: how James Salter set the standard for erotic writing," *Guardian*, February 17, 2017, [1–7].

Chris Power, "James Salter's Unreliable Genius," *Guardian*, April 14, 2017.

Jeffrey Meyers. "James Salter." *Resurrections: Authors, Heroes—and a Spy.* Charlottesville: University of Virginia Press, 2018. Pp. 84–100.

Kay Salter, "My Husband's Choice to Be a Writer," *Literary Hub*, November 13, 2018.

Steve Lukits, "Fictions of Frustration: Two Novels About Cold War Fighter Pilots," *War, Literature and the Arts*, 32 (2020), 1–11.

Antonio Díaz Oliva, "An Interview with James Salter," *Asymtote*, 2022.

Noreen Tomassi, "James Salter Interviewed," *Center for Fiction*, no date.

Reviews

George Barrett, *The Hunters*, *New York Times*, March 4, 1956.

A Sport and a Pastime, *Kirkus*, March 3, 1967.

Stanley Kauffmann, *Sport*, *New Republic*, 156 (March 25, 1967), 24.

Webster Schott, *Sport*, *New York Times*, April 2, 1967.

Anatole Broyard, *Light Years*, *New York Times*, June 25, 1975.

Robert Towers, *Light Years*, *New York Times Book Review*, June 27, 1975, pp. 6–7.

Vance Bourjaily, *Solo Faces*, *New York Times*, August 15, 1979.

Francis King, *Solo Faces*, *Spectator*, February 16, 1980, p. 22.

James Wolcott, *Sport* and *Light Years*, *Esquire*, 98 (July 1982), 120.

A. R. Gurney, Review of *Dusk*, *New York Times*, February 21, 1988.

Ned Rorem, *Dusk*, *Washington Post*, March 6, 1988.

Samuel Hynes, *Burning the Days*, *New York Times Book Review*, September 7, 1997, p. 9.

Gerald Howard, *Hunters, Sport* and *Burning, Nation*, 265 (October 6, 1997), 46, 48–50.

James Morris, *Burning, Wilson Quarterly* (Autumn 1997), 100–101.

A. Alvarez, *Burning, NYRB*, January 15, 1998.

D. T. Max, *Cassada, New York Times*, February 11, 2001.

Anita Brookner, *Light Years, Spectator*, 289 (August 31, 2002), 36.

Tobias Grey, *Last Night, Financial Times*, May 20, 2005.

Joyce Carol Oates, On 9 books, *NYRB*, July 14, 2005.

Sebastian Smee, *Burning the Days, Spectator*, 305 (October 6, 2007), 55–56.

Jeffrey Meyers, *Life is Meals, Gastronomica* 7 (Winter 2007), 116.

Geoff Dyer. "James Salter: *The Hunters* and *Light Years.*" *Otherwise Known as the Human Condition.* Minneapolis: Graywolf, 2011. Pp. 156–161.

J. D. Daniels, *Solo Faces, Paris Review*, April 12, 2011.

Jonathan Dee, *All That Is, Harper's*, April 2013.

Daniel Edward Rosen, *All That Is, Observer*, April 9, 2013.

Malcolm Jones, *All That Is, New York Times*, April 26, 2013.

Jeffrey Meyers, *All That Is, Standpoint*, 52 (May 2013), 63.

James Lasdun, *All That Is, Guardian*, May 11, 2013.

Geoff Dyer, *All That Is, Independent*, May 13, 2013.

Michael Saler, *All That Is, Times Literary Supplement* (TLS), May 31, 2013, p. 19.

Michael Dirda, On 4 books, *NYRB*, June 6, 2013, pp. 30–32.

Rob Sharp, *All That Is, Independent*, June 8, 2013.

James Meek, *All That Is* and *Collected Stories, London Review of Books*, June 20, 2013.

Clarissa Hyman, *Life Is Meals, TLS*, January 23, 2015.

James Campbell, *There & Then, TLS*, July 3, 2015.

Jeffrey Meyers, "The Sexual Novel: James Salter's *A Sport and a Pastime,*" *Style*, 51:4 (2017), 564–573.

Declan Ryan, *Don't Save Anything, TLS*, May 18, 2018, p. 5.

BACKGROUND

Bellow, Saul. *Letters.* Ed. Benjamin Taylor. NY: Viking, 2010. Pp. 338, 357–358, 415–416, 520.

Benitez, Mike, "The Korean War and the Phoenix of Flight Leadership: The Fighter Pilot, Part II," *War on the Rocks*, October 23, 2017.

Callan, Michael Feeney. *Robert Redford*. NY: Knopf, 2011. Pp. 139–141, 155–156, 160, 180.

Feifer, George. *Tennozan: The Battle for Okinawa*. NY: Ticknor & Fields, 1992.

Hamilton, Ian. *Writers in Hollywood, 1915–1951*. NY: Harper & Row, 1990.

Hastings, Max. *The Korean War*. NY: Simon and Schuster, 1987.

Hillary, Richard. *The Last Enemy*. 1942; London: Pan, 1956.

Kael, Pauline. "[*Downhill Racer*.]" *Deeper Into Movies*. NY: Bantam, 1974. Pp. 57–59.

Leader, Zachary. *The Life of Saul Bellow, 1965–2005*. NY: Knopf, 2018. Pp. 148–154.

Lumet, Sidney. *Making Movies*. NY: Vintage, 1995. Pp. 8–9.

Meyers, Jeffrey. *Hemingway: A Biography*. NY: Harper & Row, 1985.

Meyers, Jeffrey. *Scott Fitzgerald: A Biography*. NY: HarperCollins, 1994.

Saint-Exupéry, Antoine de. *Wind, Sand and Stars*. Trans. Lewis Galantière. 1939; London: Penguin, 1969.

Tenderini, Mirella. *Gary Hemming: The Beatnik of the Alps*. [Holyhead, Wales:] Ernest Press, 1995.

INDEX